You Shall Tell Your Children

You Shall Tell Your Children

Holocaust Memory in American Passover Ritual

>─┤◄►─˙Ο˙─◄►┤─◄

Liora Gubkin

Rutgers University Press
New Brunswick, New Jersey, and London

Library of Congress Cataloging-in-Publication Data

Gubkin, Liora, 1970–
    You shall tell your children : Holocaust memory in American Passover ritual / Liora
Gubkin.
        p. cm.
    Includes bibliographical references and index.
    ISBN-13: 978–0-8135–4193–8 (hardcover : alk. paper)
    ISBN-13: 978–0-8135–4194–5 (pbk. : alk. paper)
    1. Haggadah.   2. Seder—Liturgy.   3. Judaism—Liturgy.   4. Holocaust, Jewish
(1939–1945)—Influence.   5. Holocaust (Jewish theology)   I. Title.
BM674.79.G83 2008
296.4'53710973—dc22   2007006034

A British Cataloging-in-Publication record for this book is available from the British Library.

"Passover," from *Collected Poems* by Primo Levi, translated by Ruth Feldman and Brian
Swann. English translation © 1988 by Ruth Feldman and Brian Swann. Reprinted by
permission of Faber and Faber, Inc., an affiliate of Farrar, Straus and Giroux, LLC.

Visit our Web site: http://rutgerspress.rutgers.edu

Manufactured in the United States of America

CONTENTS

ACKNOWLEDGMENTS

When I was an undergraduate at the University of Missouri–Columbia, the local rabbi, Harvey Rosenfeld, taught a course on the Holocaust. Every time it was offered, he encouraged me to take the course, and every time I politely and steadfastly refused—usually with the excuse that 8:40 A.M. was too early in the morning for any class, let alone one on the Holocaust. I have the sneaking suspicion that karma (to borrow a concept from another tradition) has played a key role in keeping my attention focused on questions of Holocaust memory for more than a decade. Fortunately, I have been blessed with many wonderful conversation partners, as well as people who have offered comfort and support while thinking through the issues that occupy this book. I am especially indebted to my parents, Jan and Janet Gubkin, my brother, Josh Gubkin, my dear friend Michelle Brotzman and my husband, Richard Malicdem, for their love and generosity.

I finally did take a course on the Holocaust. "The Holocaust and Representation" forced a confrontation with the theoretical material that sparked this project and shaped its key concerns. Fellow classmates Michelle Friedman, Tania Oldenhage, and Claudia Schippert continued conversations with me long after the semester ended. In particular I want to thank Laura Levitt, who taught the course. She recognized I had a valuable project and insights worth sharing long before I believed it and has continued as my on-call mentor ever since. In keeping with my reputation for brevity, a simple "thank you" expresses an immense debt of gratitude to her.

The final version of this book was strengthened by the assistance of many people who read various incarnations of the manuscript. Many thanks to: Rachel Adler, Daniel Boisvert, Jared Chapman, Shauna Eddy-Sanders,

David Ellenson, Michelle Friedman, Sara Horowitz, Adi Hovav, Debra Jackson, Beth Kressel, Björn Krondorfer, Laura Levitt, Kristi Long, Donald Miller, Paul Newberry, Tania Oldenhage, Michelle Palmer, Michael Renov, Marian Ronan, Oren Baruch Stier, Jan Titus, and Tim Vivian. The library staff at California State University, Bakersfield and Hebrew Union College, Los Angeles made challenging research tasks much easier. Thank you as well to Lorna Clymer, Bruce Jones, and Ted Slingerland, who all gave helpful advice at a crucial moment. From this list, special thanks are due to Marian Ronan, a classmate from Temple University, whom I had the good sense to befriend our first semester. She read multiple versions of portions of this manuscript, and the book is far better for her input. My life is enriched by her friendship. Debra Jackson deserves special mention for having read multiple versions of every chapter as my research partner at California State University, Bakersfield. She provided challenging and insightful comments on an almost weekly basis. I am fortunate to count her among my colleagues and friends.

Writing can be a difficult and lonely process regardless of the topic, and writing about the Holocaust compounded the emotional toil. Swasti Bhattacharyya and Glenn Libby, colleagues at the University of Southern California, offered ongoing support. Anne Duran, founder of the Interdisciplinary Research Group at CSUB, brought together writers and researchers from across campus to provide a place to focus on scholarship amid the daily teaching tasks. Outside of academia, the swing dance community of Lindy-by-the-Sea brought an affirmation of life and pure joy when it was desperately needed. Dance continues to sustain me, and I especially want to thank Darcy Bowen, Jes Densmore, Chris Eisenberg, Rhyss Leary, Lee Anne Lynch, Jim Ma and Diana Sharp Ma for their ongoing encouragement.

When I became an assistant professor at CSUB, the book was greatly enhanced by research supported by start-up funds from Marla Iyasere, Dean of Humanities and Social Sciences. Research at the Survivors of the Shoah Visual History Foundation (now the USC Shoah Foundation Institute for Visual History and Education) profoundly impacted the shape of this book. Special thanks to Dan Yavolsky, former Coordinator of Archival Access, for guiding me through the testimonies. Douglas Ballman, Manager of Online Access of the Shoah Foundation, tracked down additional biographical references.

For me, the various stages of this project are tied to a series of moments from the concluding years of my grandmother's life. In my dissertation, I discussed her move to an assisted-living facility as an illustration of the material presence of memory. Sophie Rice Kellerman moved on her eighty-first birthday, and I returned to Los Angeles with lace shawls, photographs, and prayer books. Tellingly, an early draft of the chapter accidentally described her new home as "an assisted-leaving facility." At the celebration of my dissertation defense, I was confronted with the dementia she had feared for many years before its onset; she passed away at the age of eighty-eight as I was making final revisions to the manuscript; and my mother and I chose the inscription for her headstone ("her memory is treasured by all who knew her") the same day I completed review of the copy edits. Her astute mind and sense of humor are well-captured by the beginning words of her unpublished autobiography, written as part of a freshman composition assignment: "What I shall turn out to be, has yet to be foreseen. But to begin at the beginning I was born (as I have been informed and believe) on a September morn 1917. Disappointment reigned throughout the household, as they were all wishing for a boy to carry on the family name. But, nevertheless, I received a warm welcome." While in college she also helped form the Amergers, a name that combines "Americans" and "Germans." She describes the Amergers in later additions to her autobiography as "a social group to help Americanize the boys and girls who had come to the U.S. from Germany or wherever they were persecuted by the Nazis." May her memory be for a blessing. This book is dedicated to Sophie Rice Kellerman.

You Shall Tell Your Children

Introduction

LISTENING TO VOICES FROM THE KILLING GROUND

><--+--+>--0--<+--+--<

$\mathcal{B}$e very, very careful, for we are prone to forgetting fast. That which our ancestors suffered in Egypt today has become only a few minutes' hasty reading of the *Hagada* in anticipation that the matzos dumplings are to appear on the table as soon as possible."[1] More than a decade ago, these words from an anonymous survivor of the Nazi doctor Josef Mengele's "experiments" inspired the book you have before you. In this message of warning, the survivor makes a comparison between remembering the horrors endured through the Holocaust and remembering the suffering of the ancient Israelites, the ancestors of present-day Jews, when they were slaves in Egypt. Memory of slavery is ritually performed by contemporary Jews during the holiday of Passover, when Jews use a text called the *haggadah,* literally "the telling," to conduct a *seder,* the ritual meal traditionally held on the first and second nights of Passover. The intent of the holiday is to remember, but the survivor notes that often the telling of the story is forgotten as participants focus attention upon the special foods that accompany the celebratory meal. Reading the survivor's words, I was reminded of a Jewish joke that regularly circulates through the Internet: "A short summary of every Jewish holiday: They tried to kill us. We won. Let's eat."

I was also reminded of *A Passover Haggadah,* the haggadah of my childhood. Reading the idealistic words of Anne Frank during the seder every year forged an indelible link in my mind between the ancient slavery and the recent genocide as sites of remembrance. When I looked back at the haggadah, I discovered that the excerpt from Anne Frank's diary was one of six texts memorializing the Holocaust, and all six texts were marked "optional." I was stunned (and horrified) by the discovery. How could remembrance of the Holocaust be voluntary? Of course, no malice is intended by the label. *All* additions to the traditional text of the haggadah are marked as optional in

A Passover Haggadah so that "variant readings and interpretations are distinguishable from the basic text."[2] Still, I was struck by the contrast between the power of the survivor's words, "we are prone to forgetting fast," and the force of "optional" memory.

During the course of my research, I discovered many other *haggadot* (plural of haggadah) published in the United States that enfolded the Holocaust into the narrative of slavery and redemption. I focused my attention on *how* the two events were brought together. Whose voices were included? Whose voices were missing? Where in the haggadah did the Holocaust appear? When were the Holocaust passages read during the seder? What kinds of remembrance were enabled by the conjunction of the Holocaust and the Exodus from Egypt? What forms of remembrance were foreclosed? My reading of haggadot and the Holocaust texts within them constitutes a textual embrace, a term used by Laura Levitt to describe a Jewish feminist reading practice whereby one self-critically reads others as oneself.[3] I enact this methodological turn, which expresses the desire for the text, and yet maintains the distinct voices of author and text, self and other, in the chapters that follow. To embrace is to hold on to in a gesture of affection. The term *embrace* suggests bodily action—to wrap one's arms around another. In a mutual embrace, one finds comfort and security. An embrace may express affection, but one may also hold too tightly. A textual embrace is also about acknowledging one's disappointments with that which one loves. For me, as for many other Jews, Passover is a site of emotional attachment to Judaism and family, and the haggadah evokes these childhood memories. I love these texts: they surprise me; they teach me; they tie me to my past. And, sometimes, they disappoint me. The textual embrace is simultaneously a gesture of affection and of letting go. Sara Horowitz, following the warning from the anonymous survivor, asks, "What will help them [contemporary participants in the seder] to tell and absorb stories about the Holocaust in a manner that will defeat forgetfulness?"[4] *You Shall Tell Your Children: Holocaust Memory in American Passover Ritual* is my attempt to suggest some answers to this crucial question.

In Every Generation: Passover and the Haggadah

Passover remains one of the most popular holidays for American Jews. The 1990 National Jewish Population Survey, the largest and most comprehensive survey of American Jews, reports that 86 percent of entirely Jewish households and 62 percent of mixed Jewish-Gentile households attend a

seder.[5] As Jews who emigrated from Eastern and Western Europe accultur-
ated to life in the United States, practices such as lighting candles on the
Sabbath and keeping kosher diminished, particularly in the lives of the im-
migrants' children and grandchildren. Seder attendance, however, remained
high, and sometimes even increased.[6] Even households with no core Jews,
where the household included individuals who converted out of Judaism or
were currently practicing another religion, reported a seder attendance rate
of 25 percent.[7] Local surveys conducted in various cities between 1970 and
2000 report similarly high rates of Passover observance.[8] If the Holocaust is
to be incorporated into a preexisting Jewish holiday, Passover remains one
of the few observances available to the majority of Jews. What accounts for
the continued relevance of Passover in American Jewish life?

One of the first and most often cited attempts to explain the high rate
of Passover observance was made by Marshall Sklare and Joseph Greenblum
in *Jewish Identity on the Suburban Frontier.*[9] In *America's Jews*, sociologist Marshall Sklare expands on five criteria for ritual retention and focuses
on the fit between Jewish tradition and acculturation. He brings attention to
the ways Passover allows one to remain distinct without being separate or
isolated—different, but not too different. Sklare argues that ritual practice
will remain high when a ritual "is capable of effective redefinition in modern
terms."[10] In the case of Passover, the themes of slavery and redemption are
made meaningful in light of contemporary events, including the experience
of freedom and security for most Jews in the United States and its contrast
with the Holocaust. Sklare's second and third criteria add important qualifi-
cations to the first. Although the ritual is meaningful in modern terms, it does
"not demand social isolation or the adoption of a unique life-style" and "ac-
cords with the religious culture of the larger community."[11] Just as important,
according to Sklare's analysis, it offers "a Jewish alternative when such is
felt to be needed."[12] In other words, different, but not too different. Fourth,
people will retain ritual when it is centered on the child; the rabbis articulate
a rationale for Passover that focuses on continuity, and the haggadah says
one celebrates Passover in order to "tell your children." Ritual activities place
children at the center of the celebration: the youngest child recites the Four
Questions; all the children search for the hidden matzah (the *afikomon*), and
the one who finds it can ransom it to the seder leader so he or she can complete the seder; boisterous songs also keep children engaged in the holiday.
In addition parents often see the seder as an opportunity to transmit Jewish
identity to their children. Finally, Sklare suggests that rituals like Passover
succeed because they are performed annually or infrequently.[13]

Some Jews celebrate Passover as a way to affirm their status as Americans and to harmonize their American and Jewish identities. As sociologist Charles Silberman notes, through the process of redefinition, "American Jews have turned Chanukah and Passover into holidays that subtly underscore their Americanness as well as their Jewishness." Silberman suggests that, for many Jews, attending a seder is "an ethnic far more than a religious act; it is a way of asserting cultural and national identity."[14] Joel Gereboff, who has traced the process of "Americanization" in contemporary haggadot, sees in contemporary U.S. haggadot "various ways in which Jews are defining themselves, their place in America, and their notions of what America is and ought to be."[15] On the other hand, for some Jews, celebrating Passover is a vehicle to express one's Judaism. The authors of the 1998 study *Jewish Choices: American Jewish Denominationalism* offer an alternate view of how Passover works as an expression of Jewish identity. Bernard Lazerwitz and his co-authors cite the "five criteria of ritual observance" in their analysis of differences between the 1971 and 1990 National Jewish Population Surveys to claim that Jews are using the seder and other home observances to define Judaism in religious, not ethnic or cultural, terms. They argue that the home has become a privileged site for religious expression and argue that religious expression in the home, as exemplified by the Passover seder, has come to take the place of other forms of Jewish identity that were prominent in previous generations, such as involvement in Jewish voluntary organizations that work to raise money for Israel or provide social services for Jews in need in the U.S. and abroad.[16] Whether the seder is negotiating a religious, cultural, or social identity, to the extent that the Holocaust is a significant aspect of contemporary Jewish identity, it is not surprising that commemoration of it would appear in the haggadah.

Celebrating Passover can also create belonging and identity on a more intimate scale. The family celebration is a potent site for personal meaning. According to Arnold Eisen and Steven Cohen, co-authors of a study based on in-depth interviews, "family is thus not only the site and vehicle for holiday observance but its most important meaning and motivation."[17] Eisen and Cohen conclude that the source of this feeling often is memories of childhood.[18] This is especially the case for Passover, which features prominently in most of their respondents' interviews. They offer the following analysis for its immense popularity: "The reason is perhaps that Jewish *memories* seem to revolve around Passover more than any other single observance. Indeed, it was striking to us that few individuals, when asked about their Passover observance, responded primarily in terms of the themes of the *haggadah,* universalist or particularist: liberation, plagues, redemption, and the like (all of which loom large in recent retellings of the Passover story). They seemed, rather, to take these themes for granted—as if they knew about them, and that *we* knew about them—and were eager to describe more *personal meanings* that they found in the holiday. These meanings were almost invariably connected to family."[19]

Finally, Passover can be a site for a participant's spirituality, or individual quest for meaning and fulfillment. The seminal study by Sklare and Greenblum focused on the continued popularity of Passover for modern American Jews. At the turn of the century, scholarly attention turned from the.modern to the "postmodern Jewish self." With the publication of *The Jew Within: Self, Family, and Community in America,* Cohen and Eisen look outside of Jewish sociological studies and ask how the contemporary Jewish-American experience compares with larger trends of religion and spirituality in America. They find that, similar to their Christian neighbors, Jews are on a spiritual quest for meaningful experience. Furthermore, Jews also validate their experience as authentic by individual, internal, often emotive, criteria. If it feels good, right, or meaningful, it is.[20]

For many contemporary Jews a meaningful haggadah must include the Holocaust. By the early 1950s, insertion of texts in remembrance of the destruction of European Jewry had been noted by scholars. In a 1960 article Beatrice Weinreich writes, "Ever since the murder of six million Jews in World [War] II, a need has been felt by many Jews to amend the various *Haggadoth* [*sic*] to include a passage about this catastrophe, thus giving Passover an additional memorial function."[21] The 1973 monumental compilation of haggadot, *Haggadah and History,* also notes the presence of the Holocaust in the haggadah.[22] Since the early 1970s, Holocaust commemoration in haggadot has proliferated with newer haggadot often incorporating Holocaust material from older ones. Of the close to one hundred nontraditional haggadot published between 1970 and 2002, approximately 25 percent incorporate Holocaust texts, but there are *thousands* of different versions of the haggadah. The earliest extant versions date to the ninth and tenth centuries C.E., when instructions for a Passover seder were included in the daily prayer book. The first free-standing haggadot are illustrated manuscripts from the thirteenth century, and the earliest printed haggadot date back to the late fifteenth century. The authoritative *Bibliography of the Passover Haggadah* published in 1960 listed 2,713 printed editions, but a 1965 addendum brought the total to 3,404.[23] However, in the United States alone, close to three hundred haggadot were published between 1970 and 2000, and this number does not include those that are self-published or posted on the World Wide Web, each of which would increase the count considerably.

The focus of this study is the incorporation of the Holocaust into the haggadah, but it should be noted that the Holocaust is not the only contemporary event to prompt a new version of the haggadah. Each of the major liberal denominations within American Judaism—Reform, Conservative, and Reconstructionist—has at least one haggadah that expresses the assumptions and values of its elite through their telling of the Exodus story.[24] Many groups of secular Jews with a heritage of socialism from pre–World War II Eastern Europe have haggadot written in English and Yiddish. Feminists, peace activists, "New Age Jews," and even vegetarians have published haggadot. Other haggadot recognize specific causes, for example the effort in the 1970s and 1980s to free Soviet Jews, Black-Jewish relations, and Palestinian-Israeli dialogue. There is even a haggadah in honor of the American bicentennial. Creation of new haggadot continues to this day as individuals and groups adapt the text to make the experience of slavery and freedom significant to their lives.

Most of the haggadot presented here are from liberal rather than Orthodox Jewish communities. Orthodox and liberal are both umbrella terms. Several hundred groups of Orthodox Jews live in the United States today. Generally, Orthodox Jews hold a broadly shared set of theological assumptions. Orthodox Jews affirm a divine revelation of Torah. Orthodox Jews read and interpret the Torah through the perspective of generations of rabbis and understand their writings to be "words of the living God" and, hence, authoritative for the Orthodox Jew. Haggadot published by Orthodox groups, with a few significant exceptions, do not include recent non-rabbinic commentaries, and thus will not incorporate the Holocaust. Of course, this does not mean that Orthodox Jews do not commemorate the Holocaust. Remembrance can take the form of oral traditions incorporated into the family seder. In addition, *Tisha B'Av*, the traditional holiday for mourning tragedies throughout Jewish history, is observed by the majority of Orthodox Jews, and includes the Holocaust as the most recent event in a long history of suffering. Like Orthodox, liberal is also an umbrella term. In this study, it is a catch-all category for non-Orthodox communities and their haggadot. It includes all the remaining "denominations" or movements within American Judaism: Conservative, Reform, and Reconstructionist, as well as secular and humanist haggadot. These groups operate out of a different set of theological premises from those of the Orthodox, and one result is greater latitude in the written text of the haggadah. In varying ways and to varying degrees, liberal groups encourage contemporary Jews to add written commentary and even create new haggadot to fulfill the task of making the story of the Exodus meaningful "in every generation."

You Shall Tell Your Children

Throughout this introduction, I have used the term Holocaust exclusively, but throughout the rest of the book when referring to the events between 1933 and 1945, I will follow the example of historian and survivor Saul Friedländer: "Various synonyms for the extermination of the Jews of Europe will be used here: Holocaust, Shoah, 'Auschwitz,' the 'Final Solution.' All of them are currently utilized, but none seems adequate."[25] Chapter one reviews the film *The Devil's Arithmetic* to introduce a set of problems that can impede transmitting knowledge about the Holocaust to the next generations. In the film, Passover plays a crucial role in the formation of an American teenage girl's Jewish identity as she grows to understand the importance of the Holocaust in her own life. The film deliberately evokes *The Wizard of Oz,* and Dorothy's recognition that "there's no place like home." In this case, home is where the seder is. A pivotal scene in *The Devil's Arithmetic* depicts a Passover seder in a concentration camp. Chapter two begins with the oral testimonies of Holocaust survivors who commemorated Passover in the camps. Analysis of both the choices they made during the Holocaust within the limited range of options available and the assessments of their own actions made decades later in narrative testimony highlights agency as an important concept to privilege in the search for ways to tell stories of the Holocaust that "defeat forgetfulness." Chapter two concludes by presenting one of the first haggadot published after the Holocaust in order to examine the processes of creating group memory and the role of memory-work in the formation of identity.

Chapter three confronts the challenge posed to remembrance when a haggadah incorporates the Holocaust. Passover is a holiday that celebrates redemption, but "redeeming the Holocaust" constitutes a dangerous form of forgetting. After laying out the various forms of redemption operative in celebrations of Passover and remembrances of the Holocaust, the chapter concludes with a critique of two popular haggadot that construct a memory of Holocaust-redemption. Chapters four and five address the question that concludes chapter three: "How can Jews remember and memorialize the *Shoah* during the celebration of freedom-redemption without adding redemptive value to the 'Final Solution'?" through an analysis of passages that invoke Anne Frank (chapter four) and the Warsaw Ghetto Uprising (chapter five). "You shall tell your children" is not simply a command to tell a story, or even a desire to remember. To tell the children requires ritual enactment, which in the case of the Holocaust means to draw on the performative to learn about an event marked by trauma. Fittingly, *You Shall Tell Your Children* concludes with consideration of witnesses, those who choose to learn about the Holocaust, to bear witness to stories from the killing ground, and to incorporate them as meaningful in their own lives.

CHAPTER I

Passover and the Challenge of Holocaust Memory

>+ +>+ O +<+ + +<

We tell the story not only to preserve the memory. We tell
the story because Egypt was not only one physical place.
The Exodus was not just one moment in time. We step into this
story because it is both our story and the story of all people
who have experienced oppression and liberation.
—A Night of Questions: A Passover Haggadah

*S*even days you shall eat unleavened bread, and on the seventh day there shall be a festival of the Lord. . . . And you shall explain to your son on that day 'It is because of what the Lord did for me when I went free from Egypt'" (Exod. 13:6, 8). These words from the book of Exodus establish the Jewish celebration of Passover as a remembrance of when God redeemed the Israelites from slavery. Mishnah Pesachim, a rabbinic text that elaborates on how to tell the Exodus story during the Passover celebration, further instructs that parents should tell their children according to each child's level of understanding (Pesachim 10:4). The words from Exodus are reiterated in the haggadah immediately preceding the core section of the telling. To the child "who does not know enough to ask," who cannot express her wonderment about the strange foods and ritual actions that govern the evening meal; who cannot ask, "why is this night different?" To that child: "You shall explain to your child on that day, 'It is because of what the Eternal One did for me when I went free from Egypt.'"[1] The title of this book, *You Shall Tell Your Children: Holocaust Memory in American Passover Ritual* deliberately evokes these powerful words that resonate with generations of Jews to whom parents and grandparents, aunts and uncles told the story of slavery and redemption year after year. But in this text the subject of our telling includes both Passover and the Holocaust, or—more specifically—the insertion of the Holocaust into American Passover celebrations.

9

How do these two tellings fit together: one a story of joyous liberation; the other a story of unbearable destruction? The tellings are symbolized on the front cover by an image of two glasses: one whole; the other shattering. Glasses filled with wine figure prominently during the Passover meal. The book of Exodus employs four verbs to describe God's salvific actions: "I will free you (*v'hotzati*) from the burden of the Egyptians and deliver you (*v'hitzalti*) from their bondage. I will redeem you (*v'galti*) with an outstretched arm and through extraordinary chastisements. And I will take you (*v'lakachti*) to be My people, and I will be your God" (Exod. 6:6–7). During the Passover seder, each of these promises of redemption is recalled by a cup of wine drunk at a particular time during the highly structured ritual meal. Like the wine sanctified and drunk during celebration of the Sabbath, these glasses are symbols of joy. A fifth cup filled with wine for the Prophet Elijah occupies a central place on the seder table. In a ritual moment filled with drama, participants fill Elijah's cup with wine and a child opens the front door to welcome the prophet, who—according to legend—visits every seder on Passover night. On many present-day seder tables, Miriam's cup resides next to Elijah's. A glass filled with water, it symbolizes Miriam's well, which sustained the Israelites during their long journey in the desert. The unbroken glass contains the fullness of joy, freedom, liberation, and redemption experienced at the Passover seder.

The broken glass carries other meanings. *Kristallnacht.* "The Night of Broken Glass." On November 9, 1938, the Nazis organized and encouraged a wave of violence against Germany's Jews. Within a few hours, thousands of Jewish homes, synagogues, and businesses were destroyed. That night and the following day, Nazis arrested approximately thirty thousand Jews and sent them to concentration camps. These actions signaled a change from the previous five years of discriminatory policies to an adoption of full-scale violence and the end of German Jewry's hopes that the anti-Semitism directed toward them would be tolerable. Illusions of safety shattered. The event became known as Kristallnacht because shards of glass from broken windows covered the streets of Germany. The broken glass and the whole glass rest ill at ease side by side, and contemporary American Jews live with an uneasy dual consciousness as they commemorate the Shoah during the Passover seder. After examining the challenges of Holocaust memory to contemporary American Jewish identity, this chapter turns to a detailed introduction to Passover through Passover's primary text, the haggadah, and its central ritual, the seder.

The Devil's Arithmetic: "I Will Always Remember What Happened. Always."

In 1999 Kirsten Dunst portrayed an American-Jewish teenager thrown back in time from her family's Passover seder in present-day New Rochelle to a small village in Poland in October 1941, just as the Nazis also arrive to disrupt Jewish life there forever. Hannah from New Rochelle becomes Hannah in Janow via Lublin and experiences the horrors of life in a concentration camp. Hannah sustains other women in the camp with her "imaginative" stories of life in America, and, ultimately, sacrifices her own life so her cousin Rivkah/Aunt Eva may live. *The Devil's Arithmetic* frames Hannah's brutal immersion into the Holocaust with a family gathering to celebrate the Jewish holiday Passover at the ritual dinner, the seder.[2] Because the film powerfully brings these two Jewish touchstone events together, it provides an apt entry point into a Jewish-American historical and cultural phenomenon: the insertion of Holocaust texts into the haggadah. The following reading of *The Devil's Arithmetic* serves to introduce some of the complex issues that emerge when Holocaust stories are recounted during Passover, the holiday when Jews are commanded to tell the Exodus story of slavery and freedom to their children—the next generation.

Viewers first meet Hannah in a tattoo parlor where she asks her two girlfriends for advice: Should she get the butterfly tattoo or the one with angel's wings? Her friend recommends the butterfly because it matches her "Dracula red" lipstick. The setting is laden with meaning for the viewer, although not for Hannah. She is a Jew getting a tattoo, although traditional Jewish law forbids it. Moreover, the tattoo does not trigger a "Holocaust consciousness," even though the next images of tattoos in the film will be numbers on the arms of her aunts and uncles. Tattoos are Holocaust symbols, used by the Nazis to replace names with numbers and meticulously track how many Jews still lived and how many had died. The film's title, *The Devil's Arithmetic*, reflects this precise and disturbing equation, the reduction of a human life to a number. Primo Levi presents a succinct analysis of the significance of the tattoo: "The operation was not very painful and lasted no more than a minute, but it was traumatic. Its symbolic meaning was clear to everyone: this is an indelible mark, you will never leave here; this is the mark with which slaves are branded and cattle sent to the slaughter, and that is what you have become. You no longer have a name; this is your new name."[3] Writing forty years after the trauma, Levi says the tattoo is a part of who he is; it has become a marker rather than an erasure of identity. When he is asked why he does not have the tattoo removed, Levi replies, "Why should I? There are not many of us in the world to bear this witness."[4] While the prospect of a tattoo seems to make no difference to Hannah, its meaning is often fraught for post-Holocaust Jews who carry on the legacy of the witness.

The cover of *Generation J,* a recent memoir by thirty-something American Jew Lisa Schiffman, provides a telling example. In bright red, green, and yellow the front cover proclaims, "Call us a bunch of searchers. Call us post-Holocaust Jews. Call us Generation J."[5] These phrases are superimposed over a black-and-white image of a young woman's back, and tattooed on her shoulder blade is a star of David threaded through a vine. A close reading of the back cover, however, reveals that the "tattoo" is actually henna and will disappear with the passage of time, unlike the faded tattoos that mark Hannah's aunt and uncles.[6]

The henna is effective as a reminder of a Holocaust consciousness that marks Schiffman and other Jews of post-Holocaust generations. Schiffman describes her consciousness in relation to another Holocaust image, one which also plays a key role in *The Devil's Arithmetic,* a shower that dispels poison gas instead of water. "I'm a post-Holocaust Jew," writes Schiffman, "and that makes my unconscious only a few degrees of separation away from images of the Holocaust. It's paradoxical but the past rises up to the surface, even for those of us who were never there. It pollutes the present, perverts holy moments. It reminds us to remember."[7] The shower. The tattoo. Oren Stier uses the term "icon" to describe these images that embody the past and stand in for a larger history beyond themselves.[8] In Schiffman's memoir, and for viewers of *The Devil's Arithmetic,* tattoos and showers function as icons establishing a relationship between the reader/viewer and the events of World War II that came to be known as the Holocaust. Stier notes that Holocaust icons are symbols with a strong narrative quality. Effective icons connect to the past and leave an awareness of the gap between past and present even as they allow us to "discover our relationships to the past."[9] Hannah, however, does not recognize a relationship to this history; the history of the murder of six million Jews by the Nazis during World War II "means nothing" to her, and thus the tattoo holds no iconic status. For the viewer, on the other hand, this lack of meaning is itself meaningful.

As Hannah awaits her turn with the tattoo artist, the three girls chat about their plans for Friday night. They lament the lack of cool things to do, call the guys gawking outside the parlor window "losers," and generally act like superficial teenage girls. Suddenly, Hannah realizes she is late and has to go to Aunt Eva's for Passover. One girl asks, "What's that?" The other replies, "It's the cracker thing" referring to *matzah*, the unleavened bread eaten on Passover. The opening scene of *The Devil's Arithmetic* presents pertinent information about Hannah's Jewish identification, or lack thereof. Clearly, she is not a particularly religious Jew: she makes social plans for Friday night, the Jewish Sabbath; traditional Jewish understandings of the body as ultimately the property of God prohibit any permanent markings such as tattoos. Perhaps even more significant, many Jews associate tattooing with the Holocaust because at several concentration/extermination camps Jews who survived the first selection upon arrival had identification numbers carved into their forearms. Thus, tattoos have become taboo for many nonreligious as well as religious Jews, but this general aversion does not seem to affect Hannah. Overall, viewers get the impression that Hannah's Jewishness does not play a prominent role in her daily life.

Hannah leaves the tattoo parlor, drives home, and rushes into the house to change clothes for the seder. She makes several last-minute, futile attempts to be excused from this family obligation. "Do I have to go?" she asks her mother. When her mother does not reply favorably, Hannah turns to her father: "Why do I have to go? It's a waste of time." Her father replies, "Some things you have to do because you have to do them." But Hannah is persistent: "Come on, Mom." Her exasperated mother replies, "It's important because I say it's important," and the conversation is over. The answers given to Hannah by her parents do not inspire enthusiasm, nor impart any great wisdom or understanding. They do, however, make clear that Hannah must attend the seder. She changes out of her black jeans into a demure pale blue dress, and the family sets out for Aunt Eva's house.

Klezmer music, evoking images of nineteenth-century Jewish culture from Eastern Europe, plays in the background as the door to Aunt Eva's opens. Hannah's eyes light up and she hugs her aunt. At the moment of the hug, the camera focuses on Aunt Eva's arm, and the careful viewer catches a glimpse of the faint remains of a tattoo. The conversation that follows presents a few of the difficulties inherent in transmitting Holocaust memory to the next generations, especially American youth who are separated from the Holocaust by both time and place.

> *Eva:* Every time I see you, you look more like her.
> *Hannah:* And every time I see you, you say the same thing.
> *Eva:* Well, the shape of your mouth, the color of your eyes. You are blessed with her beauty.

Hannah: And her name.

Eva: If her name lives on in you, nothing can give me greater pleasure.

Hannah: Why don't you tell me more about her?

Eva: Shh, shh, shh. You wouldn't understand.

Hannah: Understand what?

Eva: What it was like in the camps. What we lived through, if we lived.
What it was to be a Jew. This experience is so far from your world.
I am afraid, though I want to tell you what happened, it will mean
nothing to you. And that would hurt me very much. You see?

Hannah: Hmmm hmm.

Eva: Good. Now come.

"You Wouldn't Understand"

Several important ideas emerge in this exchange. The first set of ideas
is expressed in Aunt Eva's words, "You wouldn't understand," which point
toward the limits of understanding and encapsulate a series of assumptions
about the nature of the Holocaust and the roles experience and language
play in coming to understand it. We can parse this apparently simple declaration into three overlapping parts: the Holocaust as otherworld; the primary
role of experience as a reliable form of knowledge; and the inadequacy of
language to communicate experience. These facets reflect some of the difficulties that can complicate the act of transmitting memory and telling others
about the Holocaust.

Although the Holocaust was enabled by a series of far-reaching, complex historical events, it is often signified by Auschwitz-Birkenau, the labor
and death camp that functioned from 1940 through 1944. In discussions of
the Holocaust, the word "Auschwitz" often serves as a metonym, representing the whole of the destruction of the Jews during the Shoah. Auschwitz is a significant icon for the experience of the concentration camps
and the evil acts committed in them. As Sidra Ezrahi notes, "Pronounce-
ments on the poetics of (or after) Auschwitz tend to establish a symbolic
geography in which the camp represents both the center and the periphery:
it constitutes the very center of evil but is located in a realm just beyond the
border of civilized speech and behavior."[10] The ruins of Auschwitz reside
in Poland; "Auschwitz" as icon for the horrors of the Holocaust resides at
the limits of our experience. Aunt Eva evokes this language of limits when
she describes her experience to Hannah as "so far from your world." While
this language effectively points toward the tremendous gap between Aunt
Eva's and Hannah's experiences, the phrase "so far from your world" also

inaccurately suggests that genocide is not part of Hannah's reality on our increasingly globalized planet. As a privileged American teenager, Hannah has the ability to close her eyes to the ongoing acts of genocide in her world. In her relation to the Holocaust, it is only when Hannah, to use the words printed on the video cover, "saw the truth with her own eyes," that she could understand the experiences of the past.

This theory of knowledge serves as the implicit premise of *The Devil's Arithmetic,* as Hannah comes to understand what it was to be a Jew during the Holocaust only by being there. However, dependence on the primacy of experience is complicated because viewers of the movie are watching and not experiencing this (fictional) event first-hand. I place the term "fictional" in parentheses to note that while the specific storyline of Hannah Stern is fiction, the contours of her Holocaust experience are not. Viewers are presumably acquiring some sort of knowledge of what those who actually lived through the Holocaust experienced. We are, in an important way, transported there through the mediating work of film and fiction. In "Memory: The Problems of Imagining the Past," Lore Segal, novelist and child survivor of the Shoah, makes an analogy between fiction and theater. She offers the following to understand the "work" fiction strives to accomplish: "Whereas the essay sets out to discuss its idea with you, fiction wants to stage the idea in your imagination. Essay wants to explain its thought; fiction wants the thought to happen to you."[11] In Segal's provocative observation, thought takes on an active, embodied quality; it is not the passive object in the transmission of knowledge from one source to another. In fact, the subject, "you" seems to be more passive—the thought should "happen to you." Knowledge through fiction requires a willingness to open oneself up and be receptive to an experience. Ultimately, however, the subject remains the facilitator of her own experience; she must actively engage her imagination, set the "stage" for the idea to have impact. The subject's experience is the site for transformative knowledge.

Those who lived through the Holocaust draw on firsthand experience, but are also limited by their particular position. Each has an individual story; none presents the whole. Anne Frank's diary from her life in hiding; Elie Wiesel's fiction-memoir of a religious adolescent in Auschwitz; Charlotte Delbo's trilogy as a partisan in Auschwitz and afterward; Primo Levi's scientific and humanistic observations on the disintegration of man in the Lager—each of these celebrated authors gives a crucial, partial perspective based on his or her own experience of the Holocaust.[12] Primo Levi's notion of the "privileged observer" also speaks to the issue of the representative nature of survivors' narratives. Levi notes that most prisoners could hardly take time to reflect on their position, or gain an overall perspective for postwar reflection: "Surrounded by death, the deportee was often in no position to evaluate the extent of the slaughter unfolding before his eyes. . . . In short the prisoner felt overwhelmed by a massive edifice of violence and menace but could not form for himself a representation of it because his eyes were fixed to the ground by every single minute's needs."[13] And as all of these survivors emphasize in their work, the living cannot speak for the dead.

Furthermore, as many scholars analyzing post-Holocaust narration have noted, the traumatic nature of the Holocaust often creates a block, so that knowledge of the event is inaccessible even to those who did experience it. In his essay "An Event Without a Witness: Truth, Testimony and Survival," Dori Laub argues that, "what precisely made a Holocaust out of the event is the unique way in which, during its historical occurrence, *the event produced no witnesses.* Not only, in effect, did the Nazis try to exterminate the physical witnesses of their crime; but the inherently incomprehensible *and* deceptive psychological structure of the event precluded its own witnessing, even by its very victims."[14] The Holocaust was so radically different from what had previously occurred that attempts to understand it in relation to previous events blocked meaningful comprehension by those in the midst of it.

For those who did not directly experience trauma, language further heightens mediation, the distance between the experience and our knowledge of it. If we can truly know only through experience, then, at some level at least, the event is incommensurable, or inexpressible through language. An unbridgeable gap remains between the event and the telling of the event. In fact, language itself can be problematic, suggesting a bridge to understanding that is only a mirage. This idea of language as hindrance rather than help regularly appears in the memoirs of Holocaust survivors. In *Useless Knowledge,* the second part of her trilogy *Auschwitz and After,* Charlotte Delbo describes an incident where she almost dies from thirst: "I'd been thirsty for days and days," she writes, "thirsty to the point of losing my mind, to the point of being unable to eat since there was no saliva in my mouth, so thirsty I couldn't speak, because you're unable to speak when there's no saliva in your mouth."[15] She describes the risk her friends take to get her water, quench her thirst, save her life. Delbo concludes the chapter simply titled "Thirst" with the following observation: "There are people who say, 'I'm thirsty.' They step into a café and order a beer."[16] Delbo uses language to point her reader toward the insufficiency of language, a dilemma that plagues many who attempt to communicate the gap between the Shoah and pre- and post-Holocaust daily lives.

In his introduction to *Probing the Limits of Representation: Nazism and the "Final Solution,"* Saul Friedländer sets out a series of difficulties raised by representation of "Nazism and the extermination of the Jews of Europe." What makes the Shoah an "event at the limits?" Friedländer claims that the Holocaust as "the most radical form of genocide encountered in history" brings forth an obligation from the victims to bear witness, as well as an effort by the perpetrators to efface their actions. These contrary forces have created a desire for some to establish truth claims as to the character of the event. Friedländer continues, "It may be that we feel the obligation of keeping the record of this past through some sort of 'master narrative,' without actually being able to define its necessary components. The reason for the sense of obligation is clear, but the difficulty in establishing the elements of such a master-narrative (except on the simplest factual level) may stem from the impression that this event, perceived in its totality, may signify more than the sum of its components."[17] The extremity of the event itself, in conjunction with the myriad and contradictory responses to it, constrains our traditional narrative resources: "On the one hand our traditional categories of conceptualization and representation may well be insufficient, our language itself problematic. On the other hand, in the face of these events we feel the need of some stable narration."[18]

In "Representing Auschwitz," Sidra Ezrahi examines this tension between the desire to communicate, this obligation to bear witness, and the limited capacity of everyday language to express situations of extremity. Regarding representation and, especially, the question of limits, Ezrahi identifies "clusters of attitudes that can be reduced to a fairly simple but far-reaching dichotomy between absolutist and relativist positions; between disruption and continuity in reconstructing the traumatic past; and between incommensurability and commensurability as aesthetic principles."[19] The first, found in the work of authors as diverse as Tadeusz Borowski, Paul Celan, Berel Lang, and Lawrence Langer, posits "a non-negotiable self in an unyielding place whose sign is Auschwitz."[20] For these authors there is an absolute disruption and discontinuity between Auschwitz and "after" that cannot be communicated to those who "were not there." Other authors, including Primo Levi, emphasize the commensurability, at least a partial ability to communicate or witness. With commensurability, representation becomes a site for discussing "a construction of strategies for an ongoing *re*negotiation of that historical reality."[21] The extent to which we view the Shoah as a communicable event greatly impacts how we understand the role of witness and how one can read the representations and ritualizations of the Holocaust in Passover haggadot. My readings of haggadot draw from the insights of both absolutist and relativist positions. If the Shoah were completely incommensurable, we could not read from the position of a witness and there would be little point in a project analyzing various representations of the "Final Solution." Nevertheless, the language of incommensurability, and of limits more generally, serves an important function, signaling that a key aspect of any one person's experience of the Holocaust remains incommunicable.

Aunt Eva's comments, along with survivors' accounts, suggest that the Holocaust resides at a limit of representation. Key aspects of any one person's experience of the Holocaust remain incommunicable, or, as Aunt Eva says to Hannah, "you wouldn't understand." Historian and Holocaust survivor Saul Friedländer makes a similar claim when he argues that Holocaust historians, as those engaged in the profession of understanding, should render "as truthful an account as documents and testimonials will allow" yet remain attentive to the aspect of experience that "remains indeterminate, elusive and opaque."[22] The adjective "opaque" serves as a helpful qualifier to the work of historians—and, indeed, to all interpreters who come after. It acknowledges that the primary texts are not transparent; they do not provide complete, direct access to the Shoah. Even more strongly, it acknowledges that our understanding will necessarily remain incomplete. Finally, to remain attentive to the "opaque" suggests that representations of the Shoah should acknowledge this incompleteness, the absence as well as the presence of meaning.

"What We Lived Through, If We Lived"

The second theme from the doorway conversation emerges as another caveat for us, encapsulated in Aunt Eva's words: "what we lived through, if we lived." The "if" in Aunt Eva's remarks is salient because survivors such as Aunt Eva are, in an important way, not representative of the experience of the majority of Jews, or other deportees, sent to Auschwitz or one of the other five concentration/extermination camps equipped with gas chambers. In Auschwitz alone, approximately 400,000 people were placed in the camp and its sub-camps, and more than 50 percent of the registered prisoners died. But these figures record only "registered" inmates. On most transports 70–75 percent of the Jews who survived the trip were never registered; they were sent to gas chambers immediately upon arrival. As many as 2,700,000

Jews, and tens of thousands of Gypsies, Soviet prisoners of war, Poles, and others, were murdered at the six camps.[23]

Dustin Hoffman, one of the producers of *The Devil's Arithmetic,* alludes to these numbers, and the history behind them, in his introduction to the film. Hoffman concludes his introductory remarks with an invitation to watch "a young woman's extraordinary journey of discovery where friendship, love, and courage are the rewards of caring for others, where each day the faces of evil determine who will live and who will die—*The Devil's Arithmetic.*" An eerie scene early in the film also alludes to the impact of the Nazis' arithmetic and provides a portent of what is to follow. Hannah has just ignored her uncles' attempts to talk about the past when the camera zooms in on her Uncle Morris. His tone is abrupt: "It was in the book, the arithmetic, the numbers. You add, you subtract, and there are no more Jews."

"I Am Afraid . . . It Will Mean Nothing to You"

A third theme encapsulated in the exchange between Hannah and Aunt Eva is expressed through the words "I am afraid, though I want to tell you what happened, it will mean nothing to you." Aunt Eva fears her stories will fall on deaf ears, which would further her pain. Aunt Eva suggests that the risk involved in telling is greater than the cost of keeping silent. The act of telling is marked by both fear and desire. Primo Levi describes this fear of not being heard, of being silenced, as one of the common fears he and his fellow prisoners endured: "I had dreamed, we had always dreamed, of something like this, in the nights at Auschwitz: of speaking and not being listened to, of finding liberty and remaining alone."[24]

Levi's recounting of the dream speaks to his audience on several levels and gives insight into what is at stake in listening to survivors. First, there is the original location of the dream itself. While in the camps, the prisoners dreamt of reconnecting with humanity and feared they would be alone. Readers receive a window into the dreams, hopes, and fears in the camp. The grammar of Levi's narrative, the shift from "I" to "we," moves beyond his own personal nightmare and includes his fellow prisoners.[25] Secondly, there is the situation which prompts the telling of this dream. Levi is describing an event that occurred within the first months of liberation. The narration begins with a conversation about shoes. His companion, the Greek, is appalled that Levi does not have serviceable shoes. When Levi tries to defend his deplorable situation, the Greek reminds him that in a time of war one first needs shoes and then food. With proper shoes one can walk and search for food. Levi objects, pointing out that the war is over. The Greek responds with words that foreshadow what is to come: "There is always war," he says.[26]

The next day, while stopped at a small town, Levi encounters a Polish lawyer, a man who lived outside the world of the concentration camp. Levi describes the man as "the messenger, the spokesman of the civilized world, the first that I had met."[27] When the lawyer translates Levi's story to the crowd that has gathered around, however, he describes Levi as an Italian political prisoner rather than as an Italian Jew, a sympathetic but unfaithful translation, according to Levi. "I asked him why, amazed and almost offended. He replied, embarrassed: '*C'est mieux pour vous. La guerre n'est pas finie.*'"[28] [It is best for you. The war is not over.] The first audience, the original messenger of civilization, failed to truly hear Levi's story. There is, however, another audience: each reader of *The Reawakening*. Levi writes with the hope that this implied audience will respond differently, that we will be messengers and spokespeople of a more civilized world, a world where the war, with all its attendant dehumanization, has truly ended.

In *The Devil's Arithmetic,* viewers are the implied audience, but Hannah is the present audience to her aunt's and uncles' stories of life during the war, and the scene that immediately follows Hannah's conversation with Aunt Eva suggests that the latter's reluctance to tell her story to Hannah is justified. In contrast to Aunt Eva, Hannah's uncles attempt to tell their stories, to make her understand. As Hannah walks into the room, two of her great-uncles approach and try to tell Hannah about life in their small village before the Holocaust and about a failed escape attempt that took place at the concentration camp: "Did I tell you, Hannah, about life in Janow before the war?" Hannah's response is dismissive: "Lots of times, Uncle Morris. It's an interesting story." Her tone belies the content of her words. When her other uncle begins to describe a failed escape attempt in the camp, Hannah interrupts: "I think they're starting the seder now, Uncle Abe. You can tell me the rest of the story later." Hannah thwarts their attempt to recount their memories. They are effectively silenced.

Everyone sits at the table, and the seder, the ritual meal traditionally conducted on the first and second nights of Passover, begins. Ritual foods, prayers and blessings, songs, poems, and commentary tell the biblical story of the Exodus from Egypt. The theme of the evening is slavery and redemption: the Israelites were slaves; God freed them. But the seder is not merely recollection of an ancient past. It is an elaborate staging of the past for both present and future. Furthermore, both slavery and redemption are to be personally meaningful. One of the few texts from the haggadah recited in its entirety in the film expresses this central theme of the seder. Uncle Abe begins, "We were slaves of pharaoh and the Eternal Our God brought us out. Now, if God had not brought us out, our children and our children's children would still be enslaved in Egypt." Hannah's mother continues, "Therefore, even were we all wise, all men of understanding, and even if we were all old and well-learned in the Torah, it would still be our duty to tell the story of the departure from Egypt."

A Duty to Tell the Story

The duty to tell the story begins in the book of Exodus. After the final confrontation between Pharaoh and Moses, just before God brings the tenth plague down onto the Egyptians, God says to Moses and Aaron, "This day shall be to you one of remembrance: you shall celebrate it as a festival to the Lord throughout the ages; you shall celebrate it as an institution for all time. Seven days you shall eat unleavened bread; on the very first day you shall remove leaven from your houses, for whoever eats leavened bread from the first day to the seventh day, that person shall be cut off from Israel" (Exod. 12:19). The Exodus from Egypt becomes the moment that defines the Israelites as a separate people who live in a covenantal relationship to the God who redeems them from Egypt. Although the Exodus becomes the defining moment for the Jewish people, remembered in daily prayer, weekly observance of the Sabbath, and the yearly reenactment during the Passover seder, no independent record of the event exists. For some, this lack of independent corroboration calls the historicity of the Exodus into question. For Jewish remembrance, however, the historicity of the event is secondary to its paradigmatic status as a permanent reminder of redemption.

Remembrance of God's saving acts is so crucial that Israelites who eat leavened bread during the Passover celebration place themselves outside the community. In the biblical text, the beginning of the seven-day-long Festival of Unleavened Bread coincides with Passover, the Feast of the Paschal Lamb. In addition to eating unleavened bread and abstaining from leavened bread, the Israelites are told to slaughter a lamb and "eat it roasted over the fire, with unleavened bread and with bitter herbs" (Exod.12:8). During the time of the First (c. 960 B.C.E–586 B.C.E.) and Second Temple (515 B.C.E.–70 C.E.), the slaughtering and consumption of the lamb was central to the Passover celebration, as Israelites made pilgrimage to Jerusalem for the festival. Second Chronicles records the giving of large sacrifices by the kings Hezekiah and Josiah as part of their renewal of the covenant. According to the biblical text, Josiah donated 30,000 lambs and goats and 3,000 cattle so all those present in Jerusalem could participate in the Passover sacrifice, which is described in detail as the central rite of the Passover celebration.

"Elaborate the Story": The Rabbis Create a Post-Temple, Diaspora Judaism

Rabbis in the generations after the destruction of the Temple faced a dilemma. Could Judaism survive without the Temple and outside the Land of Israel? The rabbis who developed the practices Judaism is based upon today, including the Passover seder, answered in the affirmative. The paschal sacrifice, once synonymous with the name of the holy day, is remembered during Passover today through the presence of a shank bone on the seder plate, but the telling of the story is the central practice. Instructions for how to tell the story are found in the Mishnah, a foundational rabbinic text from the third century C.E. In the Mishnah's reworking, the Exodus takes on a more mythic quality than its previous description as unique past event.[29] The Exodus story is not only the particular events of slavery and freedom in ancient Egypt recounted in the book of Exodus; these events are also read as prototype, the paradigm through which to understand the contemporary situation and its ultimate resolution. Whether or not the Exodus from Egypt is historically true, whether or not its depictions in the book of Exodus and the haggadah are accurate, the story functions as a lens through which to understand our individual spiritual journeys and Jewish communal history. This paradigmatic reading of Exodus, which is characterized by a strong narrative trajectory of past redemption and an explicit desire for future redemption, shapes the haggadah. Baruch Bokser describes how the rabbis who compiled the Mishnah reworked the Exodus story: "they had been redeemed but they had also been slaves. . . . As they had experienced redemption once, so they would experience it again. In innumerable situations, Jews could 'remyth' or adapt the paradigm to include their own situation."[30] The rabbis reworked the biblical text in the Mishnah, but they did not see themselves as creating something new. For the rabbis, as for traditional Jews today, the Mishnah is part of Torah, God's revelation. Both the written Torah (the five books of Moses, the Prophets, and the Writings) and the Oral Torah (the Mishnah and its commentaries from rabbinic authorities through the seventh century C.E., which together are called the Talmud) come from Sinai.

The haggadah tells the story through use of biblical narrative, rabbinic commentary, symbolic foods, songs, psalms of praise, and ritual action.

The central narrative and commentary in the haggadah is called the *Maggid,* which means "telling." The Maggid consists of a verse-by-verse exposition of four verses from the book of Deuteronomy. The Mishnah does not specify the content of the exposition or commentary. Instead, we are given the contours of the telling, the redemptive narrative trajectory, which appears in instructions given to a father regarding how to teach the story of the Exodus to his son: "He begins with disgrace and concludes with glory, and he expounds from 'A wandering Aramean was my father' (Deut. 26:5), until he concludes the whole portion" (Pesachim 10:4).

Briefly consider what we are told and what we are not told in these instructions. First, the Mishnah describes the overarching framework of the telling; this Exodus story should begin with "disgrace" and conclude with "glory." Second, the passage includes a biblical verse from Deuteronomy and tells the reader to "expound" upon the verse, to set forth or explain in great detail. Third, this passage from the Mishnah does not tell us exactly what constitutes "the whole portion." The verse following it does not provide an answer either. Instead, the Mishnah discusses the three symbols: a shank bone, a piece of unleavened bread, and bitter herbs, which Jews must discuss in order to fulfill the obligation to recount the Exodus from Egypt.

Up until this point in the Mishnah's tractate on Passover, references to the biblical text have focused on the book of Exodus. At this discussion of the central section of the seder, arguably the most important segment of the entire evening, the rabbis shift to verses drawn from Deuteronomy: "My father was a fugitive Aramean. He went down to Egypt with meager numbers and sojourned there; but there he became a great and very populous nation. The Egyptians dealt harshly with us and oppressed us; they imposed heavy labor upon us. We cried to Adonai, the God of our ancestors, and Adonai heard our plea and saw our plight, our misery, and our oppression. Adonai freed us from Egypt by a mighty hand, by an outstretched arm and awesome power, and by signs and portents" (Deut. 26:5–8). This may seem odd given the preceding emphasis on Exodus. Nevertheless, their decision—when viewed in its historical and liturgical context—illustrates a deliberate choice by the rabbis to maintain continuity with Temple ritual while creating new tradition. These verses were part of the celebration of the First Fruits Festival. When the Temple was standing, Israelite men were obligated to bring their offering from the harvest to Jerusalem. This was a central and familiar ritual for Israelites in an agrarian society, so incorporation of these verses into the Passover celebration establishes continuity with previous Israelite traditions.

However, the rabbis did not transport the entire portion from the First Fruits Festival ritual into the Passover ritual. Although the Mishnah instructs the father to begin with Deuteronomy 26:5 and expound upon it "until he concludes the whole portion," the Passover midrash concludes with verse eight rather than verse ten, the concluding verse in the First Fruits Festival. Deuteronomy 26:9–10 picks up the Exodus narrative after God rescues the Israelites from Egypt: "He then brought us to this place and gave us this land, a land flowing with milk and honey. Wherefore I now bring the first fruits of the soil which You, Adonai, have given me" (Deut. 26:9–10). As the liturgical recitation for the First Fruits Festival, this passage, in keeping with the social context presented in Deuteronomy, applies to an agrarian society tied to the land. But after the destruction of the Temple and the exile from the land, the text no longer "fit" its readers' social context. The rabbis refashioned the text, told a different story to fit their changed circumstance, and concluded the ritual recitation after verse eight. By referring to verses five through eight as "the entire portion," the rabbis deliberately emplot their new story on a truncated selection from the ritual component for the First Fruits Festival. The selection of this text preserves a sense of loss with its clear deletion of reference to the land of Israel and the Temple. It preserves continuity with the past and acknowledges, albeit only implicitly, a traumatic loss.

Midrash—A Rabbinic Mode of Making Meaning

In addition to the selection of the text from Deuteronomy, Mishnah Pesachim 10:4 establishes a model for reading that text. The rabbis transform the exposition of text into ritual action. They set out two distinct obligations: during the seder one must both tell the story and expound on it. Expounding, making midrash, becomes sacred, ritual action. The term midrash comes from the biblical Hebrew *lidrosh,* which means to "to search" or "to examine." The word midrash can refer to a particular story, to one of the many collections of rabbinic stories written down between the fifth and thirteenth centuries C.E., or the word midrash may more generally refer to the process of using a story for searching out meaning in a text. Traditionally, *midrashim* (the plural of "midrash") are explorations of biblical texts that attempt to search out meaning from the biblical story. Most often, midrashim revolve around a textual problem in the biblical verses. Barry Holtz offers a useful description of why midrash developed and how it works: "Primarily we can see the central issue behind the emergence of Midrash as the need to deal with the presence of cultural or religious tension and discontinuity. Where there are questions that demand answers, and where there are new cultural and intellectual pressures that must be addressed, Midrash comes into play as a way of resolving crisis and reaffirming continuity with the traditions of the past."[31] The rabbis privilege midrash as a mode of holiness. In the haggadah, a midrash called the Maggid takes center stage. Additional midrashim often surround the Maggid to create an interpretative text with new meanings uncovered or created in each generation. Midrashim fill in gaps in the text, and filling in the gaps can take many forms. A midrash may create theological innovation, present contemporary values, derive a point of law, or fill in character motivation.

Reading a text for meaning or comprehension is a common task, but the rules of reading employed in midrash differ from those we use every day. The rabbis look at the biblical text as if every word—and even every letter—contains a potential midrash. Several assumptions made by the rabbis enable this method of reading. A comparison of how two scholars of rabbinic literature understand rabbinic reading methods, particularly where they locate the impetus for interpretation, reveals the possibilities and limits of creating midrash as a meaning-making activity. Daniel Boyarin focuses on the relationship between the reader and the biblical text, which he describes as "gapped and dialogical." In this view, the text is meant to be read as incomplete, a record of a continuing conversation where the gaps invite, and even demand, a response. "Into the gaps the reader slips," says Boyarin, "interpreting and completing the text in accordance with the code of his or her culture."[32] Meaning is not predetermined by the text; rather, meaning is indeterminate and dependent on the particularity of a reader and her cultural and ideological context. In the process of reading or writing midrash, the reader slips into the gaps through the use of quotation of other texts from the Bible. Boyarin uses the term "intertextuality" to describe how the rabbis use Torah to interpret Torah. He argues that "the verses of the Bible function for the rabbis much as do words in ordinary speech."[33] Verses from one part of Torah, which may seem to be part of a completely unrelated narrative, can be combined with the verse being expounded to create meaning. The rabbis engage in non-contextual reading. This is one of the key differences in the rules of reading that may be jarring to a contemporary audience. Boyarin emphasizes the cultural component, the role of the reader and his or her cultural and ideological context, in the intertextual interpretation of text. A reader's current location and contemporary needs ultimately determine how the texts are brought together to offer a new interpretation.

But is the meaning truly new? Are possible meanings indeterminate or even infinite? If we take only Boyarin's emphasis on the cultural context for creating midrash, we may inadvertently underemphasize one of the key ideological commitments of the rabbis: the divine authority of the biblical text, which, according to David Stern, places limits on the number of legitimate interpretations of the biblical text. Stern emphasizes that the rabbis "always undertake their study of the Bible with the assumption that every word in Scripture is both necessary and significant."[34] According to Stern, the text itself constrains the range of possible meanings, but some interpretative room within midrash is available if one accepts the ultimately anchoring divine authority of the text. In the rabbinic period, the reaffirmation of this certainty of divine authorship made midrash a successful response to trauma. As the biblical text was divinely revealed so was the midrash that brought forth a layer of meaning already in the text. For liberal Judaisms today, the haggadah and its multiple midrashim carry the authority of a traditional text, even if the notion of the divine authority of the text is rejected or simply ignored. Cultural codes and current needs of the reader shape readings of the story of slavery and redemption, and they are vested with an authority granted by the weight of tradition. This gives the haggadah a persuasive power even as it remains open to readings inspired by contemporary cultural concerns.

In a traditional haggadah, each verse of Deuteronomy 26:5–8 is interpreted through creative citation of other biblical verses. Each verse serves as an anchor and touchstone for the maggid. All of these verses are woven together to fulfill the obligation to "expound" the story. *Feast of Freedom,* the haggadah published by the Conservative movement, provides an example of how the process of midrash works. The Conservative haggadah holds to a traditional understanding of midrash and its editors include an explanatory introduction that describes the midrash as "the heart of the Haggadah."[35] Following the explanation of what is to come, the haggadah cites Deuteronomy 26:5–8. The phrase "consider these verses" precedes the four verses. Then each verse appears separately, along with commentary on particular words and phrases. A closer examination of one of the four verses along with the commentary of its opening phrase demonstrates the close textual analysis characteristic of midrash. First the verse appears in bold-face type in its entirety: "'We cried out to Adonai, the God of our ancestors; and Adonai heard our plea and saw our affliction, our misery, and our oppression' (Deuteronomy 26:7)." Then the haggadah repeats the opening phrase in boldface, "We cried out to Adonai." An explanation through citation of Exodus follows: "As it is written, 'It came to pass in the course of time that the king of Mitzrayim [Egypt] died. The Israelites groaned under their burdens and cried out, and their cry to be free from bondage rose up to God' (Exodus 2:23)."[36]

Thus far the haggadah draws upon a verse from Exodus to expound upon the verse from Deuteronomy. But this is just the beginning of how the editors make use of midrash to dig deeper and "search out" the meaning of the biblical text. The margin of the page in the Conservative haggadah offers commentary on phrases from the commentary. An exposition on the phrase "the king died," reads "With the death of the tyrant who had enslaved them, the Israelites hoped for the annulment of the evil decrees. When the new ruler renewed the edicts, they realized that the persecution was a matter of national policy. Despairingly, they appealed to God." The commentary slips into the gaps in the text and responds to questions that remain unanswered by a sur-face-level, contextual reading. Neither Deuteronomy 26:7 nor Exodus 2:23 explicitly reveals the emotional state of the Israelites, nor do these verses explain what pushed them to cry out so they could be heard. What was their emotional state? After so many years of enslavement what pushed them over the edge? For those whose identity is shaped by the Exodus, these are impor-tant questions. The midrash fills in back story and character motivation, and we become privy to some of the inner life of the Israelite slaves.

The next piece of margin commentary expounds upon the phrase "the Israelites cried out." The first midrash explains why the Israelites cried out, but we are still left wondering how. Did not the Egyptians ruthlessly suppress dissent? How did the Israelites manage to wail in despair? The second midrash provides an answer: "To prevent them from mobilizing against their oppressors, the Israelites were forbidden to complain, even to each other. However, under cover of the national mourning for Pharaoh, the Israelites were able to express their anguish." The final commentary on the opening phrase from Deuteronomy 26:7 expounds on the phrase from Exodus 2:23, "their cry rose up." At first glance it appears that the previous commentary already addressed that aspect of the story, but if we look care-fully at Exodus 2:23 we see a repetition: the noun "their cry" follows the verb "they cried out." If every word is significant, then this second appear-ance demands interpretation as well. A midrash excerpted in the left margin provides our explanation. This cry is specifically the cry of the children: "When there was a shortage of construction materials, the Egyptian over-seers would seize the children of the laborers and bury them alive inside the walls of the buildings. The children wept within those terrible tombs. And God heard their weeping."[37]

The page design of *Feast of Freedom* mimics the format of the Talmud, the rabbinic text that includes the Mishnah and commentary upon it. Additional commentary lines the outside margins of the pages, which is how the Talmud is structured as well. One way to imagine the relationship between text and commentary, margin and center, is through an analogy with the World Wide Web. Jonathan Rosen makes an extended comparison between the World Wide Web and the Talmud in *The Talmud and the Internet*. Rosen looks at the Talmud and sees an "uncanny resemblance to a home page on the Internet, where nothing is whole in itself but where icons and text boxes are doorways through which visitors pass into an infinity of cross-referenced texts and conversations," including "the student himself, who participates in a conversation that began over two thousand years ago."[38] This margin commentary allows additional contemporary glosses on and interpretations of the traditional midrash, which is itself a conversation bridging many generations. *Feast of Freedom* exhibits a self-conscious appropriation of the process of midrash in one of its opening margin commentaries, where it describes the process of midrash as "a never-ending journey into inner space, a voyage of discovery, for untold treasures lie beyond the tantalizing reaches of the text. . . ."[39] In the Conservative haggadah, the body of the page and the margins work together to bring multiple voices into the conversation, and the readers of the haggadah add their voices as well. Midrash brings contemporary voices into the conversation; ritual performance through the seder brings the conversation to life.

Bringing Text to Life—The Role of Ritual

The Devil's Arithmetic accurately depicts a Passover seder. We see Aunt Eva light candles to sanctify the holy day. Uncle Abe recites a blessing over the wine—one of four cups imbibed during the course of the ritual. Hannah's uncle then raises the matzah (the "cracker" mentioned in the tattoo shop) and says "this is the bread of affliction," which refers back to the unleavened bread in the biblical story. The Israelites fled so quickly, fearful the pharaoh would change his mind and once again deny them their freedom, that their bread had no time to rise. The film then shows one of the younger children at the seder ask the Four Questions. These are traditionally recited by the youngest son or child at the table and point toward the distinctive ritual actions that govern the evening meal: "Why is this night different from all other nights? On all other nights we eat leavened or unleavened bread. Why on this night do we eat only matzah? On all other nights we eat various kinds of vegetables. Why on this night do we eat bitter herbs? On all other nights we need not dip our vegetables even once. Why on this night do we dip them twice? On all other nights we eat either sitting up or reclining. Why on this night do we eat reclining?"[40] As the evening continues and the family gathered reads from the haggadah, many answers, and even more questions, appear through ritual event.

The haggadah includes biblical verse, commentary, instruction for ritual performance, prayers, questions, answers, stories, praise, songs, psalms, and, often, illustrations. These set the parameters for any particular seder. They are the guidelines for the performance of the story of slavery and redemption. Consider the seder a dramatic performance, and the haggadah its script. On the first and second nights of Passover, Jews enact the drama of slavery and redemption. One could consider the haggadah stage directions that establish a basic structure for the seder through a series of fifteen ritual actions. The elements in Table 1 are the standard components of a seder.

This is the traditional "order" (the literal meaning of *seder*), and at its core is the account of the Exodus from Egypt. One could argue that it is this play of structure and freedom that characterizes the text, accounts for its success, and contributes to its continued powerful influence on contemporary Jewish self-understandings. The ritual dimension also includes what lies "beyond the text."[41] Yosef Yerushalmi writes about the challenge of understanding ritual in *Zakhor,* his classic study of Jewish memory: "Holy days, rituals, liturgies—all are like musical notation which, in themselves, cannot convey the nuances and textures of live performance."[42]

To work with Yerushalmi's metaphor for a moment, consider a page of sheet music: the notes on the page provide instructions denoting what pitch a performer should play, but much depends on the conductor's and performers' interpretation in each performance. Should the sound be loud or soft? Is there vibrato? Should the note stand out like a solo, or blend unobtrusively with the other instruments? The notes on the page communicate the rhythm. But should the musician hold each note to its full value, or syncopate so that the note is stressed unexpectedly? Is the emotion of the music best expressed by staccato—short and sharp notes—or legato, long and smooth notes? Most often the answers to these questions are not found on the page; they lie beyond the text with the interpretation of the notes by the players or conductor in each performance. The written text is only a beginning. So too, the performance of ritual depends on embodied enactment of text. And every performance is unique. To think about the ritual as performance emphasizes the interaction between text and body. These interactions constitute meaning; affirm and display cultural values.[43]

TABLE I   *Ritual Actions of the Passover Seder*

Ritual action	Instruction
1. *Kadesh*	Say a blessing to sanctify the festival. Drink first cup of wine.
2. *Urchatz*	Wash hands.
3. *Karpas*	Dip celery or parsley, often understood as a sign of spring, in salt water, which represents the tears shed by the Israelites.
4. *Yachatz*	Break the middle matzah from the three pieces of matzah that have been placed on the table. An adult hides half of the middle matzah, which children search for at the end of the meal.
5. *Maggid*	Recite the story of the Exodus. This is the central telling of the story of slavery and redemption. Drink second cup of wine.
6. *Rohtzah*	Wash hands and recite blessing.
7. *Motzi*	Recite blessing for eating bread. Matzah is unleavened bread.
8. *Matzah*	Recite special blessing for eating matzah.
9. *Maror*	Dip bitter herbs, which represent the bitterness of slavery, in haroset, a food that symbolizes the mortar used by the slaves.
10. *Korech*	Eat matzah and bitter herbs together. Again this ritual emphasizes the bitterness of slavery.
11. *Shulchan-Orech*	Eat the holiday meal.
12. *Tzafun*	Eat the afikomon, the piece of matzah hidden earlier, at the end of the meal.
13. *Barech*	Recite grace after the meal. Drink third cup of wine.
14. *Hallel*	Recite psalms of praise. Drink fourth cup of wine.
15. *Nirtzah*	Conclude the seder.

Hannah's Seder—More Lessons from *The Devil's Arithmetic*

This chapter has introduced two narratives that shape contemporary American Jewish identity—the Exodus from Egypt and the Shoah. The Exodus from Egypt, a narrative about slavery and redemption, is told through midrash and ritual action during the seder in order to make the events of the past meaningful in the present, and to every generation. This chapter concludes with a return to *The Devil's Arithmetic* and Hannah's seder to illustrate how both the Exodus and the Shoah become meaningful to her. By the end of the film, Hannah is transformed, and her dedication to preserving memory of the Holocaust is intended to inspire viewers, this current generation. In the film, the seder serves as a sign of her transformation. As the seder begins, Hannah's performance is decidedly unenthusiastic; one would hardly describe it as "meaningful." Her mother reads that it is everyone's duty to tell the story, but Hannah refuses to read aloud. Her father reads in her place: "It is told that Rabbi Eliezer, Rabbi Joshua, Rabbi Elazar ben Azariah, Rabbi Akiva, and Rabbi Tarfon sat all night telling the Exodus from Egypt," which further highlights Hannah's lack of participation. As the seder continues, Hannah rolls her eyes when the younger children show enthusiasm, and she drinks a significant amount of wine. When her mother scolds her for drinking too much, Hannah says, "Mom, give me a break. I'm trying to be religious." Aunt Eva asks if she is all right, and Hannah replies, "I'm loaded." Nonetheless, Aunt Eva asks Hannah to open the front door during the ritual to symbolically welcome the prophet Elijah, who suggests the coming of redemption.

Uncle Abe reads from the haggadah, "the cup of Elijah the prophet who visits each Jewish family and drinks a drop of wine." He asks, "Who will open the door and let Elijah in?" The younger children eagerly volunteer, but Aunt Eva asks Hannah. As we hear the song *"Eliahu Ha-Navi,"* Elijah the Prophet, in the background, Hannah walks through the door, out of the present, and into the Polish village of Janow. It is October 1941. Before, the door was closed; now another door opens, a threshold to understanding and a sign that transformation is possible. Hannah meets her cousin Rivkah and Aunt Mina. We learn that Hannah has recently arrived from Lublin and is recovering from the illness that killed both her parents. Rivkah takes Hannah on a tour of the village and to a series of prenuptial rituals for Leah and Shmuel, who are to be married that afternoon. Viewers glimpse a nostalgic vision of pre-Holocaust Eastern European Jewish life. The Nazis arrive as the rabbi rushes to finish the ceremony. The Jews of Janow are taken to a concentration camp, where most of the rest of the film takes place.

Hannah's Jewish consciousness is transformed through her experience in the camp. She calls herself "a stupid girl" and is ashamed that she almost got a tattoo. Her guilt and remorse over her previous behavior provide a sign of her changing consciousness: "I was thinking about how much help I could be to all of us. I had a history teacher. We spent a whole semester talking about the Jews during the war. You know what I was doing? I was writing notes to my friends. I have no idea what my teacher said. The only thing I remember is that no one paid any attention to the Holocaust." These words also provide a warning to the viewers, presumably young Americans, who should pay attention. Rivkah says, "You have a very vivid imagination, and it is causing you much needless pain." Hannah, however, knows otherwise: "I wish that was true."

Hannah's imagination, her ability to tell stories, becomes a valuable component of survival. After the rabbi's wife and daughters are taken to be killed, Rivkah requests one of Hannah's stories. Hannah demurs, "I'm not in the mood." Rivkah persists, and Hannah recounts to a growing crowd of girls and women stories about life in America where Jews will survive, find safety, and eat pizza. Rivkah repeats her earlier observation, but this time with admiration: "You have a vivid imagination." Of course, Hannah and the viewer know she is not imagining at all. "Tell us another story! More!" the gathering of women and girls clamors. Hannah begins with the classic beginning of a fairy tale, "Once upon a time" and tells the story of Dorothy and the *Wizard of Oz,* an interesting choice for us to consider as there are several parallels between Dorothy's journey and Hannah's own. At the beginning of each film, neither heroine appreciates her family. Both are bored, and, unexpectedly, are transported on a fantastic journey of self-discovery where good must triumph over evil for the journey to be complete. Each comes to realize, "There's no place like home."

Hannah's transformation continues as she tells stories that give life in the camp meaning. One sees just how far she has come when Hannah is demoralized after the brutal hanging of a group of young men who attempted to escape, including the rabbi's son with whom she has had a platonic romance. It is the same escape attempt her uncle tried to tell her about before the seder. The irony is dramatic and agonizing. "I don't want to live like this anymore. It's too painful. I wish I was. . . ." Rivkah quickly interrupts, "Shhh! Don't! Don't say that. What you have been doing has been so wonderful." Hannah looks puzzled. "What have I been doing?" "Your stories," Rivkah replies. "They've been keeping us alive. Me alive . . . They give us hope. They help us think about the future." The most dramatic sign of Hannah's transformation is when she asks the town rabbi to teach her how to conduct a seder. "Just tell me what to do," she says. "I want to do it for Rivkah. Ever since they took Mina away she's always depressed. Please—and also for me." The same girl who pleaded not to attend the seder now pleads for the knowledge and ability to lead one. And when her cousin Rivkah asks her to open the door for Elijah, Hannah expects her journey to be complete. The film cues reinforce this expectation that New Rochelle is just on the other side of the door. Expectations are dashed, however, when Hannah opens the door and finds the concentration camp commandant waiting on the other side.

Hannah returns only after she has made the ultimate sacrifice. Rivkah is chosen to be gassed, and Hannah goes to the shower in her place. She wakes to her present-day family in New Rochelle, but her knowledge from her Holocaust experience remains. She now knows, in the words of her Aunt Eva, "What it was to be a Jew." And presumably, knowing what it was to be a Jew also gives her some understanding of what it is to be a Jew. Hannah is transformed by her experience; it changes her understanding of the past as well as of the present. She tells Aunt Eva, "I will always remember what happened. Always." Hannah's experience in the camps has given her a new appreciation for the Passover seder. The film concludes with the family gathered once again around the seder table. This time, however, Hannah's voice can be heard singing "Had Gad-Ya," a song often understood as an allegory for the persecution of Jews throughout history and their ultimate triumph, joyously above the rest.[44] Hannah learns about the Holocaust and is changed by that knowledge only when she is able to personally experience persecution by the Nazis. Her newfound, hard-won knowledge changes her relationship to the Jewish past. But time travel is a fiction. How does the Holocaust became a meaningful part of Jewish identity for those who were not there? How does it become part of Jewish collective memory? It is to these questions we now turn.

CHAPTER 2

Collected Memories

>—⊢—◆⟩—◆——◇——⟨◆—⊢—◁

Experience at once motivates, defies, and defeats representation,
and the complex inaccuracies of remembered experience deepen
with time. Acts of shaping loss produce cultural memory,
but at the same time they entail an incomplete justice.
—Julia Epstein and Lori Hope Lefkovitz,
Shaping Losses: Cultural Memory and the Holocaust

$\mathcal{T}$he previous chapter utilized the
1999 film *The Devil's Arithmetic* in order to set out some of the difficulties involved in talking about the Holocaust to those who did not directly
experience it and then introduced Passover's textual and ritual dimensions. To return to that film once again, whereas Hannah of New Rochelle
disdains the seder, Hannah in the concentration camp risks her life to have
one. The seder is no longer simply a recounting of someone else's boring
story but a catalyst and sign of her personal transformation, even, perhaps,
the source of her own salvation. As we saw in chapter one, Hannah wants
the seder because Rivkah is depressed and thus at great risk; without the
will to live, death is almost certain. Hannah's personal transformation is
emphasized in her final words of request to the rabbi—she wants the seder
for Rivkah "and also for me." To prepare for the seder, Hannah trades a
pair of wedding stockings to a guard in exchange for some flour, which
she then hides under a floorboard in the barrack. The Passover night scene
begins with Hannah removing two matzahs, each about the size of the
palm of her hand, from a fire in the barrack. "The matzahs are beautiful,"
she says, "I can't believe we made them." As six other women gather at
a table in the center of the room, Rivkah and Hannah have a brief, private conversation. Rivkah reveals that she will use the name Eva, from
Hannah's stories, "when all this is over." Hannah is joyous as she exclaims, "You will be my Eva" and realizes that Rivkah will survive the
Nazi genocide and eventually be Aunt Eva, whose Hebrew name, *Chaya*,
not coincidentally, means "life."

The seder begins as one of the women recites the blessing over holiday candles. The cinematography of the seder scene lends a bizarre sort of beauty as the women gathered are bathed in soft light, presumably from the two candles in the center of their seder table. (The film gives no explanation of how they procured the candles.) A teenage girl next to her asks, "What happens next?" and the woman replies, "The wine." When the girl notes, "but we don't have any wine," the woman declares, "Then we must eat the matzahs next." The eight women gathered at the table share the two small matzahs and a vegetable that serves as the bitter herb. Then the seder leader continues, "Since we don't have anything for dinner, we must pretend we've already eaten. We will open the door for Elijah."

A seder in a concentration camp! The scene from *The Devil's Arithmetic* seems far-fetched, the pinnacle of Hollywood kitsch. And yet, more than one hundred videotaped oral testimonies at the USC Shoah Foundation include stories of Jews marking Passover, sometimes at great risk, even in concentration camps. These testimonies include accounts where survivors remember, reflect, and retell their experiences of Passover fifty-plus years after. The memory of the seder embedded in that time and place also appears in a haggadah created by a survivor who spent four years in various concentration camps. The haggadah was reproduced in 1946 by the United States Army of Occupation and used at the first post-liberation seder in Munich, Germany. Together, these oral and written texts provide a window into some of the ways victims-survivors understood Passover in light of the Holocaust and how Passover was or was not meaningful during the Nazi genocide and in its immediate aftermath.

"And in All This Madness": Passover in a Concentration Camp

When I first viewed *The Devil's Arithmetic*, I assumed that the seder scene was pure Hollywood fiction. If I hadn't "heard with my own ears," to adapt an earlier phrase, the 126 testimonies from survivors describing Passover experiences in concentration camps—from transit camps in Holland and France to labor camps in Poland, Germany, and Czechoslovakia, to extermination camps in Poland—I would not have believed it. The survivors who recorded these descriptions were primarily, but not exclusively, Orthodox and Hasidic Jews. A cluster of topics emerges in these testimonies: whether or not to eat bread during the eight days of Passover (often referred to during the testimonies by its Hebrew name *Pesach*), or at least during the first two days when the seder is held; fulfilling the command to eat matzah; and holding a seder. Even a cursory investigation of these testimonies reveals the wide range of decisions made within the narrow range of choices available. This pushes us to consider the importance of agency, especially in the situation of the Final Solution, where one's autonomy was greatly diminished. A review of these testimonies sets the groundwork to begin to think about how to preserve the plurality of voices and decisions in a communal ritual.

The Challenge of *Chametz*

Hunger was an overriding concern in the concentration camps, and almost all written and oral testimonies discuss, sometimes in obsessive detail, the constant hunger that accompanied daily life. Rations were often inadequate for survival, let alone satiety. Each meager piece of bread, slice of potato, or bowl of watery soup was crucial in the effort to stay alive. Passover presented a special challenge to this effort as traditionally Jews do not eat bread (*chametz*) during the eight-day holiday. In fact, Jews are supposed to clean their homes of chametz, and not have any bread in their possession. On the one hand, it may seem obvious that giving up bread was not a viable option in the concentration camps. But Passover is a particularly meaningful holiday, which Jews tend to maintain even as they assimilate into secular society. Thus, it would be expected that for a significant number of Orthodox, Hasidic, or traditional Jews, the decision whether or not to eat bread would be fraught. The following section explores how a number of camp inmates perceived the limited options available to them, weighed the factors, and justified their decisions.

Making Arrangements. In some cases, Jews who decided not to eat chametz were able to exchange their bread ration for some other nourishment. For example, Ester R., who was in a concentration camp for three Passover holidays, explains how she was able to exchange her ration when she was in Parschnitz, a camp in Czechoslovakia: "I went over to the Lagerführer [head of the camp] and said, 'Listen. I give up my bread for this eight days, but instead give me another two potatoes or two red beets.' And she accepted."[1] Ester's case is unusual; most survivors who spoke during their testimony about exchanging their chametz made private arrangements with Jews who chose not to observe the prohibition against eating bread. Nevertheless, in at least one case the decision was made among the Jews as a community in the camp. Abba B., who was a young child when he was in Deblin, a camp in Poland not yet under the auspices of the SS, describes how the observant and non-observant Jews worked together. In his testimony, he uses the Yiddish terms *frummeh* and *frum* to refer to observant Jews and describes non-observant Jews as irreligious: "So some *yiddin* [Jews] ate matzahs during Pesach. They did not eat chametz. So afterwards my mother told me and my father that what happened was this: Many yiddin became irreligious during the camp. So the frum yiddin, the religious and the irreligious, made a deal. All the non-*chametzke* products, what it is, whether it's peels, especially, or maybe some eggs would be given to the frummeh yiddin, and the frummeh were supposed to give to the irreligious the bread. Or whatever was *chametzick*. Apparently there was a meeting where they decided this."[2]

Views from the Tradition. Although Abba B. uses the term "irreligious" to distinguish those Jews who ate chametz during Passover, there was not unanimity from within even the most observant communities regarding whether to eat or to abstain from bread. The following two testimonies describe the actions of religious authorities—a young rabbi's wife from Hungary and the Chief Rabbi of Rotterdam. Together, they illustrate the diversity of positions even among traditional Jews. Halina L. was in Porta Westfalica, a German concentration camp. Among the new arrivals just before Passover "there was this group of Hungarian girls. The oldest sister was married to a rabbi. She was a rebbetzin, and she was very young. She misunderstood her position. . . . She forbid them to eat the bread because it was . Passover. So we told her, 'sweetheart the soup is not kosher either so what difference does it make?'" Halina disapproves of the young rebbetzin's advice and argues that there is no point in trying to observe the commandment because even if they do not eat bread, they will still be eating food that is forbidden by Jewish law. When this argument proves unpersuasive, Halina draws upon other authorities: "Plus I remember that even in the Tomászow ghetto when the Germans once gave us all horse meat, the rabbi said it's all right to eat because in case of emergency it's all right to eat anything. The real laws are put aside."

Halina describes the daily food rules, known as *kashrut*, as "the real law" and suggests by implication that the accepted practices "in case of emergency," or in times of extremity, are illegitimate. Jewish law includes important provisions for cases of emergency, including the concept of *pikuach nefesh* [where life is at stake]. Dating back to early rabbinic interpretations of biblical texts, pikuach nefesh says that for the preservation of life almost all other Jewish laws are suspended. Preserving human life takes precedence. Leviticus 18:5 states, "You shall keep My laws and My rules, by the pursuit of which man shall live." The rabbis who wrote the Talmud, a primary work of Jewish law, took that to mean that when it comes to the laws "'You shall live by them,' and not die by them" (Yoma 85b). There are only three situations, according to the rabbis, where death is preferred to violating Jewish law: when one would have to murder an innocent person, perform an act of idolatry, or engage in a forbidden sexual act. Jeopardizing one's survival by fasting or giving up the limited nourishment available in the concentration camp clearly does not fall into any of these three exceptional categories. Nevertheless, Halina concludes her recollection of the young rebbetzin, "But I don't think she let them eat the bread."[3]

We see this rationale articulated explicitly through the words and actions of Rabbi David Shapiro, Chief Rabbi of Rotterdam, who was sent to Bergen-Belsen shortly before Passover. Irma H., whose husband was a dentist in the camp and became friends with the rabbi, relays the story. Irma worked in the camp as a dental assistant to her husband. She remembers, "It was a few days before Passover, and he told my husband that he had brought matzah along for himself, but for the camp it's impossible. The barracks had to be darkened and closed at eight o'clock. He came before and made kiddush [a blessing of sanctification] in every barrack. And as we had no matzah, we had only bread. He said a bracha [blessing]. And if you say bracha then you have to do it. And he ate bread." We hear from Irma that the rabbi recited prayers for the holiday, including the prayer over the matzah. In Judaism, reciting blessings is a way of giving thanks to God. If one thanks God for creating the fruit of the vine, one needs to sip the wine that comes from the vine. If one thanks God for giving a command to light candles at the beginning of the holiday, then one has to light the candles. This is the only thanks that God requires. Irma continues the story with a conversation between the rabbi and her husband: "So the next morning he came to our dentist station. 'Rabbi Shapiro I have to ask you something. You brought matzah along for yourself but why did you eat the bread?' He said, 'As the rabbi it's my duty to save the people from starvation, and if I would not have eaten the bread the people maybe would have thought 'I may not eat it,' but I wanted to show them they need to eat everything.'" Jewish law is meant to enhance life, not diminish it.[4]

Matters of Life and Death.   Both Rabbi Shapiro and Halina L. recognize that survival was at stake, and Abraham T. justifies his decision on these grounds as well. He was in Ganacker but was sent outside the camp during the day to work in a field where he mixed cement, supposedly to build an airport to support the German war effort. The farmer who brought the water for the cement mixing would often give Abraham and his co-workers a bit of extra food when the guards were not looking. During Passover, he continued to eat the extra food: "We didn't dream of not eating bread because even though it was Pesach coming, we were lucky to have these portions." Although Abraham recognizes his good fortune, relatively speaking, to receive additional food, reflecting back fifty-plus years later, his testimony is tinged with remorse: "The only Pesach I ate chametz in my life. I can't forget it, but it wasn't my fault of course." Although he knows it is morally unjustifiable to blame himself, he still regrets his actions. He "can't forget" that he was forced to eat bread during Passover in order to stay alive.[5]

Margaret G., by contrast, chose not to eat chametz when she was transferred from Auschwitz II-Birkenau to work in a factory. She remembers working ten- and twelve-hour days under close watch and gradually receiving less and less food. But, she says, "from Auschwitz this was heaven." At the factory, the women received a small ration of sugar each week: "A few weeks before Pesach we started saving that sugar for Pesach. OK. But you can still not live on a little sugar and maybe a baked potato. But you know if you want to do something, somehow God helps you." Margaret recounts that on the second day of Passover the SS asked for volunteers to unpack crates of vegetables. Seizing the opportunity to get extra food, she volunteered: "The SS was watching us. But maybe not close enough. So when it came time for lunch we hid some rutabagas wherever we could under our clothes." Margaret points to each of her underarms as she describes their secret activity: "And we took it upstairs and put it under the mattress. And then we went back down and we did it again and we had food for the rest of Pesach. We ate it raw. But we had something to eat."[6]

Margaret G. survived and was able to eat her hidden stash of bread after Passover, but not everyone was so lucky. The cost of not eating bread could be very high. The testimonies of Andrew G. and Natan L. bear witness to this fact. Andrew remembers how weak he was by Passover, 1945. He was in Ebensee in Austria "in very, very bad shape" during one of the endless roll-calls he endured. "At Pesach I know we were standing again. Counted. There was a very religious fellow standing next to me, a very nice fellow. He decided that he's not going to eat chametz. He will not touch the bread even if we get it; he only will eat if we get any food which is not bread, and is not infected with *chametzin*. He was so weak; he was even weaker than me or anybody else. We supported him to stand there for an hour outside, and he suddenly collapsed from exhaustion. Lying on the floor, he said, 'I'm still not going to eat chametz.'" Andrew concludes his narration of the episode in almost a whisper, "And he died in front of us."[7] Natan L., a Conservative Jew, who was in Fünfteichen, Germany, speaks with a tone bordering on disdain about Jews who traded their bread for a potato: "They would cut small slices and bake on the oven. You know. Flake-like. And eat that instead, and not eating bread. And this was wrong because how much you got for one potato or two potatoes; the piece of bread was the only food, which was something. And people did it and they died." He looks away from the camera as he continues his testimony, "My brother did it . . . and he didn't survive. He lived until the end of '44."[8]

Choiceless Choice.   These testimonies reveal the terrible constraints of what literary critic and scholar of Holocaust studies Lawrence Langer refers to as "choiceless choice." In "The Dilemma of Choice in the Death-camps," Langer uses this term to categorize situations "where critical decisions did not reflect options between life and death, but between one form of 'abnormal' response and another, both imposed by a situation that in no way was of the victim's own choosing."[9] Langer's examples include some of the most painful situations in the camps: a mother "allowed" to choose which of her three children she could save. Women who killed newborn babies in an attempt to save the mothers, who, if discovered, would have been sent to their deaths along with the newborns. Langer employs the term "choiceless choice" as part of a vehement argument against judging these actions by the criteria of traditional ethics. Langer's description helps illuminate the decisions we have examined thus far about whether or not to eat chametz. The concentration camp placed these Jews in a situation of extremity, where death was the norm, without the freedom to make choices, as the vast majority of their lives were determined by forces outside their control. If we heed Langer's plea, looking at their choices from a time and place far away, we should withhold judgment. Our task is neither to praise nor to blame, but to try to understand—to the extent understanding is even possible across this vast distance.

Although Langer's analysis is compelling, it is open to criticism. Historian Joan Ringelheim critiques "choiceless choice" as a viable concept for analyzing action made by victims in the concentration camps. In "The Unethical and the Unspeakable: Women and the Holocaust," Ringelheim rightly notes that the issue is not choice as much as power. She argues that

Langer's term "obfuscates the very material conditions Langer wants to illuminate. The situation constructed in the camps is one of oppression and domination; it is about power and the lack of power to act meaningfully, not about choice or freedom."[10] Ringelheim's argument moves beyond "choiceless choice" to look at the constraints of choice due to the limited power of those in the concentration camps. A second, perhaps even more important, reason to not completely remove the aspect of choice from discussion and analysis of victims-survivors' actions exists in our present moment. Within the formidable constraints these Jews faced, they still attempted to act in ways they found meaningful, given their circumstances. Furthermore, the narratives within the oral testimonies suggest that after the Holocaust, survivors are constructing stories that preserve or establish these actions as meaningful. Actions men and women found meaningful either during or after the Shoah should be given serious consideration. In the following set of testimonies about whether or not to eat chametz, recollections from four Orthodox women suggest it was meaningful to make a choice at the time, regardless of outcome. Moreover, a recognition of choice remains meaningful in how survivors construct their sense of self afterward in telling their stories.

Belief, faith, and tradition play a prominent role in all four women's testimonies. Helen R. was in Oederan when she decided not to eat chametz. She remembers the incident after being prompted by the interviewer about Jewish holidays: "I'm trying to think back. I was in Oederan. We had left Oederan just after Passover. I did not eat the little bread that I had received. I did not. Now that you mention it, I had completely forgotten about that." She continues with a bit of irony and a statement of faith: "Of course, matzahs were not given to us. I did not eat it. I so strongly believed although I was so hungry. But somehow we managed with the other things we had received. I'm sure that that wasn't kosher for Passover neither. But just the thought of eating bread on Passover was something I was unable to do." Her choice comes from a strong belief and a visceral reaction. She dismisses even the thought of eating bread. Helen's response speaks to the embodiment of memory, the action of eating bread, that serves as the receptacle of her belief. Her faith is not simply cerebral or even a matter of the heart. Faith is shaped by, sustained through, and embedded in action. Helen concludes her testimony about Passover with an affirmation of her faith in the midst of adversity: "And I always prayed to God. I mean that's all I had to turn to, especially when I was alone. There was no one else to tell your problems to. And there were plenty of times I felt sorry for myself, and I couldn't understand why God did what He did. But in a way I never lost faith in Him. For whatever the reason."[11]

Zuzi B. also places her decision in the context of hunger: "You were very hungry—constantly hungry. Constantly." We hear her clear evocation of the constraints of choice. In the midst of this deprivation at Schatzlar in Czechoslovakia, she also chose not to eat bread. However, her evaluation of this decision differs quite dramatically from Helen R's. She says, "Now it's supposed to be Passover. We didn't have matzah. We said, 'Well we're not going to eat bread.'" She does not attribute their decision to belief or faith. Rather, as she looks into the camera, Zuzi B. slaps her hand up to her head and exclaims, "How stupid we were! We were hungry. Dying for hunger." Looking back, some fifty-plus years later, she suggests it was not a smart decision. However, she softens her evaluation, "But we had a tradition. That tradition kept us."[12]

The language—"that tradition kept us"—is evocative. Zuzi's testimony points to the sustaining role of tradition. Although psychologist Abraham Maslow's classic "hierarchy of needs" states that the basic need for food must be met before any other need can be addressed, Zuzi's testimony, along with others we have heard, suggests human needs may not be so hierarchical. According to Maslow, the need to belong, or as psychologist Erich Fromm describes it, "rootedness" can only be met, in fact can only be recognized as a need, once the more primary needs of hunger and safety are satisfied.[13] Hunger is a more fundamental need than belonging to a community or maintaining self-esteem, according to this hierarchy. Yet, as we have seen, often needs other than hunger propel decisions, even at the expense of satisfying hunger, to the extent that may have been possible. As Zuzi describes it, turning to tradition fulfills a primary need and sustains her.

Food keeps us alive, but Helen K. also attributes her survival to prayer early in her discussion of Passover. As Helen gets further into her recounting of spending Passover in the concentration camp, her testimony moves beyond any simple dichotomy of physical versus spiritual survival and gives insight into the complexity of her decision-making process within the constraints of choice: "It was Pesach. We were in concentration camp. Pesach. Never ate bread on Pesach, and there were some girls who sold the bread, exchanged the bread for soup, for a few potatoes." She considers whether she also should give up bread but decides against it because it could impair her health and dramatically lessen her chance for survival. Helen says, "I just thought back. Oh, my mother wouldn't want me to do that. She would want me to eat everything. Pesach or no Pesach. We weren't exactly sure when it is, but we had a hunch this is Pesach. But now it might hurt my health." Her reflections on how she lived with this decision, rationalized it for herself, are remarkable. "You have to do it [eat bread], and I done it. I ate whatever. I just made believe. OK. It's not Pesach. I don't know when Pesach is. And these girls don't know what they're talking about." In her testimony, Helen K. acknowledges the self-deception she used to live with her decision. Like Helen R., Helen K. cannot bear "just the thought" of eating bread on Passover. So instead of giving up bread, she gives up Passover.[14]

Finally, Edith K., a Hungarian Jew who was separated from her community while in the hospital at Ravensbruck, gives a thoughtful examination of her rationale for giving up chametz: "It suddenly dawned on me that it must be Pesach, and I wasn't together with anybody else who was in any way observant and just quietly by myself I decided I'm going to keep Pesach. Well, how can you keep Pesach in Ravensbrück? In the hospital? There was only one thing I could do, according to my mind, is not to eat bread. I mean I couldn't get a hold of anything at all, any Pesach requisites." She struggles with the constraints, the limited parameters in which she can make her choice. She eschews bread but continues to eat other food that is not kosher for Passover. Also, she does not remove the bread from her possession: "The soup which we were given daily, obviously contained food which we are not allowed to eat on Pesach, but I decided I've got to eat something, but I couldn't bring myself to eat bread on Pesach. Strangely enough, although I realize that you're not allowed to eat bread on Pesach, you're not allowed to have or possess bread on Pesach. But I couldn't bring myself to part with the bread. So I just collected it. I was fully conscious of it, that it was not the right thing to do. But nevertheless, I felt I must do something. And I collected—I'm not even sure I knew the exact date of Pesach—I decided now I'm going to keep eight days Pesach, which I did." Whereas Helen K. decides it must not be Passover, Edith decides it must be Passover.

In retrospect Edith K. surmises that her decision was not correct in terms of Jewish law. She says, "Had I been in the position to ask anyone in authority, I probably would have been told in no uncertain terms that I was not to deprive myself of bread. But I had nobody to ask." Edith possesses nuanced insight as she looks back, "And you know, in the circumstances, I'm not even sure if this was really a religious gesture." Instead, she describes it as "a gesture of defiance." In Edith's experience and in her explanation of her motivations, the religious and the defiant exist in an either/or relationship to one another, even though the story of Passover itself can be read as one of religious defiance: the Egyptian midwives help birth the Israelite children, Moses and Aaron stand up to Pharaoh to secure their right to worship, rabbis under Roman rule surreptitiously plot a revolt while celebrating the seder. Religious and defiant are not necessarily mutually exclusive descriptions of their actions—or of Edith's. Vigorously shaking her head up and down, Edith continues, "you know I really felt that all of a sudden our religious practices became so much more precious than they had ever been before." Edith then shifts back to a religious characterization of her actions: "And having been together with all these assimilated Jewish women, it suddenly dawned on me what a precious heritage is my religion."[15]

Making and Eating Matzah

The obligations for Passover are both negative and positive. One is forbidden to eat leavened bread (chametz) and commanded to eat unleavened bread (matzah). Some Jews took extraordinary measures in their attempt to fulfill this positive obligation. Matzah is a simple food—the poor man's bread, the bread of affliction. Its ingredients are simply flour and water. What makes matzah distinctive is that it is not allowed to rise. In other words, there is no leavening, echoing the biblical passage: "And they baked unleavened cakes of dough that they had taken out of Egypt, for it was not leavened, since they had been driven out of Egypt and could not delay" (Exod. 12:39). Moreover, "Whoever eats what is leavened, that person shall be cut off from the community of Israel" (Exod. 12:19). Traditional Jews eat "guarded matzah," which is carefully watched during the baking process to make certain it does not leaven. Obviously, guarded matzah would be almost impossible to make under the constraints that governed life in the concentration camps. However, several testimonies include stories of Jews who ate a particular food—kohlrabi [a turnip-like cabbage], beets, even crackers—as if it were matzah. Abram H. was in a concentration camp during Passover when someone stole a vegetable that resembled "a big black radish—four times as big," which he later identifies as a beet. He and his companions cut the beet into slices to look like matzah, and in the middle of the night put the slices of beet on the hot pipes that transported steam through the barracks. They did this at great risk because no one was allowed to be out of the bunk at night. Abram concludes the dramatic story simply: "We ate a piece of beet. This was our matzah."[16]

Survivors who came out of Flossberg, Krakau-Plaszow, and Deblin recount how Jews used flour to make matzah. Thomas S., who was a child in Bergen-Belsen at the time, expresses sheer amazement that some Jews made matzah: "And in all this madness and wild, unbelievable hell, there was this—I can't believe this—but we made matzah for Passover. Not we. I mean there were a couple of weirdoes." He pauses at this point in the testimony and rolls his eyes, "saints who kept bread and they dried them . . . They made flour from the bread, again put it in water. They rolled them and they made matzah." He laughs as he concludes this description. The interviewer follows-up and asks, "Did you actually have a seder?" Thomas responds, "Well, yes and no. We couldn't—we did as much as we could. Well, yes we did have a seder—a sawed-off seder like because we didn't have all the ingredients. We did the praying, we did the talking, we did the recounting, and we did the praying that we should be saved from this hell."[17]

Tova F's. testimony poignantly captures the hell that was Starachowice, a labor camp in Poland. When her family was deported from a ghetto to the labor camp, her entire world changed: "At four-and-a-half I had to grow up. . . . The reason I remember so much is because she [Tova's mother] insisted on talking to me and telling as much as possible what is going on. She felt that ignorance is death. You have to have as much information as possible." That information dramatically shaped the young girl's perception of the world: "One of the things I remember, my first seder was there. I must have had others but I have no memory of that. And somehow we got a little bit of flour to make the matzah . . . and we were making the matzah. We were told to put a little water mixed with the flour. There was a young woman who was supervising us. She was saying to do it quickly, do it quickly. You know from a kashrut [Jewish food law] point of view the matzah has about eighteen minutes for you to make it; otherwise, it rises. But I didn't know that. When she said do it quickly and quickly, I was positive that if we don't do it quickly, we'll be shot because we did it outside, and the Germans were still in the towers." Tova's eyes pop open with surprise, or perhaps with fear, even a half-century later: "They were sitting there, and they were with their guns really pointing to us, to anyone that was there. And I was so sure if I don't do it as quickly as I'm told to do it, we'll be dead. So that in a sense, every move that we made, we were aware of the guns."

Tova remembers that when the matzah was baked, "There wasn't enough for any of us to really eat any; it was so little. It was symbolic in a sense." In her testimony, Tova forms a small 'D' with her left index finger and right thumb and index finger and says, "Everybody got a piece about this size. And she [the young woman] told us not to eat it until our parents came home because this was the first seder, Pesach seder in 1943. So when my parents got home at night, I remember I was asleep already, but I had the matzah next to me—this little piece. I woke up because they came in. I said look, look I have matzah. I remember my mother started crying. . . . I'm not sure I knew all about the seder, or much about the holiday, but I knew this was something very special because I wasn't allowed to eat it until my parents [returned], and we all shared it. Everybody had a tiny piece. We had one bite of that matzah apiece. This was my first memory of my first seder."[18]

Holding a Seder

For Tova F., eating matzah constitutes the entirety of the seder, but a few survivors recount actually participating in a more extensive Passover ritual. William W. is about to conclude his testimony when he tells the interviewer he wants to recount an earlier experience from the time he spent in Markstädt, a labor camp, which was the first of several camps he passed through. It was Passover, and he was still with many Jews from his hometown. They asked him to conduct a seder in the barrack. He says, "I had a good voice at that time—and loud. Nice tenor." Unfortunately, the seder was interrupted by the head of the camp: "The German Lagerführer asked, who is the one singing. I was afraid to say. But then I said, why should they be blamed on account of me. I said 'I.' He told me 'Don't stop. Do it.' I started again. I don't remember what part of the haggadah I was at at that time. I was singing very good. Even better because I thought that's the end anyway, what's the use?" The camp leaders listened to the seder for a while and then the German head of the camp told William to report to him in the morning. "I knew that's the end. I'll go in; he's going to kill me. That's all. What's he going to do with me. I couldn't sleep the whole night." What he encountered in the morning was completely unexpected: "He told me you're not going out all the holiday. You have seven days not to work anymore. You're going to stay in the barrack. And you can have food; whatever you want. And that's what happened." William does not know how to account for his experience, but he knows it was arbitrary. "This was unbelievable. And it happened in other barracks the opposite. When they came in, they killed them right away. I don't know. It's just incidents like this. What they did." William speaks to the role that luck played in one's survival.[19]

The next three testimonies all include explicit comparisons between the slavery endured by the Israelites under the Egyptians and the suffering endured under the Germans in the concentration camps. Regina P. worked as a secretary in Auschwitz II-Birkenau filling out death certificates. One Passover evening she received a package, which included a box of sardines. She says it was a "miracle of miracles" that the package actually made it into her possession. She remembers using it with several other women for the seder meal. Here she describes how they recounted the story and conducted ritual acts of remembrance: "First of all by heart we knew a little bit and we just said that maror [bitter herb] we have, we do not need. And saltwater we do not need because nobody stops crying. And eggs we don't need because our life turned. And one of the girls did bring a piece of something vegetable. So we all conducted the seder." They lacked most of the foods for the ritual: no bitter herbs to represent the bitterness of slavery; no saltwater to represent the tears shed; no eggs to signify the rebirth of springtime and the transforming experience of liberation. They did have one piece of vegetable and one piece of handmade matzah. As Regina recalls what they had and what they lacked, she draws parallels between the ritual remembrance of slavery of the Israelites in Egypt and their enslavement by the Germans. Her testimony is marked by a sense of irony. During this seder the lives of the participants are the symbols of the ancient story. They do not need traditional symbols to remember their connection to the slavery of the past because they read their current enslavement within the ancient story. The distance between past and present collapses, and participants become the ancient story.[20]

Fay P.'s testimony gives a dramatically different evaluation of this comparison. Fay conducted a seder in the washrooms of Sosnowiec, a labor camp in Poland. She received a package with three matzahs and then worked with other girls to get some beet soup and potatoes. Whereas the physical text is absent in most of the other testimonies, the actual haggadah plays a crucial role in Fay's testimony. She begins this episode in her testimony by asserting she has the text: "I had my haggadah that my saintly father give me in 1939 for my upcoming birthday. . . . It was twice in oven, and twice I went to take it out because I just found out they took it to the oven. So I went into the kitchen and took it out. I scalded my fingers. But I have the haggadah to show from before the war. That's the only thing I have from before the war." At this point, Fay asks the interviewer if she would like to see it, and she is visibly disappointed when the interviewer explains they will be able to look at it at the end of the interview, but not at this moment. Fay's description emphasizes the material presence of the text and the lengths she went to preserve it. The physical haggadah takes on additional meaning as a tangible reminder of her life before the war, in particular her Jewish literacy. As a young girl, Fay attended Bais Jacob, an Orthodox school for girls. From the interview, it is clear that Fay took pride in her Jewish education and the presence of the haggadah serves as a sign of her knowledge. In addition, the haggadah functions as a symbol of Fay's defiance. Even as the Nazis attempt to make Jews and Judaism part of the past, Fay holds onto this central text of Jewish identity. Throughout her testimony, Fay emphasizes moments where she was able to resist or fight back against the Nazis. Her preservation of the text at high risk to herself is another act of defiance.

Fay then begins to tell the Exodus story as part of her testimony, a surprising addition to an interview focused on her experience during the Holocaust. The fact that Fay stops to narrate the Exodus story suggests that the Exodus story itself, or at least this particular telling of it, plays a significant role in her understanding of her Holocaust experience. She begins by saying she conducted the seder in Sosnowiec "for an hour" and then gives the central plotline told during the seder. Given that the Exodus story itself is well known, why would she tell the story within her testimony? She does not tell us. One plausible interpretation is that the haggadah connects her to her father; another is that recounting the story demonstrates her Jewish literacy and connects her to her childhood. Of course, both of these reasons could be valid. She begins with the well-known recitation: we were in bondage and God took us out; God selected Moses to lead the Israelites out from Egypt; bitter herbs represent the bitterness of slavery; matzah is the bread of affliction. Her interactions with the other girls play a crucial role in her testimony: "I start to explain what Passover is and everybody is asking me: How do you remember this? I have a haggadah from home, but I don't want to keep it outside because I don't want that they should see it. I studied it before." Fay affirms her legitimate claim to the text and then continues her testimony: "So I told them all about the Egyptians. The bondage they did. The work that they had to do. The lime, and later they had to look for straws to make the bricks, and they had to make the bricks." As she continues, her narration takes a stunning turn, a deviation from the familiar story, which Fay seamlessly weaves into the narrative: "If they don't have the full bricks to put into the wall, they put the kids into the wall, or sometimes the father and the mother had to be baked into the wall. That was a very heavy bondage." Baking children into the wall! What are we to make of this disturbing addition to the narrative?

Perhaps this is a post-Holocaust addition to the story, a reading of her own experience of horror into the Passover story. Dori Laub, a psychoanalyst who spent many years collecting Holocaust testimonies for the archive housed at Yale University, suggests displacement and misremembering are ways traumatic knowledge may appear within a narrative and speak to a truth that breaks the framework of ordinary, historical understanding. In

Testimony: Crises of Witnessing in Literature, Psychoanalysis, and History, Laub describes a woman's testimony about the uprising at Auschwitz: "A sudden intensity, passion and color were infused into the narrative. She was fully there. 'All of a sudden,' she said, 'we saw four chimneys going up in flames, exploding. The flames shot into the sky, people were running. It was unbelievable.'" According to Laub her affect was intense as if "a dazzling, brilliant moment from the past swept through the frozen stillness of the muted, grave-like landscape with dashing meteoric speed, exploding it into a shower of sights and sounds." And when she finished recounting this episode, Laub continues, "she became subdued again and her voice resumed the uneventful, almost monotonous and lamenting tone."[21] Laub's hyperbolic description matches the woman's hyperbolic account of the uprising. We learn that the woman's testimony was historically inaccurate; only one chimney was blown up, not all four. Some would argue that this discrepancy invalidates the entirety of her account. Laub suggests, however, that the woman testified "not to the number of the chimneys blown up, but to something more radical, more crucial: the reality of an unimaginable occurrence. One chimney blown up in Auschwitz was as incredible as four. The number mattered less than the fact of the occurrence. The event itself was almost inconceivable. The woman testified to an event that broke the all-compelling frame of Auschwitz, where Jewish armed revolts just did not happen, and had no place. She testified to the breakage of the framework. That was historical truth."[22] Conceivably, Fay's testimony should also be understood as traumatic testimony that speaks to the historical truth of the horrors she experienced and witnessed.

Perhaps Fay really did recount the story this way at the seder in Sosnowiec, repeating the story as she remembered it from her childhood seder. An eleventh-century midrash accuses the Egyptians of using Hebrew children as mortar. The legend presents a dialogue between God and the angels, including Uzza, the angel of the Egyptians. Uzza pleads with God to show mercy rather than justice to the Egyptians. God appears almost convinced until the angel Michael sends the angel Gabriel to Egypt who returns with "a brick for which a Hebrew child had been used as mortar" as evidence of the extreme cruelty of the Egyptians.[23] God's attribute of justice prevails, according to the midrash, and the Egyptians are drowned in the sea. A version of the legend may have been recounted during Fay's childhood seders. Although this midrash does not appear within the central story and does not seem to be well known today, we cannot rule out the possibility that a tale of children used as bricks was fixed into her childhood memory. Regardless of the source, it is a critical component of Fay's midrash on the intersection of Holocaust and haggadah.

Continuing the Exodus story, Fay returns to the familiar: "God took us out from Egypt with Moses." God sustained the Israelites in the desert with manna. The Israelites accept God's covenant and agree to keep the Sabbath holy. With the addition of baking children or their parents into the wall, perhaps Fay made an implicit comparison between her experience and the Exodus story. In the following segment, she makes the comparison explicit. Fay says, "And everybody was looking at me and smiling. Now we are in a bondage from the Germans. We have to do our work, what is expected of us. God willing we gonna be also liberated from this bondage. So everybody said, 'Shut your mouth. Don't talk so loud because you gonna not be liberated if you're gonna talk like that.'" The comparison is rejected as the response by the other women is shaped by fear. Talk is dangerous, and these words cannot be said. Fay gives her response: "So I said, 'Please I didn't say nothing. You didn't hear nothing.' And I took away my words. And they said, 'Because it's you we believe you. And we don't want to repeat it, but don't say those words no more.'" Fay concludes this narrative as it began: "And I conducted it for an hour." Fay's word choice is striking: "*I took away my words.*" The primary purpose of the haggadah is to tell the story. The term means "the telling." Yet here we have a story that could not yet be told. Perhaps, the implicit addition of the Holocaust story into the Exodus emerges because the explicit comparison was so forcefully denied.[24]

The last testimony to consider bridges past and present commemorations. Alfred P. was a teenager when he was in Dornhau with his father. Toward the conclusion of his testimony, he says, "Let me mention one other incident for camp life, which several years ago I decided to be the starting point of my seder because I just feel that members of my family, and thank God, at almost every seder we have new family members—kids at our seder table, and I really want this to really survive in my family, this story to survive and not be forgotten in my family." Alfred tells this story yearly, and his recounting reads well without editorial comment.

> It was the Passover of 1945 about a month away already from our liberation which we didn't know when it would take place. But there were rumors in the camp. There were always rumors about all sorts of things, but there were rumors in the camp that say the Russians are so close already. We might be liberated at any time. Except the Germans don't allow camps to be liberated with inmates still in place.

They usually either kill off the camp or they march them towards the inside of Germany. We heard rumors of the so-called death marches, which truly indeed were death marches. We also heard that one of the reasons they turn into death marches is because practically there is no food, or very, very little—a lot less than even what we were getting in the camp. So we decided, with my father, that from that really, truly meager portion of bread that we were receiving in the camp, everyday we are going to slice off a tiny, tiny piece. And we are going to save it up for the march.

After a few weeks, we already had what was considered in the camp a huge fortune because we may have had three or four pounds of very dried up bread. Nevertheless, that certainly didn't matter there, and we had it hidden in our bed; it gave us a little bit of security that might be instrumental in our surviving the march. Now one day I came in from work, and my father sat me down and said, "now I hope you will understand what I'm about to tell you. You won't like it, but you will understand it I'm sure. I gave away all the bread we saved because a small new transport arrived to the camp, and I found out that one of the men somehow managed to smuggle in a prayer book, an old, small prayer book he smuggled in. It was unbelievable, and I bought it. I gave him all the bread we saved up."

Alfred's testimony continues, "I started to cry. But finally, as always, I eventually always understood my father's actions and accepted it, and approved of it. In my eyes he had never really done anything wrong." Alfred pauses at this point in the testimony as his eyes tear up: "So a few days later when it happened to be Passover night my father held a seder because this little book contained the entire haggadah, and I will never, ever forget the scene. There were hundreds of inmates sitting on the bunks, on the floor, in silence, listening to my father reading the haggadah from the beginning." Once again Alfred pauses. He is choked up and tearing. He clears his throat and concludes the story: "I'm sure that this instilled some hope and courage and added a little extra strength to these people. And he helped a tiny bit for them to survive."[25]

The seder scene in *The Devil's Arithmetic* is no longer merely kitsch. Hannah pleads to the rabbi to tell her how to conduct a seder to help ensure Rivka's survival. Alfred P. begins his seder every year with the story about the trade of carefully saved bread for a haggadah and asserts this also helped people survive. The previous testimonies expressed the numerous ways

Jews in concentration camps commemorated Passover as survivors reflected back on their experiences. Their reflections contain multiple, sometimes contradictory, assessments. Clearly, we can derive no single meaning from analysis of these testimonies. In fact, if one central principle emerges from these testimonies, it is that memory of the Shoah in the haggadah should preserve the multiplicity of meanings held by survivors. This includes both the choices they made at the time, within the very limited range of options available, and their assessments of those choices preserved in these testimonies for future generations. For some, commemorating Passover, whether through avoiding chametz, making matzah, or holding a seder, was a life-affirming act. For others, commemorating Passover was life-negating, a senseless act in the struggle for survival. All of these testimonies, however, come from people for whom marking Passover in a concentration camp was worth remembering more than fifty years later.

We have seen the pivotal role the haggadah played in several testimonies from Holocaust survivors, ways in which their Holocaust experiences shaped their telling of the Passover story, and how the Exodus impacted their testimony about their experiences during the Shoah. Now we shift from oral to written text, to a haggadah written immediately after the war by Yosef Dov Sheinson, a Jew who survived four years in the concentration camps. *A Survivors' Haggadah* was used at a seder in Munich, Germany, in 1946. Abraham Klausner, the U.S. Army chaplain who presided over the seder, wrote a preface to the version of the haggadah examined here. Both the preface and the haggadah present lessons learned from the Nazi genocide, lessons that shape the telling of the story. Moreover, both authors use the haggadah as a vehicle to persuade their audiences to take particular action in light of these lessons learned.

Liberated But Not Free: Holocaust Memory in *A Survivors' Haggadah*

For many of the surviving Jews of Europe, freedom did not come with liberation. In camps such as Dachau, the U.S. Army came and locked the camp so that former prisoners were still confined behind barbed wire. In the context of the aftermath of World War II, people use the term "liberation" to refer to the turning over of the camps to the Allies, but the process of being truly free and experiencing freedom took much longer. During the course of the war, many Jews had been transported far from home. Survivors were often in poor health, and many thousands succumbed to disease and malnutrition after the end of the war. Between 1945 and 1952 more than 250,000 Jewish Displaced Persons lived in camps and urban centers in Germany, Austria, and Italy under administration by Allied authorities and the United Nations Relief and Rehabilitation Administration. Immediately following the war, Jews were a minority in the Displaced Persons (DP) camps. However, while repatriation of non-Jewish former concentration camp inmates, prisoners of war, and Eastern European nationals proceeded relatively smoothly, return of the liberated Jewish population to their previous residences proved much more difficult. Many Jews had no homes to return to, or no desire to live among those who either collaborated with the Nazi regime or stood by while Jewish lives were destroyed. Others returned only to encounter virulent anti-Semitism. Thus many Jews remained in, or returned to, the American and British Allied zones. From there, Jews engaged in the often arduous process of trying to leave Europe and emigrate to the United States or Palestine.

Prior to May 14, 1948, with official recognition of the state of Israel, Jewish immigration to Palestine was illegal. The British government controlled Palestine and refused entry to Holocaust survivors, who organized and referred to themselves as *she'erit hapletah,* the surviving remnant, a biblical reference to the Israelites who returned to Jerusalem after the Babylonian exile in the sixth century B.C.E. (Ezra 9:14; 1 Chronicles 4:43). Throughout the first four decades of the twentieth century, fierce debates raged in Western and Eastern Europe regarding the desirability of a Jewish nation-state. After the Nazi genocide, almost all Jewish survivors, including those who had been staunchly anti-Zionist before the war, recognized the necessity for an autonomous Jewish state. The illegal organization *Bricha,* the Hebrew term for "escape" or "flight," brought Jews from Eastern Europe via Hungary or Czechoslovakia to the DP camps and surrounding areas in Germany. In September 1945, the U.S. Army estimated that approximately two thousand Jews lived in Munich; by April 1946, estimates ranged from six to seven thousand, the increase due largely to the efforts of Bricha.[26]

Yosef Dov Sheinson, an active Zionist who survived four years in various slave-labor concentration camps, created *A Survivors' Haggadah* in this context. The following analysis uses a facsimile published in 2000 by the Jewish Publication Society with introduction and commentary by Saul Touster, an emeritus professor at Brandeis University, who discovered the haggadah while sorting through his father's papers. Sheinson wrote the text of the haggadah, designed its page borders, and selected the art, woodcuts by Miklós Adler, another Holocaust survivor. Sheinson was already an ardent Zionist before the war, and *A Survivors' Haggadah* was first published by two Zionist organizations active within the DP camps.

The version reproduced by the Jewish Publication Society was published by the United States Army of Occupation, which raises the question: How did a Passover haggadah written by a European Holocaust survivor become an official publication of the U.S. Occupying Army? The republication of the haggadah and the seder in Munich, Germany, at which it was used in 1946, were due largely to the efforts of Abraham J. Klausner, who served as an American Jewish military chaplain in the U.S. Occupying Army. Klausner's efforts to help survivors at the end of the war were enormous. He was instrumental in improving the situation of survivors in the DP camps by making certain that Earl G. Harrison, who was sent by President Harry Truman to investigate the status of DPs under the U.S. Army, personally saw the problems Jews faced in the camps after liberation. The response to the resulting Harrison report ended some of the most egregious conditions facing European Jews in camps controlled by the U.S. Army. Klausner also compiled lists of names of survivors, assisted the efforts of Bricha, and advocated for Jewish self-government in the DP camps. According to Klausner and several attendees, approximately two hundred participants, most of whom were Holocaust survivors, participated in the seders in Munich on April 15 and 16, 1946.

Klausner's preface to *A Survivors' Haggadah* is the only part of the haggadah written in English. In these two pages, Klausner sets forth several key ideas. First, he establishes the parallel relationship between Pharaoh and Egypt and Hitler and Germany that runs through the haggadah. He notes that although the participants "spoke of Pharaoh and the Egyptian bondage . . . in their hearts they felt very close to all that which was narrated. Pharaoh and Egypt gave way to Hitler and Germany."[27] Even more significant than the similarity is the recognition of a crucial difference: while the seder celebrates the liberation from slavery, the she'erit hapletah, while liberated from the Nazis, are not completely free. Liberation remains incomplete, especially for those Jews who want to emigrate to Palestine. Moreover, he pointedly argues that the Allied powers have an obligation to guarantee the complete liberation of the survivors. Klausner writes the preface as if its primary readers, attendees of the seder, were Jewish members of the U.S. Army, "the khaki-clad sons of Israel," although the vast majority of the attendees were survivors who lived in and around the camp.[28] He describes the situation of the survivors and suggests that "just beyond the sounds of the Seder" survivors celebrate their first Passover after liberation. Klausner's words are poignant as he describes the gap between liberation and freedom: "The former slave sat in company with his tantalizing memories and celebrated his first Passover since liberation. He fumbled his life-giving gift, trying as best he could to understand this miracle of freedom. It was not all that he had dreamed of." Klausner places blame with the Allies who prevent "complete liberty," referring primarily to the inability of survivors to emigrate to Palestine. He concludes the preface with a warning to the world that "in the slavery of a single human being the world would find itself enslaved."[29]

The parallels between Pharaoh and Hitler and between Egypt and Nazi Germany also appear in Sheinson's border art. The cover page of the haggadah shows a clear trajectory from slavery to freedom. Touster notes this as well in his commentary on *A Survivors' Haggadah:* "The border designs in the right column contain traditional imagery of the slavery in Egypt, while in the left column the celebration of the Seder (wine, matzah, Paschal sheep) suggests that *that* slavery is long over."[30] The next page begins Klausner's preface, and the border moves from past to present. The traditional iconography of the pyramid and slave driver is replaced by a Nazi figure standing on a dead body. Bearded Israelites in loincloths weighed down by heavy loads become skeletal Jews in striped prison garb weighed down by heavy loads. In the left column, the elements of celebration are replaced by imagery that suggests a journey in progress. The boat sails to Jerusalem where "the trowel will build and the sickle will harvest."[31] This imagery leads the reader from past to present, and from Egypt to Germany, where the remainder of Sheinson's Exodus narrative takes place.

A Survivors' Haggadah maintains a direct, sustained analogy between slavery in Egypt and the Holocaust in Germany, but the emphasis of this story is not the past. The central telling, the maggid of this haggadah, is not the slavery of the distant past imagined as one's present, but rather the very recent past, as well as the present moment of the survivors. The page following the preface, the last text in English, presents a single line, which clearly completes the temporal and geographic shift: "We were slaves to Hitler in Germany . . ." The shift is maintained by the border art as well. Surrounding this solitary line of text is a border that graphically depicts the violence of the Nazi genocide: flames consuming a man, an axe in the midst of a decapitation, a knife slitting a throat with two drops of blood dripping from the knife, the gas showers that led to the crematoria, a skull peering out from behind barbed wire, and smokestacks.

FIGURE 2.1 The Violence of the Nazi Genocide. *Reprinted from* A Survivors' Haggadah, © *2000 by Yosef Dov Sheinson and edited by Saul Touster, published by The Jewish Publication Society, with the permission of the publisher.*

Following this brutal introduction to Sheinson's representation of the experiences of "slaves to Hitler in Germany," Sheinson uses the language of the traditional haggadah to tell the story of Jews during the Holocaust. His concise telling is rife with echoes of traditional haggadah language. For example, after describing the inaction of the Allies, the horrendous suffering inflicted by "that evil man" Hitler, and the various motives of Christians who hid Israelite children, Sheinson writes, "the children of Israel groaned and cried out," a direct repetition of the language of the haggadah. His next sentence echoes the haggadah as well: "And they cried to the Lord, the God of their fathers, who saw their suffering and oppression, and their cry went up." Sheinson also uses the language of the haggadah to describe the saving actions of the Allies: "Finally, the enemies of that evil man grew indignant, and they girded themselves and unleashed against that man of evil and his people great wrath, rage, fury, disaster, and a band of avenging angels, afflicting them with two hundred and fifty plagues." The Allies, and not God, are the agents of redemption, although "God hardened Hitler's heart," as God did to Pharaoh so many centuries before. Sheinson concludes the maggid with the Allies coming to the rescue; finally "the Holocaust survivors in the camps are rescued and redeemed."[32]

In the traditional haggadah, the cause of slavery is attributed to the rise of a Pharaoh "who knew not Joseph" and feared the increase in the number of Israelites. In Sheinson's contemporary analysis, Jews who chose to live in the diaspora must take some responsibility for their own situation. In *A Survivors' Haggadah,* the diaspora is the underlying cause of slavery. We see this most strikingly in Sheinson's presentation of the second of the Four Questions. The graphic border depicting Nazi brutality appears for the second and final time. Within it is the question, "Why do we eat this bitter herb?" along with Sheinson's answer:

> Because we were intoxicated by the incense of *Galut* [Diaspora],
> because we fled from one *Galut* [exile] to another,
> because we reassured ourselves saying: Ours will not be the fate that
>   befell our people before us.
> Because we did little to help ourselves and reestablish our destroyed
>   homes and country.[33]

If diaspora is the cause of slavery, then *aliyah,* emigration to Palestine, is required for freedom. Following the central narration of slavery and redemption, the rest of the haggadah presents the case for aliyah. Sheinson puts the need for emigration in the strongest possible terms: "The sorrow is great and so is the pain, such that the survivors swear to make an illegal *Aliyah,* no matter what, and go to the Holy Land at any cost; for it is hard for them to remain in lands that are soaked with their blood, and they long for Zion and their brethren there."[34]

Sheinson builds the case for aliyah as he presents the horrors of exile. His version of Dayenu, a text of praise in the traditional haggadah, serves as a striking example of this approach. In a traditional haggadah, the passage Dayenu lists the many gifts God has given the Jews, with the idea that any one of them "would have been sufficient" [Dayenu]. Sheinson writes a bitter, ironic text that turns Dayenu on its head, which begins with a harsh critique of God's acts in Jewish history: "Had He scattered us among nations but had not given us the First Crusade, we would have been content." Each line of Sheinson's Dayenu draws upon a legacy of suffering to demonstrate how awful it would be to remain in diaspora. Sheinson's version reads as an anti-Dayenu that recounts a legacy of horror in exile. The First Crusade is just the beginning. Included in Sheinson's Dayenu are the Second Crusade, the Blood Libel, the Third Crusade, the requirement to wear the yellow star in the Middle Ages, persecution following the black plague, the Inquisition, the pogroms of the seventeenth century, and the slaughter in Ukraine in 1919. The second half of this Dayenu lists horrors specific to the Nazi genocide: Hitler, the ghettos, gas chambers and crematoria, torture of wives and children, hard bondage, hunger, disease, and torture. For Sheinson, the lesson to be learned from this history is clear: Jews cannot live anywhere but the Promised Land. He concludes Dayenu with the admonition: "[S]ince all these have befallen us, we must make Aliyah, even if illegally, wipe out the Galut [diaspora], build the chosen land, and make a home for ourselves and our children for eternity."[35]

Sheinson clearly advocates direct action by Holocaust survivors on their own behalf, but God's role in Sheinson's text is not as clear. Sometimes, it seems that God shoulders some of the blame: Dayenu seems to hold God, not the nations, responsible as the ultimate cause of suffering. When the Children of Israel "groaned and cried out," for example, God did not hear them. And later, the nations who in "their great sorrow decided to keep silent" give God as one justification for their inaction when they lament, "perhaps this is the hand of God, and who are we to interfere in the conduct of the world."[36] At other times, God appears incapable of saving action. Sheinson's line in the maggid, "Babies were being killed and still no one knew what to do about it," could be read to include God amongst the clueless. Moreover, redemption comes from the Allies, not from God. The absence of God appears most powerfully in Sheinson's version of Nirtzah, the praises to God that conclude a traditional haggadah. Sheinson omits the praises and includes only the opening words: "Therefore we are bound . . ." These appear underneath one of Miklós Adler's woodcuts, which includes a disturbing image of three faces—a man, woman, and child—wafting up through the top of a smokestack, presumably the chimneys of the crematoria.[37] At the very top of the woodcut, above the chimney in black lettering imposed on white smoke, appears the phrase "*lech-lecha . . . al-ha-aretz*" echoing the emphatic command God gives to Abraham in Genesis "go forth . . . to the land that I will show you" (Gen. 12:1). The interactions of allusion and art by both Sheinson and Adler provide an ironic commentary. Perhaps the praises are absent in this Nirtzah because God is also absent. Despite this, before attributing a completely secular, atheistic view to Sheinson, consider the fact that the final page of *A Survivor's Haggadah* presents "Pour Out Thy Wrath." This traditional text pulls together passages from Psalms and Lamentations in a cry to God asking for acts of retribution upon the nations under whom the Jews suffered: "Pour Out Thy Wrath upon the nations that know Thee not, and upon the kingdoms that do not know Thy name. For they have devoured Jacob and laid waste his habitation. Pour out Thy indignation upon them, and let the fierceness of Thy anger overtake them. Pursue them in anger and destroy them under the heavens of the Lord."[38]

Memory Work and the Work of Memory

The haggadah is a text of memory. Its impetus derives from the command to remember found in the Bible and repeated throughout the haggadah. The shift from survivor testimonies to *A Survivors' Haggadah* included a shift from oral to written text, and from the individual to the group. *A Survivors' Haggadah* is the work of three men and the product of generations. The words and art of Sheinson, Klausner, and Adler build on the work of past Jews, who, over many centuries, established the general contours for telling the Exodus story and the specific texts within it. The twentieth-century authors place themselves in conversation with the past, and, in the process, shape our understanding of the present, as well as modify how we remember the past. In "Collective Memory and Cultural History: Problems of Method," Alon Confino argues that the term memory "links representation and social experience."[39] Confino's claim illuminates one way the command to remember functions in the haggadah. A closer examination of the link between social experience and representation provides insight into the process of memory work and the functions memory work serves.

The term "social experience" acknowledges that memory takes place in a communal context. Maurice Halbwachs, a French sociologist, argued for the communal location of memory when he coined the term "collective memory" in the 1920s. Taking issue with Freud, Halbwachs argued that there is no complete individual memory separate from its "localization" in social frameworks, which are determined by our position in various social groups such as family, social class, and religious affiliation.[40] All of the narratives presented in this chapter recall memories shaped by these frameworks. The celebration of Passover itself is a memory-practice located within the family and connected to a communal religious tradition. Halbwachs's argument, however, goes beyond the evident observation that Passover is celebrated in a group. The power of his insight resides in the realization that these group frameworks shape the content and contours of memory. The individuals' memories presented in this chapter share a common thread because their participation within the Jewish community shapes their shared understanding of core terms such as slavery, freedom, and redemption. A Jewish reading of freedom, for example, could differ markedly from a reading shaped by memory of the American Revolution, which emphasizes individuals banding together and, against great odds, fighting those in power for the sake of individual liberty. Freedom from slavery in a traditional Jewish context, by contrast, emphasizes the freedom to be part of a community that can fulfill obligations given by God. Traditional Jewish memory is not about individual freedom as much as communal responsibility. The similarities in the presentation of collective memory narrated by Fay, Tova, Alfred, Sheinson, and all the other survivors whose words enrich this chapter are due, to a large extent, to their shared "localization."

Nevertheless, each memory is also singular and unique. Seventy years after Halbwachs, James Young offered the term "collected memory" to preserve Halbwachs's insight and to highlight the work that undergirds memory.[41] Young's focus is often on memorials, including the ongoing and shifting social functions they serve. My own thinking about how memory works and the work of memory was influenced by Young, and I offer the plural "collected memories" to further highlight the multiple perspectives that shape memory. The term "collected memories" can provide important correctives to the singular collective memory as long as it does not overemphasize the role of the individual. Collected memories are not simply a collection of individual reminiscences, because a dominant interpretation and an authoritative reading of memory emerges from the communal context. In other words, certain memories of events are accepted while others are rejected. In Fay P.'s memory of the Exodus, for example, the other girls at the seder reject her reading of God's act of redemption in light of her current situation. Fay's reading of the Exodus as a present ideal was dangerous memory that did not fit the group's dominant self-understanding, although they could identify with the Exodus as part of their past. Memory works to establish a common story—such as the Exodus from Egypt—that members of a community share, one that imbues them with a sense of belonging and identity. Recalling memory, often in the form of re-telling a communal story, establishes, confirms, and shores up the boundaries of group identity.

"Collected" is a verb in the past tense as well as an adjective that describes memory. As a verb, it points to an activity. Memory is something we do. Placing the activity in the past tense emphasizes that the activity is no longer visible. Hence, memory seems like a natural, passive object rather than the result of a process of selection. Moreover, the construction of social memory is not a process of recollecting the past in its entirety but of selective representation of fragments deemed significant within our social context in the present. To the extent we choose what we remember, we also choose what we forget.[42] This dynamic of remembering and forgetting is a critical component of memory work. The term "memory work" further emphasizes that memory is neither given nor natural.[43] Understanding memory as an ongoing activity, a process of representation, rather than as a static object, foregrounds the fact that the process of memory is always selective, always already an interpretation. This raises an important set of questions: Who is doing the selection? Which memories are selected and for what purpose? Which memories are excluded? A study of memory requires careful attention to context, to the specific contours of the interpretive community. One must ask: What are the community's values and norms? Where is the locus of moral authority? Who is included and who is excluded? Collected memories and memory work are important concepts for understanding how the Shoah is commemorated in American Passover haggadot. These two concepts serve as reminders that the readings and re-readings of Holocaust texts presented in haggadot make claims about what should be remembered, by whom, and for what purpose.

CHAPTER 3

Wrestling with Redemption

>⊷⊷⊶○⊷⊷⊶

In remembrance lies the secret of redemption.
—The Ba'al Shem Tov

Holocaust memory redeems only when it falsifies.
—Lawrence Langer, *Admitting the Holocaust*

In this chapter we turn to an analysis
of the motif of redemption in the Passover haggadah, especially how redemption impacts commemoration of the Shoah within the Passover ritual.
At the Passover seder, Jews are commanded to tell the story of their slavery and redemption to their children, the next generation. As Yerushalmi
writes in his compendium of printed haggadot, "Passover is preeminently
the great historical festival of the Jewish people, and the *Haggadah* is its
book of remembrance and redemption. Here the memory of the nation is
annually revived and replenished, and the collective hope sustained. The ancient redemption of Israel from Egypt is recounted and relived, not merely
as an evocation from the past, but above all as prototype and surety for the
ultimate redemption yet to come. That, indeed, is the basic structure of
the *Haggadah* itself."[1] The experience of freedom-redemption must be remembered and enacted: "Remember this day, on which you went free from
Egypt, the house of bondage, how the Eternal One freed you from it with a
mighty hand . . . (Exodus 13:3)."[2] The experience of redemption carries the
responsibility to retell the narrative: "Had God not taken our ancestors out
of Egypt, then we and our children and our children's children would still
be enslaved to Pharaoh in Egypt. And even if all of us were experienced
in the ways of the world, all knowledgeable in Torah, it would still be our
responsibility to tell about the Exodus from Egypt."[3] But when it comes to
the Shoah, redemption poses a problem. This chapter begins with an answer to the question: "What is troubling about redemption?" The rest of the
chapter takes us through the ritual elements, narrative structure, and literary
motifs of the haggadah that have made it a compelling text of liberation and

redemption for generations of Jews. The overarching narrative structure of the haggadah derives from a dictum to "begin with degradation" and "end with glory," and this chapter concludes by examining how two popular and influential haggadot incorporate the Final Solution into this powerful narrative emplotment of redemption.

The Problem with (Value-added) Redemption

The description of redemption as a problem may be disconcerting to some readers because they usually construe redemption as a positive theological concept. In many Christian traditions, redemption means that an individual receives the gift of grace, salvation from sin, through Jesus' sacrifice. For Jews redemption is also communal. In the context of Passover, God redeems the Israelites from slavery. These two moments of redemption are foundational for Christianity and Judaism; individual Christians and Jews regularly commemorate, celebrate, and witness these events and their resulting positive—perhaps even transformative—effects through narrative and ritual. In both traditions, redemption brings freedom. These are important theological understandings of redemption. Despite this, many studies of the Holocaust proffer a strong critique of redemption, particularly in regard to narratives or art about the Holocaust that imbue the Nazi genocide with some sort of meaning.

Why would anyone argue against redemption? The word *redemption* carries a distinct meaning beyond the standard theological definition when people argue against redemption of the Holocaust. In addition to the freedom-giving theological meaning of redemption, something else is going on. An analogy with recycling may help point toward this "something else." When I lived in Michigan, the state began recycling pop cans. Every can included the phrase, "Michigan redemption value ten cents." In California, one finds the abbreviation CRV, "current redemption value" on every pop can. Before recycling, the value of the can was depleted after the last gulp; one would finish the drink and throw away the can. Recycling added value to an object previously perceived as being without worth. To distinguish this from "freedom-redemption"—the primary meaning of redemption in Jewish and Christian theologies—we can call this interrelated meaning "value-added redemption." While adding value may be good for container recycling, in terms of the Shoah, the value-added meaning of redemption is cause for concern. The film *The Devil's Arithmetic* once again provides an example. A brief look at how these two kinds of redemption appear in the film illustrates the difference between value-added and freedom-redemption. It also suggests that value-added redemption hampers one's ability to hear and to understand what witnesses to the Final Solution, like those whose testimonies appeared in the previous chapter, desire to tell.

One could read Hannah's journey from New Jersey through the Holocaust and back as a story of redemption. Hannah saves Rivkah/Aunt Eva through her actions. Moreover, through her "Holocaust experience," Hannah experiences her own redemption. Hannah appears at the beginning of the film as "the wicked child," to use the language of the haggadah, the one who does not see the value of the seder, and hence will not be redeemed: "What does the wicked child ask? 'What does this ritual mean to *you?*' (Exodus 12:26). To you and not to this child. Since this child withdraws from the community and denies God's role in the Exodus, challenge the child by replying, 'This is done because of what the Eternal One did for me when I went out of Egypt.' (Exodus 13:8). For me and not for you. Had you been there you would not have been redeemed."[4] By experiencing the concentration camp and ultimately sacrificing herself to save the life of her cousin Rivkah, Hannah learns what it meant, and what it means, to be a Jew. She returns to the present as the "wise child," and Passover plays a pivotal role as the sign of her personal journey from ignorance and slavery to knowledge and freedom. The seder, a celebration of freedom in its own right, also functions in the movie as a marker of Hannah's freedom-redemption.

By making the Holocaust the catalyst for Hannah's transformation, however, *The Devil's Arithmetic* also engages in value-added redemption. Hannah comes to appreciate her Jewish identity because of her experience in the concentration camp. At the beginning of the seder Hannah refuses to read aloud and rolls her eyes when the younger children participate enthusiastically. At the conclusion of the film, she leads all the seder participants in song and promises, "I will always remember what happened. Always." The film suggests that the Holocaust was the necessary cause of her positive Jewish identity, that without experiencing the Nazi genocide, Hannah would remain "the wicked child." As a result, the Holocaust takes on a positive role in shaping her Jewish identity. This value-added approach to the Holocaust in relation to American, adolescent Jewish identity is not limited to coming-of-age Hollywood filmmaking. Jewish educational materials regularly present the Holocaust as a way to shore up the boundaries of Jewish identity and to encourage American Jewish teens to affirm their heritage as a response to their knowledge of the twentieth-century genocide against the Jews. For example, through a program known as March of the Living, thousands of young adult Jews from the United States and around the world have made a pilgrimage to Poland "to understand the world that was destroyed" and from there to the state of Israel where they observe Holocaust Remembrance Day and Israeli Independence Day. The official website for March of the Living conceives the purpose of this journey from the death of European Jewry to the rebirth of Israel as a modern nation-state as redemptive: "The mission is to create memories, leading to a revitalized commitment to Judaism, Israel and the Jewish People."[5]

How can Jews remember the Holocaust during a celebration of redemption without redeeming the Holocaust itself, imbuing the Final Solution with some sort of value or meaning? Historian and Holocaust survivor Saul Friedländer suggests communal remembrance will be difficult. His essay "Trauma, Memory, and Transference" analyzes the redemptive contours of collective memory and its implications for remembering the Nazi genocide.[6] Friedländer draws on an analysis of Holocaust testimony to posit two types of survivor memory. Common memory reestablishes the pre-Holocaust self. Deep memory is an unassimilated trauma that remains enveloped in the experience of the Holocaust and cannot be expressed in language. Charlotte Delbo's commentary on the difference in meaning for "thirst," presented in chapter one, serves as an illustration of a pre- and post-Holocaust self.[7] A pre-Holocaust self can say "I am thirsty" and grab a beer from the refrigerator, while a post-Holocaust self when confronted by deep memory cannot. The Holocaust as traumatic event cannot be fully left behind. Friedländer takes this notion of two irreconcilable types of memory and extends it from individual to group or collective memory: "Individual common memory, as well as collective memory," writes Friedländer, "tends to restore or establish coherence, closure, and possibly a redemptive stance, notwithstanding the resistance of deep memory at the individual level."[8] Friedländer suggests that collective memory resembles individual common memory, especially in its desire to move beyond the Shoah. The establishment of coherence and closure may shape collected memories of the Holocaust, but at the cost of betraying the legacy of deep memory. Imagine an attempt to synthesize Delbo's disparate images of thirst so that they do not conflict. This is an example of coherence. Closure might require leaving the Holocaust meaning of thirst behind altogether. In both cases, the Holocaust experience is forgotten, perhaps even denied. Included among these tools of collective memory is the evocative term "redemptive stance," which suggests a form of memory that overcomes the persistent loss that deep memory refuses to let go. In the conclusion to his essay, Friedländer says, "at the individual level a redemptive closure (comforting or healing in effect), desirable as it would be, seems largely impossible."[9] In other words, individual victims often suffer life-long effects from their traumatic experiences. Yet, at the collective level, redemptive closure may be possible; communities can in various ways come to terms with the past or put the past behind them. However, these various forms of closure become problematic if collective memory is to bear faithful witness to individual Holocaust experiences. Friedländer asks whether collective remembrance includes some form of memory analogous to individual deep memory: "The question remains whether at the collective level as well an event such as the Shoah may, after all the survivors have disappeared, leave traces of a deep memory beyond individual recall, which will defy any attempt to give it meaning."[10]

As collective memory of the Shoah is brought into the haggadah, attempts to give it meaning are complicated by the presence of redemption. Norman Lamm and Lawrence Langer offer two extreme formulations of the general problem. Lamm is the chancellor of Yeshiva University, the premier Orthodox institution of higher learning in the United States. His 1986 Holocaust Remembrance Day address, "The Face of God: Thoughts on the Holocaust" works within the Jewish tradition and discusses the Shoah in conjunction with classic rabbinic concepts such as *tzaddik ve-ra lo* (the righteous who is afflicted), *mi-penei chata'einu* (because of our sins), and *hester panim* (the hiding of the face).[11] An emeritus professor of English, literary critic, and co-founder of the Fortunoff Video Archive for Holocaust Testimonies at Yale University, Langer lodges his critique of redemptive readings of the Holocaust within secular institutions. In "Pre-empting the Holocaust," one of his many writings on this subject, Langer places his critique within the Enlightenment liberal tradition that gave birth to and informed much of the great works of literature that he taught in his years as an English professor.[12] Although Lamm and Langer argue from different locations and with different guiding concepts and vocabulary, they both vigorously protest any interpretation of the Holocaust as a meaningful event.

Lamm begins with the assertion that the Holocaust does not present a new challenge to the question of theodicy; it is "a continuation of the ancient question of evil and suffering." Nevertheless, the Shoah does present a new challenge to the Jewish people, according to Lamm, because it calls into question God's "faithfulness" to the covenant between God and Israel "in the decimation of one third of the Jewish people and the trauma to the remaining two thirds."[13] He then suggests that the problem Jews face is one of meaning: "In trying to come to grips with the Holocaust and to probe, haltingly but inevitably, for some scrap of understanding of this cataclysm, we are confronted with an immediate dilemma: the very relevance of 'meaning' to the Holocaust."[14] He quickly rejects any explanation that accepts the Holocaust as divine providence to bring about the state of Israel because God appears incredibly unjust.[15] Lamm also surveys the few Orthodox thinkers who have attempted to posit some meaning to the Holocaust. Each offers some variation on *mi-penei chata'einu;* according to these views, six million Jews died during the Shoah as punishment from God "for our sins." The nature of the sin varies. The Satmarer Rebbe, Rabbi Yoel Moshe Teitelbaum, the most outspoken proponent of this view, argued that Zionists who actively worked to create the modern nation-state of Israel, against the centuries-long understanding that Jews must passively wait for the messiah in order to reclaim the Holy Land, were responsible for the Nazi genocide. Lamm proclaims that all variations of a "because of our sins" explanation are "massively irrelevant, impudent, and insensitive."[16]

Lamm offers three arguments from within Jewish tradition to support his rejection of this explanatory and meaning-making approach to the Holocaust. First, Lamm looks to the book of Job. Although Job was not guilty of any crime, his "friends" insisted he must be guilty because he suffered; in the end, his friends are rebuked by God, and Job's family and possessions are restored. Lamm suggests that Jews, especially those living in safety and after the fact, who accuse European Jewry of grievous sin are analogous to Job's "friends" and are themselves guilty of "criminal arrogance and brutal insensitivity."[17] Second, Lamm uses rabbinic interpretations of several biblical prooftexts to illustrate the rabbinic principle that one should not justify the punishment of the people Israel. For example, Moses was not allowed into the Promised Land because he called his fellow Israelites "rebels" (Num. 20:10). A second prooftext Lamm uses is from Isaiah. When Isaiah embellished his own confession of sin and tried to diminish his personal responsibility with the claim that he dwelt "in the midst of a people with unclean lips," one of the angels of God placed hot coal on his mouth (Isa. 6:7). According to midrash the angel did this so Isaiah could atone for criticizing his fellow Jews.[18] Lamm also cites a story from midrash where one rabbi puts sand in the mouth of another because "the Holy One does not approve of one who slanders Israel."[19] Third, Lamm criticizes those who explain the Holocaust as "punishment for our sins" because they exclude themselves from blame. Each Jew is actually criticizing other Jews—the Zionist blames the non-Zionist, the religious Jew blames the secular Jew, and so forth. Lamm concludes his critique: "In sum, if we ask, if we may resort to the *mi-penei chata'einu* rationale for the Holocaust, my answer is a resounding no—indeed, six million times, no!"[20]

Lamm is hesitant, however, to eschew the issue of meaning altogether and offers an exploration of meaning as a framework for understanding the Shoah, rather than as rationale or explanation for the murder of six million. Lamm's framework encapsulates the entire philosophy of Jewish history, beginning with the covenantal relationship between God and Israel. Imagine a relationship between lovers characterized by trust and mutuality where each gazes longingly into the eyes of the other. When one partner is hurt by the words or actions of the other s/he will turn away, refuse to meet the partner's gaze. Eventually the partner, encountering a face which is turned away, will also turn away. In terms of Lamm's analysis of the relationship between God and Israel, the people sin against God; God punishes Israel, which causes the people to turn away as they perceive God's punishment as absence or indifference. Eventually, God also turns away and "hides God's face" (*hester panim*), which leaves the collective Israel to the fate of nature and history without divine providence:

> The *totality* of Jewish history, from the beginning, to the messianic
> end point, is the highest form of meaning, in that it represents the
> engagement of man with God; and by "meaning," I intend noth-
> ing less than the universal redemptive design of history. However,
> *within* this process of meaning there exists a hiatus, a blank, an
> empty space, a "bubble," in which meaninglessness pervades. In
> this period, which is the epoch of *Hester Panim,* the history of the
> people as such makes no sense; that is, this period taken by *itself,*
> other than the sheer survival of Israel, shows no specific responsive-
> ness to a divine plan. It is thus, in a manner of speaking, a period of
> "meaningful meaninglessness."[21]

Lamm's dramatic conclusion is that all of Jewish history from the destruction of the Second Temple in the first century C.E. through the Holocaust in the twentieth century is meaningless in terms of the overall redemptive thrust of Jewish history. This reading of Jewish history is astounding. Lamm would rather remove God from the history of the Common Era altogether than grant explanatory, value-added redemptive meaning to the Holocaust.[22]

Lawrence Langer also rejects any form of meaning-making in rela-
tion to the Holocaust. Langer argues that redemptive memory is an attempt, primarily by those who did not experience the Holocaust, to attach some meaning to the horror in a way that ultimately is a betrayal of the survivors'

experiences. Langer believes "[t]he need to make the Holocaust appear more harmless than it was has many roots, and hence many branches, leaves, and blossoms."[23] Thus, he has spent much of his career challenging redemptive readings of the Shoah. In "Pre-empting the Holocaust," he argues that the problem with redemptive readings is twofold. First, redemptive readings necessarily gloss over the particular harms suffered by individuals during the Nazi genocide. Second, in moving from particular to universal, redemptive readings minimize the key fact that Jews were the primary targets of the Nazi genocide.

Langer uses the term "pre-empting" to refer to using the Holocaust "to fortify a prior commitment to ideals of moral reality, community responsibility, or religious belief that leave us with space to retain faith in their pristine value in a post-Holocaust world."[24] Langer believes that faith in any of these universal values cannot be maintained once one takes seriously the atrocities committed during the Holocaust. To show this, he presents in graphic detail horrifying, mind-numbing, inconceivable descriptions of atrocity: a baby torn in half before its mother's eyes by an SS man when she refused to hand over her one-year-old infant to be murdered along with all the other children in the Kovno ghetto; a doctor who beheaded two young Jews, boiled the flesh off their skulls and displayed them as trophies; a Jewish community whose members were ordered by the Gestapo to strip naked and jump into a large pit where they were boiled alive. In addition to horrific suffering, in each case cherished values were shattered. Certainly, the recognition of the bond between mother and child would triumph over a desire for destruction. Certainly, a doctor trained to heal others would not glorify and take pleasure in causing harm. Certainly, the basic decency of human beings would prevail. But these "certainties" are no longer certain after the Holocaust. In Langer's view, misguided people who hold these values, and others like them, as certainties after the Shoah "evoke the redemptive rather than the grievous power of memory" in an attempt to avoid the implications of the Holocaust for humankind.[25]

Langer also notes that not only were these events horrific, but also that the Nazis targeted these horrors most directly, most intentionally, and most systematically at Jews. Those who look for universal lessons to be learned by study of the Final Solution often ignore this key fact. Langer echoes many critics who protest representations of the Holocaust that downplay the Jewish identity of the primary targets: "If Jewish experience in the Holocaust can be made to 'stand for' something else, some 'larger human experience' . . . then the intolerable may seem more tolerable through the sheer invocation of patterns or analogies."[26] The clearest example of this approach is found in Langer's critique of artist Judy Chicago. In *Holocaust Project: From Darkness to Light,* Chicago traces her own encounter with the Holocaust, including its challenge to her suppositions about the goodness of humankind. She plunged into darkness, but moves from "darkness" to "light" as she realizes that "the unique Jewish experience of the Holocaust could be a window into an aspect of the unarticulated but universal human experience of victimization."[27] The Holocaust is made meaningful for Chicago when she forges links between particular Jewish suffering and "the vulnerability of all human beings and, by extension, of all species and our fragile planet as well."[28] In this move, the particularity of the Holocaust is lost altogether, and the Holocaust is made meaningful at the price of mitigating victims' and survivors' experiences.

Freedom-Redemption in the Haggadah

The experience of redemption poses a particular challenge when Jews confront the Shoah in the context of Passover, as freedom-redemption and value-added redemption often become intertwined. While redemption is suspect in Holocaust discourse, it is the central motif of the haggadah. During Passover, Jews are commanded to remember that they were slaves and that they were redeemed. The command to remember is both communal and personal, a remembrance of past history and a recognition of current reality. The haggadah emphasizes this personal element: "In every generation, each individual should feel personally redeemed from Egypt, as it is said: 'You shall explain to your child on that day, it is because of what the Eternal One did for me when I went free from Egypt.'"[29] Another name for Passover is *zeman heiruteinu,* the season of our liberation, and the redemptive aspect of Passover, arguably its *raison d'être,* poses a tremendous challenge to Holocaust remembrance in the haggadah. Before turning to an analysis of this challenge, I will focus on how the central acts of drinking and eating performed by seder participants create and sustain embodied memory of redemption.

Wine—A Symbol of Joy

The opening ritual action of the Passover seder is Kadesh, the blessing over the first of the four cups of wine drunk by participants at designated points during the seder. Haggadot often connect these four cups of wine to the book of Exodus, which employs four verbs to describe God's salvific actions: "I will free you (*v'hotzati*) from the burden of the Egyptians and deliver you (*v'hitzalti*) from their bondage. I will redeem you (*v'galti*) with an outstretched arm and through extraordinary chastisements. And I will take you (*v'lakachti*) to be My people, and I will be your God" (Exod. 6:6–6:7). Each verb indicates God's acts of redemption. Many haggadot include commentary to make this link to the biblical text explicit. The Conservative haggadah, for example, prefaces the blessing over the first cup of wine with a reflection on the ritual action: "I am ready to fulfill the commandment of drinking the first of the Four Cups. This recalls God's promise of redemption to the people of Israel, as it says, 'I will free you from the burden of the Egyptians' (Exodus 6:6)."[30] A reflection with a similar formula precedes the other three cups as well.

In addition to the four cups of wine that commemorate past and ongoing redemption, a cup of wine is also set on the table for Elijah, the harbinger of the messiah. The seder celebrates past and current redemption, and Elijah's cup symbolizes future redemption. The Reconstructionist haggadah introduces the cup of Elijah with a description of the prophet: "Elijah, the eternal companion of the Jewish people, will herald the messianic age. In the meantime, he reminds us of the hope he carries. He reappears at moments when hope is tangible—at the seder and at the birth of children."[31] As a gesture of welcome, the front door is opened during the seder, often by a child. On the seder table, the cup for Elijah symbolizes a world-to-come dramatically different from the unredeemed world in which we now live. Some haggadot, including the Silverman edition utilized in *The Devil's Arithmetic,* incorporate a Holocaust commemoration at this point in the seder. Silverman's text, published in 1959, includes a responsive reading "to recall the bitter catastrophe which so recently has befallen our people in Europe."[32] In the film, Hannah begins her own engagement with the Shoah when the seder participants turn to this page of Silverman's haggadah. Hannah enters the past when she opens the door for Elijah. Opening the door begins the journey that allows her transformation, Hannah's personal redemption as a Jew that concludes the film.

Elijah is a symbol of hope for the future, but the ritual surrounding Elijah's cup often notes that this hope is not yet reality. In many haggadot the ritual to open the door for Elijah is preceded by "Pour Out Your Wrath," a text probably written during the Middle Ages, perhaps after the Crusades. The short text is a compilation of biblical verses from Psalms and Lamentations: "Pour out Your wrath upon those who do not know You and upon the governments which do not call upon Your name. For they have devoured Jacob and laid waste his dwelling place (Psalms 79:6–7). Pour out Your fury upon them, let the fierceness of Your anger overtake them (Psalms 69:25). Pursue them in indignation and destroy them from under Your heavens (Lamentations 3:66)."[33] Some contemporary haggadot, including the 1972 Reform version and the 1999 Reconstructionist haggadah, do not include "Pour Out Your Wrath." Others offer an alternative reading following the traditional passage. The new Reform haggadah, published in 2002, opts for this approach: "Give up anger, abandon fury, put aside your wrath; it can only harm. The call to violence shall no longer be heard in your land, nor the cry of desolation within your borders. If your enemy is hungry, give him bread to eat. If she is thirsty, give her water to drink. For when compassion and truth meet, justice and peace kiss."[34] This text parallels "Pour Out Your Wrath" in its structure by drawing from biblical texts, in this case Psalms, Isaiah, and Proverbs, and affirms the possibility of redemption by setting specific tasks in the realm of human action. In a world redeemed, one cares for one's enemies; in a world redeemed, compassion, truth, justice, and peace reign.

Rabban Gamliel and the Three Necessary Foods

In addition to wine, several foods play prominent roles in transmitting the meaning of freedom-redemption during the seder. Following the teachings of Gamliel, a political and religious leader of the Jewish community in Israel in the first and second centuries C.E., before the actual meal can begin the presence and meaning of three ritual foods must be made clear: "Rabban Gamliel would say: 'Those who have not explained three things during the seder have not fulfilled their obligation. These are matzah, maror, and the pesaḥ offering.'"[35] Each explanation ties the present meal, and the food physically present on the table, to the biblical story in Exodus. Before blessing and eating the matzah, those present ask, "Why do we eat it?" and continue with an answer, "In order to remind ourselves that even before the dough of our ancestors could become leavened bread, the Holy One was revealed to the people and redeemed them."[36] The paragraph concludes with the biblical reference to matzah in Exodus 12:39: "And they baked unleavened cakes of dough that they had taken out of Egypt, for it was not leavened, since they had been driven out of Egypt and they could not delay; nor had they prepared any provisions for themselves." While the biblical verse dramatically emphasizes that the dough did not have time to rise as the Israelites hurried out of Egypt to escape Pharaoh, the preface focuses our attention on God's actions. The preface to this passage clearly foregrounds the redemptive element of the Exodus, and the explanation for bitter herbs follows a similar format.

The text explains the pesach offering and connects it to the biblical passage: "You shall say, 'It is the Pesaḥ sacrifice to the Eternal One, because God passed over the houses of the Israelites in Egypt when God smote the Egyptians, but saved our houses'" (Exod. 12:27). God's saving actions and God's destruction on behalf of the Israelites are clear. With an understanding that sacrificial offerings may not speak to a liberal audience, the passage is flanked in the Reconstructionist haggadah by contemporary commentary. Almost every page of the Reconstructionist haggadah includes commentary along the page margins. Sometimes traditional rabbinic texts are quoted in the margins; often, new commentaries on the tradition are presented.

The two margin passages next to the presentation of Exodus 12:27 are new midrash on the pesach offering. They illustrate contemporary renderings of the pesach offering as a ritual of redemption. In the left margin, Naamah Kelman imagines the offering as an "annual gathering of Jews who were celebrating religious independence and hoping for national liberation. Hundreds of thousands of Jews would come to Jerusalem to proclaim the hope for redemption. This was our ancient 'Independence Day.'"[37] Commentary from Toba Spitzer occupies the right margin: "What is the significance of the pesaḥ, the paschal lamb? On the night before they were to leave Egypt, the Israelites were told to slaughter a lamb and paint their doorposts with its blood, a sign to the destroying angel not to take the first born in those homes. Today we no longer sacrifice an animal, but we do remember that night of terror and hope, a prelude to redemption." Up to this point, Spitzer's commentary is a fairly traditional summary of the biblical narrative. The conclusion of her commentary, however, presents a decidedly contemporary rendering of the meaning of the pesach offering with resonances of multicultural identity politics: "The pesaḥ is a reminder that freedom begins when we mark our doors, when we take the risk of speaking up and standing out. Saying no to oppression, being open and proud of our Judaism, allowing ourselves to be fully who we are, daring to believe that things will be different—this is how we mark ourselves as people on the road to liberation."[38]

"Cloud of Smoke, Pillar of Fire": Holocaust, Haggadah, and the Challenge of Redemption

Can Holocaust memory be placed within the Passover seder in a way that holds to the core truths of both events, without creating closure and without losing deep memory to the pull of redemption? No theologian has wrestled with this question as sincerely and provocatively as Irving

Greenberg, an Orthodox rabbi and the president of the nondenominational Jewish Life Network. Greenberg's opening claims in his essay, "Cloud of Smoke, Pillar of Fire: Judaism, Christianity, and Modernity after the Holocaust," set forth the dilemma. Because his essay, published in 1977, profoundly influenced how people came to understand the role of the Holocaust in Jewish life and because he focuses specifically on the relationship between the Holocaust and Exodus, his work is worth analyzing in some detail. Greenberg begins "Cloud of Smoke, Pillar of Fire" with the claim that Judaism and Christianity are religions of redemption. According to Greenberg, both Judaism and Christianity claim "redemption will be realized in actual human history."[39] Implicit in this formulation is the idea that historical events shape fundamental norms. Greenberg makes an ethical claim and argues that the Holocaust is, and should be, one such event. In other words, the standards and ideals Jews use to shape their lives today must be informed by the experience of the Holocaust.[40]

How does Greenberg develop this ethical challenge? First, he must demonstrate that the Holocaust is indeed central to Jews and to Judaism. Second, he must illustrate what a Judaism re-oriented to post-Holocaust fundamental norms looks like. Greenberg tackles the first task in two parts. His evidence is both statistical and theological. At the outset, Greenberg presents the numbers of destruction: 90 percent of Eastern European Jewry dead; one-third of all Jewry, which includes "80 percent of the Jewish scholars, rabbis, full-time students and teachers of Torah alive in 1939," destroyed.[41] "For this reason alone," Greenberg argues, "the trauma of the Holocaust cannot be overcome without some basic reorientation in light of it by the surviving Jewish community."[42] After presenting these devastating statistics, Greenberg turns to the realm of theology. He presents two traditional Jewish theological claims. One, the Exodus provides testimony that God acts in history and that God is a redeemer. The language of witness to this theological truth both in the past and the present is foundational to Jewish theology and pervades the Passover seder. The apparent lack of action by God during the Shoah serves as counter-testimony to Judaism as a religion of redemption. Second, according to the book of Genesis, all human beings are created *b'tzelem elohim,* in the image of God. Greenberg asserts that this theological claim provides each human being with infinite value and worth. The commodification of human life during the Holocaust serves as more counter-testimony in Greenberg's argument. He describes the "rational" decision made by Nazi leaders to save money by cutting back on the amount of gas used to kill Jews. With less gas, some Jews were still alive when they were transferred from the gas chamber to the crematoria. In this example, life does not hold infinite value. Each life was worth approximately "two-fifths of a cent."[43]

Responding to the Challenge I:
Moment Faiths and Voluntary Covenant

Having argued that the Holocaust is and should be an event that shapes contemporary norms and values, Greenberg develops a theological response. How is Greenberg's understanding of faith and covenant changed by his encounter with the Shoah? He begins with a description of Jewish faith that is fairly standard, and is unlikely to encounter resistance: "Faith is living in the presence of the Redeemer, even when the world is unredeemed."[44] In other words, one should live with faith and confidence in the presence of God in one's life. But Greenberg argues this faith is not possible after the Holocaust. One can have only moment faiths: "Moments when Redeemer and vision of redemption are present, interspersed with times when the flames and smoke of the burning children blot out faith—though it flickers again."[45]

"Moment faith" refers to an individual's relationship with God, and "covenant" refers to the relationship between God and the Jewish people. Greenberg's encounter with the Shoah, like Lamm's, requires him to rethink the terms of the covenant between God and Israel and God's role in history. Greenberg concludes that after the Holocaust, the covenant is voluntary. He posits a three-stage developmental model for the covenantal relationship and views the biblical period as Israel's childhood. God takes on a parental role—establishing rules, setting limits, rewarding good acts, and chastising when necessary. The rabbinic period constitutes the second stage in Greenberg's model. The Mishnah, Talmud, and later commentaries upon these central texts present a more equal partnership between God and Israel. According to traditional Jewish theology, the rabbis' words are also Torah. During this time, the rabbis write revelation alongside God's presence in the world. After the Holocaust, God is more hidden. We see evidence of God only through human activity. Greenberg argues that the creation of the state of Israel is a sign of the voluntary covenant: "Coming after the incredible destruction of the Holocaust, the creation of Israel and the rebuilding of Jewish life constitute an unparalleled reacceptance of the covenant."[46] In *Beyond Auschwitz: Post-Holocaust Jewish Thought in America,* Michael Morgan offers a helpful evaluation of Greenberg's rethinking of the covenant: "The covenantal story that Greenberg tells shows how much can be retained and how much must be revised when exposing the traditional account to the

Shoah. The key feature that remains is the human responsibility for God's redemptive goal; even if we are bewildered by God's role in the covenant now, we can still appreciate our own. And this means a voluntary assumption of obligations that we try to articulate in our world."[47]

Responding to the Challenge II: Prayer for the Fifth Child

Given the powerful argument Greenberg makes for the Holocaust as a reorienting event, how is even moment faith possible? In other words, what allows for the possibility of faith at all? Greenberg's answer can be summarized with one word: Exodus. These two events, Holocaust and Exodus, form two poles of a dialectical faith, and one can never reside at one pole or the other in the comfort of certainty or absolutes. Greenberg offers a "general principle" for faith after the Holocaust: "Every solution that is totally at ease with a dominant option is to be seen as an attempt to escape from the dialectical torment of living with the Holocaust."[48] In *The Jewish Way: Living the Holidays,* Greenberg presents "Prayer for the Fifth Child" as a ritual moment of dialectical faith. The opening verse of "Prayer for the Fifth Child" makes clear that there will be no easy solutions. Participants ask "why" on behalf of the child "who did not survive to ask." But "We are like the simple child. We have no answer."

In the second verse of "Prayer for the Fifth Child," Greenberg evokes the passage of the five rabbis from Bene Berak presented earlier in the seder, which offers an interpretation of the phrase "all the days of your life" from Deuteronomy. Each word of biblical text is significant, so as did generations of rabbis before him, Greenberg answers the question: Why is the biblical verse "all the days" and not simply "the days?" The rabbis at Bene Berak in the second century C.E. suggested that "all" refers to the nights as well as the days. Greenberg expounds upon that interpretation found in many haggadot: "'The days of your life' indicates the daylight and the goodness of life. 'All the days of your life' means even in the darkest nights when we have lost *our* firstborn, we must remember the Exodus." For Greenberg, even when smoke blots out the flame of faith, Jews must remember the Exodus. Still the child's question persists. "Why?" The only possible answer is silence. In "Prayer for the Fifth Child," memory accompanies silence, especially memory of those who "preserved their image of God in the struggle for life" and memory of "that seder night when the Warsaw ghetto rose in revolt." "Prayer for the Fifth Child" then shifts from "that dark time" to the cup of Elijah, "the cup of the final redemption yet-to-be." The verse affirms Greenberg's reading of the creation of the state of Israel as an acceptance of the voluntary covenant and "the beginning of that redemption." The prayer in-structs all seder participants to fill Elijah's cup with wine from their own cup "expressing the hope that through our efforts, we will help bring closer that redemption." The concluding verse of "Prayer for the Fifth Child" ends with Maimonides' statement of faith: "I firmly believe in the coming of the Mes-siah, and even though the Messiah may tarry, in spite of this, I believe."[49]

Emplotting Redemption

I now shift from an analysis of the ritual components of the seder to the overall narrative structure, or emplotment, of the haggadah. The term "narrative emplotment" is derived from Hayden White's concept of "his-torical emplotment." White looks at emplotment specifically in relation to the Final Solution in the essay "Historical Emplotment and the Problem of Truth." White focuses on how the discourse characterized as narrative represents the real events that are the subject matter of history and argues that when we recount history in narrative form we impose a framework of interpretation.[50] In other words, narrative itself creates order and meaning. Emplotments, or plot types, are interpretations that determine the kinds of events that can be featured and "provide a pattern for the assignment of the roles that can possibly be played by the agents and agencies inhabiting the scene."[51] What sort of pattern do we find in the telling of the Exodus from Egypt? How does it both create and constrain the possibilities for human and divine agency? Emplotment creates systems of meaning production or sets of codes at play in a text that generate a range of possible meanings. This framework "possesses a content prior to any actualization of it," and this content, which often remains unexamined, can be as full of meaning as the manifest content, the explicit subject matter, of a text.[52]

The Mishnah and Talmud present instructions for reemplotting the biblical narrative for the seder. White's insights into the ways the structure of a text possesses a meaning prior to its content apply to the haggadah it-self, the structure of which, apart from individual content, carries meaning. In addition, White's contention that there is no one privileged way to tell the story or recount the history embedded in the event itself raises ethical issues about how to narrate the Holocaust. One can ask, following White's query, is there anything inherent to the Shoah to disallow its telling as a comedy? For this project, the question is whether there is anything inher-ent in the event that disallows its telling within a narrative of redemption. The Passover story tells of the redemption of a people and culminates in the making of an everlasting covenant between God and Israel. When the Shoah is brought into this narrative the contours of the story shift and the contemporary meaning of redemption becomes uncertain.

Recognition that narrative imposes a framework occurred long before White's radicalization of its implications for historiography. As Aristotle noted in his *Poetics,* through narrative we impose a unity on human experience and order events as significant components of the whole. Aristotle deemed plot, and in particular the end or purpose of the actions recounted, the most significant component of narrative. In Aristotle's theory, art is imitation, and plot is imitation of action: "The imitation of the action is the plot . . . the combination of events."[53] The combination of actions, the construction of a plot, is guided by a set of principles that privilege action as a unified object. Aristotle writes, "The plot, since it is the imitation of an action, must be the imitation of a unified action comprising a whole; and the events which are the parts of the plot must be so organized that if any one of them is displaced or taken away, the whole will be shaken and put out of joint; for if the presence or absence of a thing makes no discernible difference, that thing is not part of the whole."[54] This view, influential for both authors and critics since the Renaissance, says that each action in the narrative should be necessary to the plot and create a harmonious whole in perfect proportion.

In the search for proportion and wholeness, particular attention is paid to the beginning and end of the narrative. Combining particular actions to form a plot means that beginnings and endings should not be arbitrary.[55] A deliberate process of selection allows us to distinguish event (the actions selected) from discourse (the form of presentation). As Seymour Chatman notes in his study of narrative structure in fiction and film: "Aristotle's discussion of the terms 'beginning,' 'middle,' and 'end' apply to the narrative, to story-events as narrated, rather than to real actions themselves, simply because such terms are meaningless in the real world. . . . Such a term [beginning, middle, end] marks out plot, the story-as-discoursed."[56] Gary Morson makes a similar observation: "The privilege of closure necessarily comes from outside the frame, from the author and reader. . . . Closure and structure mark the difference between life as it is lived and as it is read about."[57] Morson's use of the term "closure" echoes Friedländer's concern with the imposition of closure upon collective memory of the Final Solution, especially if closure creates a disjunction between life as lived and life as read, and thus may move us away from, rather than closer to, an understanding of survivors' experiences.

As literary critic J. Hillis Miller paraphrases Aristotle: "We order or reorder the givens of experience."[58] Miller's observation that we give experience a form and a meaning is a particularly useful paraphrase in this context because the seder, which literally means "order," creates a frame of meaning for the Exodus narrative. Several ordering strategies exist in the haggadah, including the rubric of ritual action examined in chapter one and the narrative trajectory established in the Mishnah, both of which function to impose or encourage a specific reading of the Exodus and interpretation of the meaning of its events. The structure of narrative—the ways its individual components work together—becomes a crucial carrier of meaning.

One important result of this structure or ordering of reality is the imbuing of events with moral meaning. Narrative assures us that our primary experience of reality is not arbitrary, chaotic disorder. White goes so far as to say that the very ordering of experience comes out of the desire to moralize reality, to invest it with value.[59] The term narrative emplotment, then, describes systems of meaning production, of how a story—whether fiction, history, or myth—is recounted in order to structure the discrete events into a unified whole that possesses moral significance. Is there any moral significance to the Final Solution? This chapter began with vehement rejections of this very assertion. Does the Shoah become part of the covenantal story—an account of the bond between God and Israel that creates a relationship of moral significance—or does it remain inassimilable? As the Shoah is interpolated into the Exodus narrative—a key episode in the larger covenantal story—it challenges the meaning of covenantal community. The basic meaning of interpolate is to insert or introduce between parts, but it can also mean "to change or falsify (a text) by introducing new or incorrect material." Addition of the Shoah is certainly new to the traditional haggadah; whether or not it "falsifies" remains the question of this chapter.[60]

Liberation after the Shoah cannot be easily equated with freedom-redemption. Many survivors have said in both oral and written testimonies that it was only after liberation that the magnitude of their losses began to set in. Primo Levi describes the moment of liberation in a memoir, *The Reawakening:* "Liberty, the improbable, the impossible liberty, so far removed from Auschwitz that we had only dared to hope for it in our dreams, had come, but it had not taken us to the Promised Land. It was around us, but in the form of a pitiless deserted plain. More trials, more toil, more hunger, more cold, more fears awaited us."[61] While there is a clear resonance between Levi's text and the biblical recounting of the Exodus, the recounting in the haggadah does not dwell long in the desert.[62] These differences in narrative emplotment hold implications for Holocaust memory. The haggadah, in contrast to the biblical narrative, does not leave room for the loss that persists after redemption. The narrative emplotment of the haggadah, which begins with degradation and ends in praise, complicates the ability to remember the Shoah within it. The haggadah is a rabbinic reshaping of the Exodus story through both ritual and narrative emplotments. A comparison of the emplotment in the biblical book Exodus with that in the haggadah demonstrates how narrative emplotment works. When one reads the haggadah with attention to characteristics of emplotment, it is clear that in terms of agency and closure biblical and rabbinic tellings of the same story differ markedly. Both traditions form strong links between memory and redemption. However, the rabbinic reframing lessens the ambiguity and indeterminacy present in the biblical text. The result is a redemptive narrative.

Emplotment in the Book of Exodus

In order to see the changes in the Exodus story in the haggadah clearly, the summary of Exodus that follows serves as a baseline for comparison. Using the tenth-century C.E. division of Torah that is standard in synagogue use today, the book of Exodus contains eleven portions, each of which is named after its first significant Hebrew word. Human characters, both before and after the Exodus, play strong roles in the narrative. The first portion, *Shemot,* sets the scene of the Exodus narrative. It locates the Israelites in Egypt with a Pharaoh who did not know Joseph and his respected status among the Egyptians. This new Pharaoh enslaves the Israelites and orders the midwives, including Shifrah and Puah, to kill all Israelite males at birth. Jocheved, the mother of Moses, sends her infant son down the Nile River where he is rescued by Pharaoh's daughter. Moses' sister, Miriam, who is nearby, offers to find a "Hebrew nurse to suckle the child," and reunites mother and child. Moses is raised as an Egyptian prince but flees to Midian after killing an Egyptian who was beating a Hebrew slave. In Midian, Moses marries Zipporah, with whom he has a son. The text continues with the phrase "a long time after that" and introduces God into the narrative as one who hears the plight of the Israelites and remembers the covenant with their ancestors. On account of the covenant "God took notice of them" (2:24).

God appears to Moses in a burning bush and appoints him to free the Israelites from bondage. Moses protests his ability to serve, and God selects Aaron to assist Moses in his task: "He shall serve as your spokesman, with you playing the role of God to him" (4:16). Moses and Aaron ask Pharaoh to let the Israelites travel three days into the wilderness to make a festival to the Lord, but Pharaoh refuses and increases the burden of the Israelites. The portion *Vaera* then begins with an invocation of the covenant as God's reason for liberating the Israelites. At this point, the narrative pauses as the text gives a genealogy of the various Israelite clans. The rest of Vaera tells the drama of the plagues, signs of God's power. God "hardens Pharaoh's heart" (9:12, 10:1, 11:10, 14:8) so that even with these awesome signs and wonders, Pharaoh will not free the Israelites.

In *Bo,* the third portion of Exodus, the plagues continue as signs of God's power. After the ninth of ten plagues, the text appears to break again from the story and presents ritual instructions for sacrificing and eating a lamb as part of the Feast of Unleavened Bread: "This day shall be to you one of remembrance: you shall celebrate it as a festival to the Lord throughout the ages; you shall celebrate it as an institution for all time" (12:14). The narrative continues with the tenth plague, the killing of all the first-born Egyptian males. The rest of Bo alternates between recounting the escape from Egypt, including the tenth plague and Pharaoh's cry "Up, depart from among my people" (12:31), and detailing ritual instructions for celebrating Passover, the Feast of Unleavened Bread.

The Exodus narrative continues with the high drama of the portion *Be-shalach.* As the Israelites leave Egypt, God's presence dwells among them as "a pillar of cloud by day and a pillar of fire by night" (13:21). Meanwhile, Pharaoh reconsiders his decision to let the Israelites go and sends his army after them. In fear for their lives, the Israelites reproach Moses for bringing them out of Egypt only to die in the desert. Moses retorts, "Have no fear! Stand by and witness the deliverance which the Lord will work for you to-day" (14:13). The Israelites successfully cross the sea and sing a song of celebration when the Egyptians drown in the waters. They have seen the wondrous power of God, which instills fear of God and confirms their faith. Their songs of praise conclude: "The Lord will reign for ever and ever!" (15:18). Miriam makes a second appearance in the narrative. All the women follow her and dance with timbrels: "Miriam chanted for them, 'Sing to the Lord, for He has triumphed gloriously; Horse and driver He has hurled into the sea'" (15:21). The two songs conclude with glorious triumph. But the songs are not the end of the story. In contrast to what those who are familiar with the telling in the haggadah might expect, the very next verse continues, "Then Moses caused Israel to set out from the Sea of Reeds. They went on into the wilderness of Shur; they traveled three days in the wilderness and found no water" (15:22). When the Israelites finally do find water, it is "bitter" and undrinkable. At this point the people express their displeasure to Moses. He cries out to the Lord who then sweetens the water. This cycle of dissatisfaction, complaint, and placation continues throughout their journeys in the wilderness.

The rest of the book of Exodus takes place while the Israelites travel in the wilderness. In *Yitro,* God gives the Ten Commandments, and human leadership is established. The next portion, *Mishpatim,* is well summarized by its opening phrase: "These are the rules" (21:1), concluding with Moses going back up the mountain. In *Trumah,* Moses receives instructions regarding how to construct the Tabernacle, and in *Tetzaveh* the role of the priests is defined. As Moses has been receiving these detailed instructions up on the mountain, however, the Israelites have once again become restless. One of their first actions after receiving the Ten Commandments is to build the golden calf. In anger, God considers destroying the Israelites, but Moses persuades God to reconsider. Instead, Moses instructs the Levites, one of the leading tribes amongst the Israelites, to "slay brother, neighbor, and kin," and as a result "some three thousand of the people fell that day" (32:27–28). Moses asks God to be present once again in the camp; God responds by revealing attributes of grace and compassion and allowing Moses to view God's back (33:18–23). Moses travels up the mountain once again and returns with a second version of the Ten Commandments. *Ki Tissa* and *Vayakhel* provide a description of the Tabernacle and instructions for its use. As Exodus concludes, God maintains a presence among the people "throughout their journeys" (40:38).

A brief analysis of this plot summary using the categories of agency and closure reveals some interesting differences between the narrative emplotment found in the biblical text and the one in the haggadah. First, several crucial agents populate the biblical narrative. Redemption is not attributed to God alone. God works through Moses, and other human beings, to redeem the Israelites from slavery. At one point, God even describes Moses' role as parallel to God's own when God instructs Moses to "play the role of God to Aaron," who will serve as spokesperson. Both Moses and Aaron become crucial participants in realizing God's plan. In addition, a host of human agents, including Shifrah, Puah, Miriam, Jocheved, Jethro, Joshua, and Bezalel, propel—and not merely populate—the plot of this narrative. (This emphasis on human agency led Mordecai Kaplan, the founder of Reconstructionist Judaism, to use the biblical text to tell the Exodus story in the first Reconstructionist haggadah.) Second, the narrative is not closed. The end of the Exodus episode does not bring closure to the story. Immediately following triumph and freedom, discontent returns. After crossing the sea, the Israelites sing two joyous songs of praise to the God who has rescued them and is like no other, but in perhaps one of the most moving depictions of human frailty, the Israelites backslide the moment they encounter hardship. After redemption their journey is ongoing. The conclusion without closure is bittersweet. On the one hand, God is present throughout their journeys. Even in the desert, God is visible by cloud and by fire. On the other hand, God is present throughout their journeys, yet they have not reached the Promised Land. In fact, none of the generation who were slaves in Egypt will enter the land of Israel.

Emplotment in the Haggadah: From Degradation to Glory

Explanation of how the emplotment of the Exodus narrative appears in the haggadah must begin with the Talmud, the rabbinic text of the fifth and sixth century C.E. The Exodus story and its ritual are embedded in a frame established by the rabbis of the Mishnah, who gave instructions regarding how to celebrate the seder. These instructions receive additional study in the Talmud and are often replicated and elaborated in haggadot as well. The rabbis instruct a father regarding how to tell the Passover story to his son: "*Matchil bigenut umesayem beshevach,*" which is translated as "begin in shame [or degradation]; end in glory [or praise]." This trajectory from shame to glory, degradation to praise, shapes the maggid, the telling, in the vast majority of haggadot. Because the implementation of these instructions has important consequences for the incorporation of the Shoah, it is worthwhile to look at the explication of these instructions in the Talmud. But first, a few words about the Talmud and its relationship to the haggadah are required.

The Talmud includes the third-century C.E. Mishnah and commentary on it by later rabbis. The resulting Talmud, compiled in the sixth century C.E., is arguably the formative text of rabbinic Judaism.[63] The Talmud, which became an object of study in its own right, is characterized by freewheeling discussion of the Mishnah. In the Talmud, a short selection from the Mishnah is presented; rabbinic deliberations on its meaning follow; differing views are often presented in the form of "give and take."[64] Ostensibly, these discussions are to determine a particular practice or point of law. Yet much of the discussion is devoted to specifics about rituals performed at the Temple, which was destroyed centuries before the Talmud was compiled. Furthermore, the issues that are examined, discussed, and debated—sometimes from every conceivable angle—often remain un-resolved. The Talmud is neither a description of existing practices of the time nor a normative rulebook of Jewish law. As Robert Goldenberg notes in his essay on the Talmud: "Its chief purpose is to preserve the record of earlier generations studying their own tradition and provide materials for later generations wishing to do the same. It is a book produced by and for people whose highest value was the life of study."[65] In its traditional con-text, reading Talmud is an act of sanctifying study. The more one studies and interprets the text, the more praiseworthy one is. Thus, the presence in the haggadah of multiple interpretations of "matchil bigenut umesayem beshevach" illustrates a classic rabbinic approach. In classic Jewish under-standing, both interpretations of degradation and glory found in the hag-gadah are worthy of study; both are words of the living God.

The first section of Pesachim 116b, the relevant Talmudic passage, says, "He commences with shame and concludes with praise. What is 'with shame'? Rav said: 'Aforetime our fathers were idolaters;' while Samuel said: 'We were slaves.'" Before focusing upon where the opinions differ, it is in-teresting to note where the rabbis agree. The story of Passover begins with shame and concludes with praise. Both parties acknowledge the redemptive frame. Regardless of how one comes to understand this trajectory, and hag-gadot offer legions of commentary on the relationship between "spiritual" (idolatry) and "physical" (slavery) degradation, the movement, or emplot-ment, of the text is affirmed. The redemptive narrative frame is the defining characteristic of the telling. Based on this brief reading, the Talmud presents a fairly closed narrative where the beginning and end are clearly marked and the end presents closure. In the Talmud, the debate is between Rav and Samuel, two of its most oft-quoted rabbis, who proffer differing opinions on the meaning of shame. Rav asserts that the shame (genut) resides in the fact that our ancestors worshiped foreign gods; Samuel argues that slavery is the cause of our shame. The Talmud presents both opinions with approval, and both Rav and Samuel appear in the haggadah. Their two interpretations of degradation and praise determine the content of the emplotment.[66] For example, the page layout of the Reconstructionist haggadah emphasizes the parallel attention to beginnings. On the right-hand side of the page, at the beginning of the Maggid section, appears the question: "How do we begin the story?" Directly underneath this question Samuel makes his first appear-ance: "The rabbinic sage Samuel began with physical enslavement." The top line of the facing page presents Rav: "The rabbinic sage Rav began with spiritual degradation."[67]

The components of the maggid that follow continue to develop these two understandings of degradation. The Four Questions, each of which draws attention to a symbol connected to slavery or freedom (matzah, bitter herbs, salt water, sitting in a reclined position), fill in the narrative from slavery to freedom. The first text presents a microcosm of Samuel's position:

> We were slaves to Pharaoh in Egypt. The Eternal One our God brought us out from there with a strong hand and an outstretched arm. Had God not taken our ancestors out of Egypt, then we and our children and our children's children would still be enslaved to Pharaoh in Egypt. And even if all of us were wise scholars, all of us were sages, all of us were experienced in the ways of the world, all knowledgeable in Torah, it would still be our responsibility to tell about the Exodus from Egypt. Whoever expands upon the story of the Exodus from Egypt is worthy of praise.[68]

Even a brief look at this text in terms of agency and closure reveals significant differences from the biblical telling. God and God alone frees the Israelites. Moses, Miriam, and the actors in the biblical text make no appearance in this synopsis. (When they do appear at other points in the haggadah their secondary position is always made clear.) The story begins and ends with the Exodus. Freedom-redemption concludes this telling. To end in praise is to praise God for the Exodus; one is worthy of praise in direct proportion to one's expansion upon God's saving action.

An analysis of Rav's emplotment of the telling leads to a similar conclusion. The Four Children introduce the questions of concern to Rav. The wise, wicked, simple, and silent child all offer perspectives on the questions: Why should the Exodus matter today? Why is Passover important? For Rav, this is a spiritual question. Degradation is not physical enslavement but the worship of idols, and Rav traces the growing realization of God's presence and the resultant commitment of the Israelites to serve as God's people. The prooftext presented in the haggadah to expound on Rav's understanding of degradation comes from the book of Joshua:

> From the beginning, our ancestors worshiped idols. But now we have been brought near to God's service. As it is written, "Joshua said to the people: 'Thus said the Eternal One, the God of Israel: In olden times, your ancestors—Terah, father of Abraham and Nahor—lived beyond the Euphrates and worshiped other gods. But I took your

father Abraham from beyond the Euphrates and led him through the whole land of Canaan and multiplied his offspring. I gave him Isaac, and to Isaac I gave Jacob and Esau . . . Jacob and his children went down to Egypt'" (Josh. 24:2–4). [69]

An examination of the verbs in these few passages reveals that God is the primary agent and the Israelites' agency is more likely to be negative than positive. We can break down the verbs in these verses into three categories: active verbs in reference to the Israelites; passive verbs in reference to the Israelites; and active verbs in reference to God. The primary activity attributed to the Israelites is worship; they worship other gods and idols. The other two active verbs with the Israelites as the subject refer to the geographic location of the Israelites: they "lived beyond" where they worshiped other gods and idols, and they "went down" to Egypt, which ultimately led to their enslavement. Again, these are not positive activities. The other active verbs refer to God's activity: God takes Abraham away from the land where idols are worshiped; God leads Abraham through the land of Canaan; God gives offspring. The one positive activity of the people takes a passive verb construction. The people were "brought near to God's service." The positive action is brought about by God. Thus, of course, it is God—and God alone—who is worthy of praise.

From Degradation to Glory after the Holocaust

What happens when the Holocaust is inserted into this emplotment? Editors of the haggadot from the Reform and Conservative movements directly address the issues regarding commemoration of the Holocaust in the haggadah. In the preface to the 1974 Reform haggadah, editor Herbert Bronstein suggests that the Holocaust need not alter the redemptive frame. In contrast, the Conservative haggadah is particularly interesting because in its introduction, the Haggadah Committee says that the events of the Final Solution require a second maggid for inclusion in the traditional haggadah. Although these positions seem to take opposite positions on inclusion of the Shoah, the approaches may not be so different as they originally appear. Some of the differences can be traced to different emphases in Reform and Conservative ideology. Classical Reform Judaism holds to an understanding of progressive revelation. The past, including its texts, rituals, and theologies, informs the present but is not privileged above it. In this view, just as the rabbis of the Talmud, including Rav and Samuel, and the great medieval commentators, including Rashi and Maimonides, were influenced by God, so are the rabbis of our own day. As Samuel Holdheim, one of the nineteenth-century creators of Classical Reform Judaism, quipped, "The Talmud speaks with the standpoint of its time and for that time it was right. I speak from the higher level of consciousness of my time, and for this age I am right."[70] Although twentieth- and twenty-first-century American rabbis may not hold to quite as strong a position, they do see themselves in the tradition of the rabbis who created the haggadah in the first place and are willing to place their contemporary commentary into the Maggid itself as a series of optional readings.

By contrast, Conservative Judaism puts more weight on the role of tradition, especially as it is lived out in the context of community. The Conservative Haggadah Committee begins its preface with the question, "Why is this Haggadah different from all other Haggadot, from the estimated 3,000 editions that have been produced during the past 500 years?" The Haggadah Committee answers its own question by claiming that *Feast of Freedom* is the first haggadah that "faithfully reflects Conservative ideology" including a strong commitment "to preserving the classic tradition."[71] Not surprisingly, then, the addition of current events would appear outside the traditional frame of the Maggid. Current references are added alongside rather than within the traditional text. In this way, this haggadah follows the model of the Talmud, in which later commentaries were incorporated by appearing around the edges of the page surrounding the original Mishnaic text. Nevertheless, this haggadah too emplots the Holocaust within a narrative frame moving from degradation to glory. In both haggadot, the Holocaust is paired with the creation of the state of Israel, death with rebirth, using the language of both haggadot.[72] This pairing is determined as much by the emplotment of redemption as by the historical chronology of the two twentieth-century events, perhaps even more so. Praise must follow degradation; shame must conclude with glory.

The Reform Haggadah (1974)

A Passover Haggadah was the first in a series of liturgical revisions by the Central Conference of American Rabbis (CCAR), published between 1974 and 1985, which responded specifically to the Holocaust and the creation of the modern state of Israel. Half a century had passed since the last revision of a haggadah for the Reform movement, and clearly much had changed for world Jewry. A. Stanley Dreyfus, a member of the CCAR liturgy committee that created *A Passover Haggadah,* described the impetus for change as a mandate: "The enormity of the Holocaust on the one hand, and, on the other, the establishment of the state of Israel brought a reawakening of faith and commitment and, for Reform Jewry, mandated a complete revision of its liturgy."[73] Herbert Bronstein, editor of the haggadah, explains in the preface to *A Passover Haggadah* how the mandate was implemented: "So this Haggadah is not a revision of the previous Union Haggadah. It is an attempt at *renovatio ab origine:* a return to the creative beginning so as to bring forth what is utterly new from what was present in the old. Throughout, we have endeavored to be faithful to the elemental structure of the Haggadah, beginning with the statement of the theme—the movement from degradation to glory—and the intentional complement of the story of Israel's own deliverance with the Messianic vision for all humanity."[74] The structure of the haggadah is the emplotment of the redemptive frame, to which this new haggadah remains faithful. Accordingly, the Holocaust must reside within the redemptive frame. According to Bronstein this place is natural, already set by previous theological understandings of Jewish history: "The Holocaust and the modern Jewish national rebirth find their place in this Haggadah because the tragedy and exaltation of our historic existence have already provided a place for them within the Seder, this story of our life whose shining conclusion is yet to unfold."[75] The Holocaust and the state of Israel are paired together and understood through the paradigm of tragedy and exaltation, another rendering of *"matchil bigenut umesayem beshevach."* When the Holocaust is incorporated into the Reform haggadah, the narrative frame of degradation to glory abets a value-added redemptive reading of the Shoah.

From Degradation.   If the inclusion of the Holocaust is a mandate, the creators of the Reform haggadah took the mandate to heart. Six passages related to the Holocaust appear within this text.[76] All six passages are located in the first half of the haggadah, early in the maggid, before the second cup of wine. Each passage is marked as an "interpretation" of the traditional text. The first two references are interpretations of the four children. Albert Einstein is the wise son. He stands before a memorial in honor of the Warsaw Ghetto fighters, which he suggests is a reminder "to remain loyal to our people and to the moral principles cherished by our fathers."[77] Separated by a single asterisk, the second passage immediately follows Einstein's words. Elie Wiesel, author of *Night* and founding chairperson of the United States Holocaust Memorial Museum, argues for loyalty to the Jewish people through the story of the wicked child who rejects her connection to the Jewish people. Wiesel chastises the wicked child and asserts "The Jew who repudiates himself, claiming to do so for the sake of humanity, will inevitably repudiate humanity in the end."[78] Although Wiesel does not explicitly mention the Shoah, as author of the most famous memoir about the Holocaust and a vocal spokesperson for the preservation of Holocaust memory, his name is inextricably linked to it.

The third passage, written by a teenage boy interned at the concentration camp Theresienstadt, serves as a modern midrash on the phrase "our plight" found in Deuteronomy 26:7, one of the four verses that forms the core of the maggid.[79] Passages five and six pair an excerpt from Anne Frank's diary with Abraham Shlonsky's poem "A Vow" as commentary on the traditional words from the haggadah: "For more than one enemy has risen against us to destroy us. In every generation in every age, some rise up to plot our annihilation. But a Divine Power sustains and delivers us."[80] The set of Holocaust readings concludes with more commentary on Deuteronomy 26:7 as Anthony Hecht offers words of caution: "These words 'more than one enemy has arisen . . . ' are likely to recall with a special and monstrous emphasis what has come to be known to the world as the Holocaust—an explicit program of annihilation of all European Jews, in which six million men, women, and children were efficiently singled out and sent to their deaths. To remember them on this evening, as ones who once shared in this service, is right. Yet we must guard against letting our bitterness at their extermination deflect our hearts from, or diminish our gratitude for, the gift of deliverance we celebrate tonight."[81]

To Glory.   Given that the emplotment begins with degradation and ends with glory, it is fitting that references to the modern state of Israel appear in the concluding section of the haggadah. "An Additional Cup Set Aside for the Future" appears as an optional, additional ritual within Hallel, words of praise. The creators of this haggadah attribute the new ritual to "the events of our time." The creation of the state of Israel requires a new ritual. However, they also place the ritual in the context of past tradition, noting that several rabbis, including Rashi and Maimonides, praised the inclusion of a fifth cup for seder participants in reference to Exodus 6:8: "I will bring you into the land which I swore to give to Abraham, Isaac, and Jacob, and I will give it to you for a possession, I the Lord." Creation of the state of Israel allows seder participants to bring the fifth aspect of God's redemptive actions into the seder. "An Additional Cup Set Aside for the Future" presents ancient and modern references to Israel, including excerpts from the

Declaration of Independence of the state of Israel.[82] Readers are encouraged to view the Holocaust in conjunction with the creation of the state of Israel through the traditional rabbinic redemptive narrative of the maggid, with its focus on freedom-redemption. Nevertheless, contrary to the impulse of the Preface, the conjoining of Holocaust and the nation-state of Israel was not inevitable; Israel as religious (rather than political) ideal was part of Jewish self-understanding long before the call for a political nation-state. In fact, the tradition of concluding the haggadah with the hope "next year in Jerusalem" goes back to the Middle Ages, whereas Zionism as a Jewish national movement has its roots in the European nationalisms of the nineteenth century. All of these precede the Shoah.

Moreover, American Jews who use the haggadot in question have made the United States, and not the state of Israel, their home. Jacob Neusner tries to make sense of this contradiction by identifying a Jewish-American sensibility common from the late sixties through the mid-eighties that encourages a reading of the Holocaust as "redeemed" by the creation of the modern nation-state Israel. In *Stranger at Home: "The Holocaust," Zionism, and American Judaism,* a collection of essays written between 1960 and 1980, Neusner critiques redemptive Holocaust discourse, what he calls "the myth of Holocaust-redemption," and its role in American Judaism. Here, the term "myth" does not mean a lie; rather myth indicates that a particular way of understanding the Holocaust has shaped the ways modern American Jews understand their place in the world. Neusner asks, "What role is 'the Holocaust' as symbol meant to serve? For it is as evocative symbol, not as historical memory, that 'the Holocaust' wins its capital H and its quotation marks."[83] Neusner argues that the Holocaust functions in American Judaism as a rationale for Jewish continuity and as a marker of ethnic identity. In this myth, the creation of the state of Israel is the marker of redemption; it is a required but also problematic component of the myth of Holocaust-redemption for American Jews since the vast majority do not choose to make aliyah, and make Israel home. Nevertheless, the myth is required, Neusner argues, because "without Zionism, 'the Holocaust' is unbearable and to be avoided except as a topic for learned books about unspeakable facts. The myth of 'the Holocaust' is complete only in the redemption of the Jewish nation."[84]

The Conservative Haggadah (1982)

As in the Reform haggadah, the Conservative haggadah deliberately pairs the Holocaust with the state of Israel. For the editors of *Feast of*

Freedom, these two events require a second maggid: "Catastrophe and consolation: each generation must endure or witness this fateful yet all too familiar cycle. Both the Holocaust and the rebirth of the state of Israel are mirrored here, for they shape our own Exodus from our own Mitzrayim."[85] The creators of this haggadah choose not to translate Mitzrayim as Egypt. Instead, they highlight the literal root meaning of the term "from the narrows," which refers to more than the specific time and place of ancient Egypt: "The violent vicissitudes of history have endowed Mitzrayim with broader connotations, so that it has come to represent repression and tyranny. . . . Mitzrayim is every place and any place in the world where people have been (or still are) persecuted."[86] The *mitzrayim* of the modern age is the Holocaust, and the trajectory for the Exodus of contemporary generations begins with Holocaust and ends with Israel. The second maggid compresses this redemptive trajectory, similar to the one observed in the Reform haggadah, to a mere eleven pages. Located between the third cup of wine and the words of praise in Hallel, the story moves from degradation/Holocaust to glory/Israel. The introduction to the second maggid, titled "In Every Generation," says that its purpose is "to enrich and intensify" participants' personal encounter with the Exodus. Art also plays a crucial role, enriching and intensifying the text. Bold, stark shapes in vibrant colors frame the passages in this section and shape the telling. The graphic layout of this material divides these passages into three parts. Passages associated with "degradation" appear first in a series of mustard-yellow boxes. The second section consists of readings and rituals associated with Elijah's cup, the symbol of hope for final redemption. The final section includes passages associated with glory, which are again placed in mustard-yellow boxes, suggesting a unity between the first and third sections with Elijah's cup functioning as a transition between the two.

From Degradation. Five of the first six passages either were written during the Shoah or are commentary on it. The second maggid begins with degradation, but, to use Langer's term, the presentation is "preempted" as these passages "fortify a prior commitment to ideals of moral reality, community responsibility, or religious belief."[87] The first passage, "*Erev Pesaḥ* [Passover Eve] 1943," memorializes the fighters of the Warsaw Ghetto Uprising: "The Freedom Fighters of the Ghetto will live for ever, fiery testimony to the love of liberty kindled by the Exodus," and concludes with the claim, "Once more the Covenant People had kept the faith."[88] The ideals affirmed are both American and Jewish. The famous query of the eighteenth-century Hasidic Rabbi Levi Yitzhak of Berditchev appears next: "I do not ask why I suffer. I ask only this: Do I suffer for Your sake?"[89] The rabbi's question could be read as an effort to place the Holocaust within the legacy of meaningful suffering that shapes some readings of Jewish history. However, the question could also read as a challenge, suggesting that the suffering endured during the Shoah has no added value.

The third passage, which follows Yitzhak's question, takes the reader once again to Passover in the Warsaw Ghetto. The concluding lines of Binem Heller's famous poem read:

> They have come here, these jackbooted pharaohs, to herd
> Israel's innocent lambs to their terrible fate.
> But never again will Jews tolerate taunts,
> Never again obey death-bearing orders.
> The doorposts tonight will be crimson with blood,
> The blood of the murderers, freedom's destroyers.[90]

Heller depicts the Warsaw Ghetto as Mitzrayim by using images from the Passover story—"Pharaohs," "innocent lambs," "doorposts," and "blood"—to describe the Nazis' actions toward the Jews, and the Jews' rebellious response. From the Warsaw Ghetto we move to the concentration camp Bergen-Belsen, where Jews offered a prayer to God before eating bread during Passover: "May [You] keep us alive and save us and rescue us speedily so that we may observe Your commandments and do Your will and serve You with a perfect heart. Amen." [91] The structure of these two passages parallels the first two. Heller's poem offers a triumphant note—the Jews will fight back. A commitment to autonomy and integrity is affirmed. The second passage is an affirmation of faith in the midst of doubt, and like the query from the Hasidic rabbi, a call to God for help. The next page includes two more Holocaust readings. The first passage describes the Jewish victims of Nazi genocide as "our martyred brothers and sisters" whose "glow illuminates our path."[92] Again, we see both degradation and its pre-empting: the Jewish victims must not die in vain. A martyr chooses to die rather than to renounce religious principles. The use of the term "martyr" suggests both agency and religious belief, neither of which was necessarily present. The final line affirms that "we will all be present at the final redemption."[93] This second maggid bears the title, "In Every Generation," and the final passages of the opening section focus upon the plight of contemporary Jewry. During the time this haggadah was edited Jews from the Soviet Union were subject to severe persecution if they lived openly as Jews, or expressed a desire to emigrate to Israel. Thus, the current mitzrayim, oppression of Jews in the Soviet Union, concludes the first part of the "In Every Generation" section.

The Conservative haggadah employs a dramatic graphic layout to place a break between the sets of passages in yellow boxes. A striking two-page spread of a bright yellow sun in the midst of solid black separates degradation and glory. On the left- and right-top corners of the two-page spread is "Ani ma'amin," the famous declaration of faith by Maimonides. The right-upper margin presents Maimonides' text in Hebrew using both Hebrew lettering and English transliteration, while the left presents a translation, "I believe with all my heart in the coming of the Messiah, and even though he may tarry, I will wait each and every day for his arrival." Underneath Maimonides' text is a corollary prayer attributed to "Jews in Germany, 1939," which reads, "I believe in the sun even when it is not shining. I believe in love even when I do not feel it. I believe in God even when He is silent."[94] "Pour Out Your Wrath" occupies the next page, followed by the cup for Elijah.

To Glory. The yellow boxes appear again after the traditional renderings of "Pour Out Your Wrath" and the cup for Elijah. These readings, immediately preceding Hallel, all take as their topic the land and state of Israel. Like the Reform haggadah, the passages draw upon both biblical and modern sources. Of the six readings, three are from the biblical prophets Isaiah and Jeremiah; two are from the modern Zionists Theodor Herzl and Rabbi Abraham Isaac Kook. The last text is Deuteronomy 26:9: "And He brought us to this place and gave us this land, a land flowing with milk and honey." This is an amazing insertion. The first maggid in a traditional haggadah expounds upon Deuteronomy 26:5–8, and deliberately excludes entrance into the land. In *Feast of Freedom,* the final verse from the First Fruits Liturgy, the verse the rabbis excised in their formation of the "whole portion," reappears. The second maggid completes the first, and the state of Israel redeems the Holocaust. By identifying the Holocaust with degradation and the state of Israel with glory, the Conservative haggadah places the Holocaust within a narrative of value-added redemption.

The question remains, "How can Jews remember and memorialize the Shoah during this celebration of freedom-redemption without adding redemptive value to the Final Solution?" The next chapter considers answers to the question through an examination of Anne Frank's appearance in American Passover haggadot.

Ani ma'amin.
I believe with all my heart
in the coming of the Messiah,
and even though he may tarry,
I will wait each and every day
for his arrival.
Maimonides, 12th century

Ani ma'amin.
I believe in the sun
even when it is not shining.
I believe in love
even when I do not feel it.
I believe in God
even when He is silent.
Jews in Germany, 1939

FIGURE 3.1 Maimonides' declaration of faith, juxtaposed with a prayer attributed to "Jews in Germany, 1939." *Reprinted from* Feast of Freedom *edited by Rachel Anne Rabinowicz (98–99), copyright © the Rabbinical Assembly, 1982. "Jews in Germany, 1939" from* The Tiger Beneath The Skin *by Zvi Kolitz. Copyright © 1947 by Creative Age Press, Inc. Copyright renewed 1974 by Zvi Kolitz. Reprinted by permission of Farrar, Straus and Giroux, LLC.*

אֲנִי מַאֲמִין בֶּאֱמוּנָה שְׁלֵמָה
בְּבִיאַת הַמָּשִׁיחַ. וְאַף עַל פִּי
שֶׁיִּתְמַהְמֵהַּ, עִם כָּל זֶה
אֲחַכֶּה לוֹ בְּכָל יוֹם שֶׁיָּבֹא.

Ani ma'amin b'emunah shleimah
b'viat ha-mashiah. V'af al pi
she-yit-mah-mei-ah, im kol zeh
ahakeh lo b'khol yom sheyavo.

CHAPTER 4

Anne Frank, Hope, and Redemption

⊱⊶⊶⊙⊷⊷⊰

> *I still believe, in spite of everything,*
> *that people are really good at heart.*
> —Anne Frank, *Anne Frank: The Diary of a Young Girl*

> *Anne Frank's story, truthfully told,*
> *is unredeemed and unredeemable.*
> —Cynthia Ozick, "Who Owns Anne Frank?"

> *What, after all, was the meaning of all this?*
> *The more I find out, the less I understand it.*
> —Harry Mulisch, "Death and the Maiden"

$\mathcal{T}$he previous chapters set forth three major issues surrounding Holocaust commemoration in U.S. Passover ritual. The first chapter explored difficulties that accompany the desire to transmit knowledge of the Holocaust to future generations through communal memory. The next identified impediments to honoring efforts made by victims and victim-survivors to assert their agency within a context of extreme dehumanization. Chapter three presented the critique of redemption in Holocaust studies and demonstrated how the problem is especially complicated given the strong redemptive frame of the Passover seder and haggadah. This chapter shifts to application, examining the placement of one individual's Holocaust experience in the haggadah, with particular attention to how freedom-redemption and value-added redemption impact one another when Passover and the Holocaust are commemorated together. Each haggadah examined in this chapter commemorates the Holocaust through the famous words of Anne Frank presented in the opening epigraph: "I still believe, in spite of everything, that people are really good at heart." Although Frank's words contain a hopeful and optimistic message, these words, when placed

96

in the haggadah, do not simply fortify the redemptive frame or affirm the emplotment from degradation to glory. The varying effect of Frank's words is shaped in part by where she appears within the traditional text: Is she the wise child or the simple child? Is she a voice of suffering "in every genera-tion," or the companion of Elijah? Does she appear as a reminder of the deg-radation suffered during the Shoah or as an affirmation of hope in spite of suffering? Each site of commemoration prompts a different interpretation. Other elements of the text such as ritual instruction, midrashic commentary, and art also shape readers' understandings. These elements can work in con-junction with the frame, or they can challenge it. Sometimes the challenge is subtle and indirect. At other times, ritual, midrash and art mount a direct, powerful, and dramatic challenge to the redemptive frame.

Anne Frank is arguably the most famous victim of the Holocaust, and the words "in spite of everything . . ." have inspired people around the world, so it is not surprising to find them in many commemorations. The three haggadot examined in this chapter all use Frank's text to honor the Jewish victims of genocide during World War II, and each text creates a different relationship between Frank's words and the redemptive theme of the haggadah. This chapter concludes with analyses of haggadot that are representative of the range of Passover Holocaust commemorations which draw on Anne Frank's diary. It begins, however, with an extended review of scholarship about the iconic status of Anne Frank and the popularization of her diary. The diary and later representations engage key questions for the formulation of collected Holocaust memories: What counts as knowledge of the Holocaust? How do post-Holocaust generations evaluate the asser-tion of subjectivity and resistance? What remains of the possibility of hope? Anne Frank's diary and its popularization raise profound questions about knowledge, memory, agency, and redemption, all of which remain relevant as her words continue to appear in American haggadot and contribute to the shaping of contemporary Jewish memory and identity.

Anne Frank and Her Diary

Anne Frank received her diary as a gift from her father for her thir-teenth birthday, June 12, 1942, approximately one month before her elder sister, Margot, received a summons for deportation to a Nazi work camp and the Frank family went into hiding in "the Secret Annex." In her opening en-try Frank sets forth her hope that the diary will be "a great source of comfort and support."[1] Frank's diary becomes her friend and confidante, whom she addresses as "Dearest Kitty." For more than two years, Anne recorded her thoughts, hopes, dreams, frustrations, and astute observations of the limited world around her. The diary entries written in hiding begin July 8, 1942, and end August 1, 1944, three days before the eight residents of the Secret Annex were captured by an SS sergeant and several members of the Dutch security police.

Much of the diary revolves around Anne's reflections on her development as an adolescent, including her relationship with Peter van Pels, the only teenage boy in hiding. She also records her vantage point on the war, especially the difficult circumstances of forced confinement with all the interpersonal disputes that result, and her reflections on Jewish suffering caused by Dutch compliance with Nazi anti-Jewish persecution. In an early entry written before they went into hiding, Anne posits that "later on neither I nor anyone else will be interested in the musings of a thirteen-year-old schoolgirl,"[2] but her sense of herself as a writer with something to contribute had clearly changed by May 11, 1944, when she confides to her diary "my greatest wish is to be a journalist, and later on, a famous writer. We'll have to wait and see if these grand illusions (or delusions!) will ever come true. In any case, after the war I'd like to publish a book called *The Secret Annex*. It remains to be seen whether I'll succeed, but my diary can serve as the basis."[3] Anne even revised the diary with an eye toward postwar publication, deleting and adding material, after a cabinet minister of the Dutch government in exile announced during a radio broadcast on March 29, 1944, that he hoped to assemble a collection of letters and diaries dealing with the war once it was over.[4]

Anne never had the opportunity to complete her diary revisions or write her book. All eight residents of the Secret Annex were sent to Westerbork, the transit camp that served as a holding station for Dutch Jews on their way to Auschwitz. The Franks, van Pelses, and Pfeffer rode the last transport of the war from Westerbork to Auschwitz. Anne and Margot were later sent to Bergen-Belsen where they both died of typhus. Otto Frank was the only one of the eight to survive the war. When it was confirmed that Anne would not return, Miep Gies, one of the four Dutch employees who protected and sustained the Jews while in hiding, gave Anne's diary to Otto. He worked with the two versions left by Anne to create a version for publication as a testament to his daughter.[5] Since then Anne Frank's diary has been translated into more than fifty languages, adapted for the stage and screen, made into a traveling exhibition, and used to teach millions of students around the world about the Holocaust.

"I Still Believe, in Spite of Everything, That People Are Really Good at Heart"

Even people who have never read *Anne Frank: The Diary of a Young Girl;* seen the 1955 or 1997 Broadway plays about her life during the Holocaust; watched the 1959 or 2001 dramatic movies based on her diary as presented in the 1955 Broadway play; seen the 1998 or 2004 television episodes about her life broadcast on the Discovery and Biography cable channels; or viewed the 1995 documentary *Anne Frank Remembered,* winner of the Academy Award for Best Documentary the following year, may be able to quote the most famous line from Frank's diary: "I still believe, in spite of everything, that people are really good at heart." This line, and the more than fifty years of debate surrounding its various interpretations, has come to shape public perceptions of Anne Frank.

July 15, 1944

Frank's famous passage appears as part of a lengthy entry written July 15, 1944, which begins as a response to an article that charges "youth today" are concerned only with superficial matters.[6] A summary of this entry reveals Frank's unflinching introspection and struggle to make sense of an external world that has forced her and her family to live hidden away for more than two years. Frank ruminates on the possibility of building her own character and how the struggle to do so has impinged on the close relationship she once had with her father, with whom she is disappointed because "he failed to see that this struggle to triumph over my difficulties was more important to me than anything else." Otto Frank, however, is not her greatest disappointment. That honor is reserved for Peter van Pels, whom she described as "loving," "strong," "brave," and "hopelessly endearing" less than four months earlier.[7] By mid-July, her ardor had cooled: "I forced Peter, more than he realizes, to get close to me, and now he's holding on for dear life. I honestly don't see any effective way of shaking him off and getting him back on his own two feet. I soon realized he could never be a kindred spirit, but still tried to help him break out of his narrow world and expand his youthful horizons."[8]

The entry then leaves Peter behind and takes up the question whether the young or the old have a harder time in hiding. Not surprisingly, the fifteen-year-old diarist notes that the young find it particularly difficult "to hold on to [their] opinions at a time when ideals are being shattered and destroyed, when the worst side of human nature predominates, when everyone has come to doubt truth, justice and God." She tells her diary that even through she possesses self-knowledge, courage, and self-confidence, "youth today," including herself, are simply too young to solve the grave problems thrust upon them. The entry's concluding paragraph brings inner and outer worlds together: "It's utterly impossible for me to build my life on a foundation of chaos, suffering and death. I see the world being slowly transformed into a wilderness, I hear the approaching thunder that, one day, will destroy us too, I feel the suffering of millions. And yet, when I look up at the sky, I somehow feel that everything will change for the better, that this cruelty too will end, that peace and tranquility will return once more. In the meantime, I must hold on to my ideals. Perhaps the day will come when I'll be able to realize them."[9]

Frank clings to her ideals as someone drowning in the ocean would cling to a life preserver. In "The Utopian Space of a Nightmare," an essay in *A Scholarly Look at the Diary of Anne Frank,* Barbara Chiarello looks to the important role Frank's optimism played in sustaining her while in hiding and argues that Frank's optimism and idealism were conscious constructions meant to "manufacture a resiliency to depression and defeat . . . She sees how despondency destroys the soul and counterattacks it with a credo she sets down in the third from final entry in her diary."[10] The credo is Frank's meditation on the difficulty and importance of ideals. Hope functions as Frank's life-preserver, saving her from despondency and despair while trapped within the Secret Annex. Rachel Feldhay Brenner, author of *Writing as Resistance: Four Women Confronting the Holocaust,* characterizes Frank's buoy against despair as resistance, but cautions readers not to adopt interpretative strategies that limit their confrontation with the impact of the Holocaust on Frank's life. Simply accepting Frank's struggle as an exemplar of character building apart from its Holocaust context, according to Brenner, "would attest to our reluctance to comprehend fully [her] desperation and fear, to our need to evade the enormity of [her] mental suffering. To perceive these attempts as the definitive evidence of the prevailing inner strength of the victims 'despite everything' would trivialize the horror of the Holocaust experience."[11]

Brenner also offers an important corrective to the slew of critiques of Frank's work that follow: "The hopeful passages do not support, therefore, the popular notion of Frank's naïve faith in the goodness of man. Rather, they disclose the subtext of an immense effort to affirm meaning in the meaningless, hopeless ordeal."[12] A similar subtext appears in many of the testimonies presented by survivors as they decided whether or not to eat bread or hold a seder during Passover. We also saw an assertion of agency in their later assessments of those choices made under the most trying circumstances. The ability to make meaning affirms agency and subjectivity, both of which were under direct attack by perpetrators of the Final Solution. Rather than read these testimonies and texts as a psychological denial of the dehumanizing and life-denying evil victims faced, one can read the testimonies as resistance to Nazi ideology, whether or not the resistance was ultimately successful in terms of individual survival.

The Anne of Broadway and Hollywood

In his comprehensive study of the "popularization" of Anne Frank, professor of Holocaust Studies Alvin Rosenfeld observes that the 1955 play "was to prove extraordinarily successful in moving mass audiences to pity and love the image of the bright young girl without, at the same time, feeling overly frightened or repelled by too stark a sense of her end."[13] The play utilized two key strategies to evoke this response. First, the playwrights, Frances Goodrich and Albert Hackett, chose to sometimes downplay and, at other times, to suppress darker entries from the diary and to highlight affirming ones, such as the famous text that concludes the play. Second, Goodrich and Hackett minimized the specifically Jewish aspects of her story, especially her understanding of suffering as part of the historical Jewish experience. By minimizing her Jewishness, the playwrights said, Frank would have more universal appeal. These two strategies worked in conjunction to create one of the earliest, most successful, and most enduring representations of value-added redemption in the Holocaust. In 1959, a screenplay adaptation, also by Goodrich and Hackett, came to the big screen. The climactic episode of the film provides a powerful value-added rendering of Anne Frank. It is August 4, 1944, the day the Franks, van Pelses, and Pfeffer were taken away, three days after Frank wrote the last entry of the actual diary, although the film depicts Anne recording her thoughts in her diary. Anne is sitting at her desk writing while her voiceover in the film presents the words as if they were from her diary: "Everyone is low. Even father can't lift their spirits. I have often been downcast myself, but never in despair. I can shake off everything if I write, but—and that is the great question—will I ever be able to write well? I want to so much. I want to go on living even after my death." The scene would be unbearably sad, but viewers are able to take comfort during what follows in the knowledge that through her writing she went on living after her death. All the members of the Annex are gathered around and increasingly agitated by the repeated ringing of the phone downstairs and the fact that no one is in the building on a weekday. Otto Frank refuses to answer the phone, although the other men think it is Miep, one of the office employees who serves as their caretaker and protector, trying to send them a warning. When Peter's parents begin to blame each other for the fact they had to go into hiding, Peter runs upstairs, and Anne follows to console him.

She begins by describing to Peter how she transports herself outside to lift her spirits when she is feeling down. "You know the most wonderful part of thinking yourself outside?" she asks. "You can have it any way you like. You can have roses, violets, and tulips all blooming in the same season. Isn't that wonderful?" Frank's words demonstrate her ability to affirm life, remain optimistic, and see beauty in the natural world, even as the human world crashes around her. She then tells Peter she wishes he could take comfort in some sort of belief system. "When I think of all that's out there—the trees and flowers—and those seagulls—When I think of the dearness of you, Peter, and the goodness of the people we know . . . all of them risking their lives for us every day—when I think of these good things I'm not afraid anymore. I find myself in God, and I. . . ." Peter interrupts her and says when he thinks he gets mad. He describes their situation in hiding as Jews who are trapped, waiting to be discovered and taken away. The camera quickly cuts to the others pacing below and then returns to Anne who has moved toward Peter. As they look out the window together, she places their suffering in a universal context: "We're not the only people that have had to suffer. There have always been people that have had to. Sometimes one race, sometimes another, and yet. . . ." Peter interjects, "That doesn't make me feel any better," and Anne acknowledges his frustration: "I know it's terrible, trying to have any faith—when people are doing such horrible—But you know what I sometimes think? I think the world may be going through a phase, the way I was with Mother. It'll pass. Maybe not for hundreds of years—but someday. I still believe, in spite of everything, that people are really good at heart."

These words seem to calm Peter. He puts his arm around her, and she rests her head on his shoulder. When he speaks again, his voice is filled with longing rather than anger: "I want to see something now, not a thousand years from now." Anne encourages him once again to adopt a larger perspective, but then stops herself and chides them for "going at each other like a couple of stupid grown-ups. Look at the sky. Isn't it lovely?" Peter's parents may argue, but innocent adolescents, like Anne and Peter, affirm what is good and beautiful in the world. They gaze out the window together as the sound of sirens grows louder. The orchestral score also builds as Anne dreams about the future: "Someday when we get outside again, I'm going to. . . ." These are the last words we hear Anne speak. The scene shifts downstairs once more and pans the anxious faces below before returning upstairs, positioning our gaze behind Peter and Anne as they look out the window. The music reaches a climax, the police van screeches to a halt, Anne and Peter embrace and share a passionate kiss before heading downstairs to join the others. Tension builds as the police ring the buzzer several times and then break into the building. Otto Frank speaks the final words before the door to the Annex is broken down by the SS officer and Dutch police: "For the past two years we have lived in fear. Now we can live in hope." The camera zooms in on Anne, who, with trembling lips and eyes brimming with tears, turns toward her father and smiles.

In the scene after the film's climax, Otto Frank, the only survivor from the Annex, has returned from Auschwitz, and is sitting on a crate reading Anne's diary. We hear the words that the screenwriters imagined written on the page in Anne's voice, "P.S. Please, please anyone. If you should find this diary, will you please keep it safe for me because someday I hope that. . . ." Otto Frank looks up and sighs, "No more." He then fills in what happened after the climactic scene, including the fact that he just learned that Anne perished in Bergen-Belsen. As he picks up her diary once again, Anne's voice is heard alongside the sound of the seagulls soaring in the sky above: "In spite of everything, I still believe that people are really good at heart." Otto Frank says with a sense of wonder, "She puts me to shame," and the scene fades to the seagulls above. The words "The Diary of Anne Frank" are imposed on the screen alongside the seagulls as the film comes to an end.

Texts are always subject to interpretation, and the idealized reading proffered by the 1955 Broadway play and 1959 Hollywood film is certainly not the only way to read the diary. For example, Jan Romain, the first critical reviewer of the diary, wrote that its ultimate message was that humanity had lost the battle to live in a just and humane world. In his 1947 review, Romain concludes, "The way she died is unimportant. More important is that this young life was willfully cut off by a system of irrational cruelty. We had sworn to each other never to forget or forgive this system as long as it was still raging, but now that it is gone, we too easily forgive, or at least forget, which ultimately means the same thing."[14] Romain acknowledges Frank's resistance and argues that "we," those who live on after the Holocaust, have failed her by forgetting. This foreboding, pessimistic reading of Anne Frank was almost completely submerged following the success of the Broadway and Hollywood versions of Anne. Criticisms of the mainstream interpretative stance of the diary and its iconic cultural representations cluster around two issues: critics disapprove of the affirmation of the universal aspects of Frank's diary at the expense of the particular and censure the redemptive strategies employed to make Frank symbolize a palatable Final Solution.

Against Universalizing.   As might be expected, Jewish critics were among the first to express concern about universalist representations of Anne Frank. In contrast to the positive general reception given to the play and film, Jewish opinion has been more reserved. As Rosenfeld notes, "Many could not sanction the serious historical compromises that accompanied the popularization of the diary. . . . Hence, the criticism that one finds expressed time and again by Jewish writers of the period frequently turned on questions of representation. Was Anne Frank being portrayed faithfully, or was her image and that of the larger Jewish tragedy she symbolized being cheapened and distorted? These questions, which remain with us still today, marked the Jewish reception of Anne Frank right from the start."[15] Three Jewish authors writing between 1960 and 1991 on the popularity of Anne Frank cite Frank's diary entry of April 11, 1944. The warehouse has been robbed, and, in the aftermath, Frank reflects on the relationship between Jewish suffering and God. Each Jewish author cites the following passage not solely for its own merit but also to serve as a counterpoint to the predominant universalizing readings of the diary:

> Who has inflicted this on us? Who has set us apart from all the rest? Who has put us through such suffering? It's God who has made us the way we are, but it's also God who will lift us up again. In the eyes of the world, we're doomed, but if, after all this suffering, there are still Jews left, the Jewish people will be held up as an example. Who knows, maybe our religion will teach the world and all the people in it about goodness, and that's the reason, the only reason, we have to suffer. We can never be just Dutch, or just English, or whatever, we will always be Jews as well. And we'll have to keep on being Jews, but then, we'll want to be.[16]

Frank certainly focuses on her Jewishness in this passage as she tries to make sense of the suffering around her. Frank attributes meaning to suffering. Is this yet another example of value-added redemption? Rather than read this passage as "pre-empting" the horror of the Holocaust, Frank's reflections should be read as an assertion of agency and subjectivity, an effort to maintain a sense of self and identity against all odds. Regardless, her entry is highly particular, linking Jewish suffering to teaching non-Jews about goodness.

Unfortunately, the 1955 play and the 1959 film replace this thoughtful entry with a practically meaningless statement: "We're not the only people that've had to suffer. There've always been people that've had to . . . sometimes one race . . . sometimes another."[17] Every element of value in the previous passage is erased in this banal platitude. All trace of Jewish particularity is gone. Jews are no longer even mentioned. This glaring absence removes from view the particularity of the Final Solution as the Nazi genocide against the Jews. The Holocaust is replaced by generic persecution, which all races and people supposedly suffer at one time or another. This simply flies in the face of the distinctive historical record of the Shoah. Furthermore, Judaism also drops out of view, as do Frank's attempts to find meaning within her experience of suffering, which depends on her analysis of Jews, Jewish identity, and Judaism.

The history of universalism and its legacy continues to shape representations of Anne Frank. On June 15, 1952, the *New York Times* published a book review of *Anne Frank: The Diary of a Young Girl* by Meyer Levin. His review of her work brought it to the attention of the world. His decades-long battle over the diary's transformation in the Broadway play helped keep the issues of "popularization" at the forefront of academic discussion. Levin believed the optimism and universalism predominant in the play betrayed the message of the diary. In 1973, Levin published *The Obsession*, an account of his battle to have his theatrical adaptation of Anne's diary performed.[18] In the 1990s, the issues raised by Levin continued to receive scrutiny with the publication of two scholarly books on the Levin-Frank legal drama.[19] It appeared that the 1995 Academy award-winning documentary *Anne Frank Remembered*, which put Frank's life back into a context that included eyewitness accounts of her final days at Bergen-Belsen, would lay to rest some of the controversies about the optimistic, universalistic image and legacy of Anne Frank, but all the familiar issues were raised anew in 1997 when Wendy Kasselman adapted the 1955 play. In a review of the play, Molly Magid Hoagland credits Kasselman for making the play darker and more distinctly Jewish: "For example, 'I still believe, in spite of everything, that people are really good at heart' is no longer its ultimate message. Now the line is heard in voiceover as the group is being seized onstage." Her review, however, ends on a critical note: "Despite the changes, this is still the same sentimental play about a luminous, flirtatious, idealistic Anne Frank that made the critics swoon 40 years ago."[20] With the "flirtatious, idealistic Anne" as their guide, people can encounter the Holocaust and simultaneously affirm universal ideals.

Against Redemption.   Universal ideals take many forms, as do the strategies to sustain them when confronted by the Holocaust. Bruno Bettelheim offered a psychological explanation for the popularity of the play and movie in "The Ignored Lesson of Anne Frank." He critiques the redemptive strategy of forsaking the public sphere and glorifying the inner world of mind and heart. According to Bettelheim, the "universal and uncritical" response to Frank's story is a manifestation of our desire to repress knowledge that would threaten our sense of ourselves as civilized human beings who live in a benevolent modern state. "The world-wide acclaim given her story cannot be explained," he asserts, "unless we recognize in it our wish to forget the gas chambers, and our effort to do so by glorifying the ability to retreat into an extremely private, gentle, sensitive world."[21] One might note the similarity to Langer's critique against pre-empting the Holocaust presented in the previous chapter. In this case, one affirms the inner life, which remains untouched by the state-sponsored, genocidal murder system. Audiences fixate on Frank's affirmation "I still believe . . . ," not only to ignore the ways in which the Nazi concentration-camp system reduced perpetrator and victim to subhuman levels and provided sites and technology for mass murder, but also to ignore the lessons to be drawn from that knowledge.

In a problematic mischaracterization, Bettelheim describes Frank's declaration as "fiction." Frank wrote these words. The fiction Bettelheim decries may be the way Frank's words conclude the play, which emplots a happy ending. In the play, Frank has the last word, and this may be what Bettelheim accurately protests as "contrary to fact" because Frank died a miserable death at Bergen-Belsen. Moreover, the problem posed by this emplotment is more than a matter of historical inaccuracy. Bettelheim protests, "her *seeming survival* through her moving statement about the goodness of men releases us effectively of the need to cope with the problems Auschwitz presents. That is why we are so relieved by her statement. It explains why millions loved play and movie, because while it confronts us with the fact Auschwitz existed, it encourages us at the same time to ignore any of its implications" [emphasis added].[22] The value-added strategy of redeeming the inner life at the expense of the outer world comes at a high price, according to Bettelheim. He ends his discussion of Frank's quotation with the dramatic claim, "If all men are good at heart, there never really was an Auschwitz; nor is there any possibility it may recur."[23]

Although Bettelheim claims his criticism is leveled at audience reception of the Frank story, he pronounces harsh judgment on the choices Otto Frank made in his, ultimately futile, attempt to save his family. Bettelheim faults Otto Frank for not confronting the problem Auschwitz presented. In other words, the lesson people living in the wake of the Holocaust ignore was ignored by Otto Frank as well, according to Bettelheim, who presents a list of the many things Frank should have known and should have done: he should have known keeping the family together greatly diminished their chance of survival; he should have known the Nazis would not stop until Holland was free of Jews; he should have emigrated from Holland; he should have placed his children with non-Jewish families; he should have created an escape route in the back of the Annex; he should have taught his children how to escape, rather than teach them academic subjects; he should have had a gun, or at least a butcher knife, to use as a weapon; he should have shot the men who came to take him and his family away; he should have fought back. Instead, they clung desperately to their old way of life and sealed their fate.[24]

This litany of blame undermines Bettelheim's adherence to his own good judgment that "it would be very wrong to take apart so humane and moving a story."[25] John Berryman's retort is indicative of the outrage that characterized early responses to Bettelheim's argument: "I am unable to make anything of [Bettelheim's] recent article in *Harper's,* weirdly titled 'The Ignored Lesson of Anne Frank,' which charges that the Franks should not have gone into hiding as a family but should have dispersed for greater safety; I really do not know what to say to this, except that a man at his desk in Chicago, many years later, ought not to make such decisions perhaps."[26] Berryman's observation regarding the vantage point of judgment is sound. Bettelheim accuses Otto Frank of "disregarding" what was happening in the world outside the Annex, when, truthfully, the most one can say is he misread the situation. Even this assessment comes from a vantage point after Auschwitz, with the advantage of hindsight and knowledge that could not have been known at the time. Thus, such a harsh judgment of Frank's actions seems unfair, or, at the very least, not helpful.[27] If a guiding principle of post-Holocaust memory is to honor attempts to maintain agency during the Final Solution, then any hasty dismissal of choices made in situations of extremity are unwarranted.

The power of the "idealistic" Anne Frank endures and continues to accompany redemptive readings of the Shoah. For example, former President Ronald Reagan's 1985 address from Bergen-Belsen illustrates that recognition of Frank's death, even standing on the very ground where she was consumed by typhus, does not guarantee a "non-redemptive" reading of her significance, or a tempering of the unadulterated optimism that shaped early American interpretations of the diary. In contrast to Bettelheim's observation, Reagan directly attempts to redeem the public domain, even going so far as to place the Nazi SS elite and Anne Frank in the same category as victims of a historical era in need of redemption. In 1985, President Reagan scheduled a visit to the military cemetery in Bitburg, Germany, where more than seventy SS officers are buried. Despite protests by many Jewish, Christian, and U.S. veterans groups, Reagan refused to cancel his visit to Bitburg prior to attending an economic summit in Germany. Instead, Reagan added Bergen-Belsen to his itinerary and suggested that young German soldiers—including, it seems, the members of the SS buried at Bitburg—acting under the sway of Hitler, were as much victims of war as the Jews and others murdered at Bergen-Belsen. Reagan used the optimistic image of Anne Frank for political effect and drew upon the most famous lines from the diary to make his point: "Just three weeks before her capture, young Anne wrote these words: 'It's really a wonder that I haven't dropped all my ideals, because they seem so absurd and impossible to carry out. Yet I keep them, because in spite of everything I still believe that people are really good at heart." After quoting from Frank's diary, Reagan draws attention to the site of his speech: "Eight months later, this sparkling young life ended at Bergen-Belsen. Somewhere here lies Anne Frank. Everywhere here are memories—pulling us, touching us, making us understand that they can never be erased. Such memories take us where God intended his children to go—toward learning, toward healing, and, above all, toward redemption."[28] In this case, healing and redemption seem to include the reconciliation of Germany and America as great economic powers.

Reagan's political rhetoric was made possible by the legacy of artistic readings, especially the first Broadway play and Hollywood film that captured the American imagination. As artistic renderings continue into the twenty-first century, so, too, do value-added redemptive representations. On April 12, 2001, I had front-row seats for the world premiere performance of *About Anne: A Diary in Dance* choreographed and directed by Laura Gorenstein Miller and performed by the Helios Dance Theatre. Immersed in debates about the various artistic renderings of Frank's diary, I was, perhaps, unfairly predisposed to be critical. I was dismayed even before the curtain rose as I read the description of the evening's program. Granted, modern dance is not a genre meant to convey historical accuracy, but why were two of the eight Jews hiding in the Secret Annex completely absent from the performance? To be fair, Miller made brilliant use of the movements of modern dance to show the effects of living in confined quarters under anxious conditions for an extended period of time. In addition, Jewishness was far more prominent than in earlier representations. Actually, this became one of the more problematic aspects of the performance as a redemptive reading of Jewish faith took center stage.

Throughout the performance, the dancers were silent with the exception of two scenes when they sang in Hebrew. The first occurred during the celebration of Hanukkah. Once again the influence of the play and film on later representations looms large. While Hanukkah occupies a pivotal scene in the film, Frank barely mentions the holiday in her diary.[29] In the modern dance Hanukkah celebration scene, the Annex residents and Miep, their non-Jewish protector, sing "*ma-oz tsur,*" a song about God as the rock whose power saves. The song was presented in Hebrew, but for those who know the meaning of the lyrics, the irony is heartbreaking: "Rock of Ages, let our song/ Praise Your saving power; You amidst the raging foes,/ Were our sheltering tower./ Furious, they assailed us,/ But Your arm availed us,/ And Your word/ Broke their sword,/ When our own strength failed us."

The second instance of singing in Hebrew comes at the conclusion of the dance after the families have been taken away. Anne returns to the stage, wraps herself in sheer white material (which was the tablecloth), and, alone on stage, lighted by two floodlights at her feet, sings the Sh'ma, a central prayer of Jewish faith: "Hear, O Israel, the Lord is our God, the Lord is One. The Lord will reign forever and ever." Although this artistic choice does address the critique of universalism in response to the ending of the original play, its indebtedness and commitment to an optimistic reading remains. The program offers an interpretation of how to make sense of the final scene: "In spite of Frank's short life, her indomitable spirit lives on. She sings the Sh'ma, a declaration of Jewish faith." Whereas Frank's reflections on Jews and Judaism tentatively place value on Jewish particularity, primarily as a form of resistance in the context of Nazi persecution, the dance wholeheartedly affirms the triumph of religious faith over adversity. In fact, the Sh'ma is also the traditional prayer recited by Jews at the moment of martyrdom. Once again, a redemptive strategy betrays the complexity of an individual's Holocaust experience.

As artistic renderings continue unabated, so do scholarly interpretations. As expected, Lawrence Langer is vocal in his critique of the redemptive use made of the diary. A short newspaper article with the lengthy headline "The Uses—and Misuses—of a Young Girl's Diary: 'If Anne Frank Could Return from the Murdered, She Would Be Appalled'" is one of several places where he criticizes common understandings of the diary: "Her journey via Westerbork and Auschwitz to Bergen-Belsen, where she died miserably of typhus and malnutrition, would have led her to regret writing the single sentimental line by which she is most remembered, even by admirers who have never read the diary: 'I still believe, in spite of everything, that people are truly good at heart.' What, she might have asked, of my other views? For example: 'There's a destructive urge in people, the urge to rage, murder and kill.'"[30] Langer evokes Auschwitz as counterpoint to the passage, "I still believe," echoing the rhetorical strategy used by Bruno Bettelheim more than forty years earlier. Leaving aside the supreme arrogance of knowing what Frank would and would not regret, and the hubris of considering himself able to speak for her, Langer's critique does point to the one-sided, optimistic reception of her work.

Fortunately, more judicious voices than those of Langer and Bettelheim also proffer critiques of redemptive strategies that make use of the diary's most famous line. In her essay, "The American History of Anne Frank's Diary," Judith Doneson responds to Bettelheim and suggests that the use made of the quote is more explicitly theological than psychological. Specifically, Doneson argues that Frank's pronouncement is used to offer religious redemption. Jews were murdered by Christians at the heart of Christian civilization, and Frank's affirmation that "people are really good at heart" functions as a sign of grace. Even though Christians failed her, Frank, and by extension all victims, still believes in them. "We might say," Doneson writes, "that this ending serves to mitigate Christian responsibility. It is not a denial of Auschwitz, but rather the forgiving of a Christian lapse of goodness."[31] Frank's text serves as a form of cheap grace.

Responsible Use—A Nonredemptive Reading of Hope

While most scholars who note Anne Frank's declaration that "people are really good at heart" launch into critique of its misuse in public consumption of the diary, a dramatically different tone characterizes several essays in Carol Rittner's collection, *Anne Frank in the World: Essays and Reflections*. In part this is due to the context and purpose of the volume. Originally developed as a companion to the traveling exhibition "Anne Frank in the World," the volume is designed for teaching in the classroom.[32] Rather than simply critiquing or dismissing the pedagogical value of Anne Frank's work, the volume looks at *Anne Frank: The Diary of a Young Girl* as a valuable entry point for learning about the Final Solution. This presents a more difficult task for it wrestles with the question: what would it mean for people today to make responsible use of Frank's hope and idealism? Certainly, responsible use must avoid value-added redemptive readings where Frank's optimism allows simple affirmation of pre-Holocaust ideals, both religious and secular. But one need not eschew Frank's words altogether. Rather, people can use Frank's optimistic words to bring attention to the gap between ideals and reality, in both her day and our own.

Victoria J. Barnett's opening essay from *Anne Frank in the World* offers an example of a responsible approach. Barnett acknowledges those who critique the prominence of the diary in Holocaust education because it offers a "more comfortable, less graphic view of history—a history we can live with."[33] She argues, however, that the more significant problem is contemporary readers' own lack of innocence: "We read these words with different emotions—cynicism? anguish? irony? But the one emotion that is impossible to recapture is the full measure of that young girl's innocence and idealism."[34] Readers know the horrors of Bergen-Belsen and other sites of humiliation, degradation, terror, and death, both past and present. Frank, had she survived, might have—probably would have—forsaken her idealism. Nevertheless, echoing Frank, Barnett argues that "despite everything" the diary should be read. "In reading Anne Frank's diary," she says, "we are reminded of our possibility to be good, of her expectation (and her right to expect) that we be good, of our obligation to reawaken a sense of goodness within ourselves."[35] In Barnett's reading, "in spite of everything, I still believe that people are really good at heart" challenges rather than comforts. Readers cannot rest assured that "people are really good at heart," but neither can they take refuge in cynicism and do nothing. Frank's text poses a challenge to us to work towards the realization of the possibility of goodness.

Anne Frank in the Haggadah: "I Still Believe"

What happens when Frank's words are placed in an explicitly Jewish context? Are they redemptive? Do they comfort with an unproblematized message of hope, or do they challenge readers to live up to Frank's ideals, to justify her idealism? Rosenfeld argues that "like others, Jewish readers of the diary know the famous passages in which the young girl speaks her belief in the goodness of man, but most Jews do not see these passages as constituting the central teaching of the text."[36] While the impassioned critiques written by Jews during the past fifty years most often support this view, Jewish ritualization presents a more complicated picture. The haggadot examined below all employ Frank's most famous words. To the best of my knowledge, every haggadah that includes Anne Frank includes the words "I still believe." This is especially interesting because other passages could have been chosen. Many of Frank's reflections on Jewish suffering, chosenness, and identity resonate strongly with central themes of the haggadah. For example, the April 11, 1944, entry with its expression of real suffering, faith in God, and affirmation of Jewish particularity could supplement the traditional text "in every generation" found in the maggid. Then again, Jewish academic critics, myself included, do not have the final word in the construction of American Jewish collected memory. All elements within the text encourage particular interpretations, but meaning ultimately comes out of the interplay between author (the creator/s of a haggadah), text (all the elements on the page), and reader (the ritual participant at the seder).

Within the Frame: **A Different Night: The Family Participation Haggadah**

A Different Night: The Family Participation Haggadah originates in Jerusalem, but is intended for a diaspora audience. The Shalom Hartman Institute (SHI), which published the haggadah in 2003, describes its mission to serve "all sections of the Jewish world that wish to enrich their dialogue with Jewish texts."[37] The SHI is particularly concerned that the bond diaspora Jews have to Israel "no longer be based primarily on the trauma of the Holocaust and threats to Israel's security."[38] Like the Conservative and Reform haggadot presented in the previous chapter, the editors of *A Different Night* place their haggadah in relation to classic Jewish tradition. For the Reform haggadah, fidelity to tradition means "to bring forth what is utterly new from what was present in the old," and for the Conservative haggadah fidelity entails commitment "to preserving the classic tradition." But, for the SHI, to be "true to the spirit of the haggadah" is to be "eclectic, building on the creative artistry and intellectual insight of others: Maimonides, Ben Gurion and I. B. Singer, Ben Shahn and Marc Chagall, gifted children's writers, cartoonists and philosophers."[39] In *A Different Night*, Frank's words are placed in Barech, the section toward the end of the seder that includes grace after meals and the third cup of wine as part of the ritual for Elijah's cup. In addition to Anne Frank, the ritual for Elijah's cup in *A Different Night* includes art by twentieth-century artist Marc Chagall, ritual directions from a nineteenth-century Hasidic rabbi, a sixteenth-century prayer "associated with the legend of the Golem, the Jewish precursor of Frankenstein," a dramatization of Passover 1943 in the Warsaw Ghetto, and commentary from the early twentieth-century Zionist poet H. N. Bialik.[40] Anne Frank finds herself in eclectic company indeed! Yet, from this dizzying array of voices a privileged interpretation emerges. The ritual instructions, midrashic commentary, and art primarily work in concert with the traditional text and its redemptive frame to promote a redemptive reading of Anne Frank's message of hope.

Frank's text appears under the bold heading "Anne Frank: I Still Believe," and is part of four pages devoted to the ritual to welcome Elijah. The section opens with artwork by Marc Chagall. The black-and-white art depicts a winged Elijah, holding a cup of wine, floating above an open door where a young woman peers out. She looks as if she might float through the air and meet Elijah. The toes of her front leg barely graze the ground and her back leg is stretched out behind, suggesting a forward motion beyond the wall of the house. Behind her a woman sits, engrossed in a book. Perhaps it is a haggadah. The sketch titled "Opening the Door for Elijah" serves as a transition from the third cup wine to the cup of Elijah and from God's saving acts of the past to the hope for future redemption. How does this imagery shape an understanding of Frank's words? There are several possibilities. Certainly, the presence of art, regardless of how one interprets it, provides a visual element that increases participants' engagement with the seder. Because Chagall's art appears to the right of Frank's text, the young woman appears to be looking at Frank's words, capturing them in her line of sight, and linking them to Elijah's promise of future redemption.

Or perhaps the young woman is Anne Frank, and the book is her diary. Perhaps the woman in the background is reading Frank's entry from December 24, 1943: "Whenever someone comes in from outside, with the wind in their clothes and the cold on their cheeks, I feel like burying my head under the blankets to keep from thinking, 'When will we be allowed to breathe fresh air again?' I can't do that—on the contrary, I have to hold my head up high and put a bold face on things, but the thoughts keep coming anyway. Not just once, but over and over. Believe me, if you've been shut up for a year and a half, it can get to be too much for you sometimes. . . . I long to ride a bike, dance, whistle, look at the world, feel young and know that I am free."[41] In Chagall's picture, the young woman's hands (now imagined as Anne's hands) break through the wall that confines her. She gazes longingly out above the skyline, where trees, houses, and the sun (or perhaps the moon) appear in the distance. This reading constitutes an act of imagination made possible by the proximity of Frank and Chagall in the haggadah. Chagall completed "Opening the Door for Elijah" in 1946, before Frank became an icon to the world. But the meaning of art is not predetermined. The surrounding context and prior experiences of the viewer also contribute to meaning.

An Open Door: A Menu of Meanings

THE OPENING of the door on Pesach is a universal custom in Jewish homes, but its explanations are as varied as can be. Here is a sample of its multiple meanings:

1. Trust in Divine Security.
While night time is generally a time of fear and vulnerability to attack, on seder night the Jews show their confidence in Divine surveillance. Seder night is called **the Night of Watching** (*leil sheemureem*) in which God protected us from the plague of the first born and the persecution of the Egyptians. Therefore, there is no reason to lock one's doors or even to keep them closed tonight. Our electronic security systems can be switched off.

2. Expectation of Redemption.
The door is opened in expectation of redemption. As Rabbi Joshua said, "Just as Israel was redeemed from Egypt in the month of Nisan (on Pesach), so are we destined to be redeemed again – once and for all – in Nisan in the future." Elijah is expected to visit, bringing good tidings of the coming of the Messiah.

3. Fear of the Blood Libel.
Medieval folklore suggests a pragmatic reason for opening the door: the fear of spies and informers who might accuse the Jews of drinking the blood of a Christian child or using it for making matza. The Jews wanted to see who might be **eavesdropping** and spreading malicious – in fact, deadly – rumors about the seder.

Anne Frank: I Still Believe

That's the difficulty in these times: ideals, dreams, and cherished hopes rise within us, only to meet the horrible truth and be shattered.

It's really a wonder that I haven't dropped all my ideals, because they seem so absurd and impossible to carry out. Yet I keep them, because in spite of everything I still believe that people are really good at heart. I simply can't build up my hopes on a foundation consisting of confusion, misery, and death. I see the world gradually being turned into a wilderness. I hear the ever-approaching thunder, which will destroy us, too. I can feel the suffering of millions – and yet, if I look up into the heavens, I think it will come out all right, that this cruelty too will end, and that peace and tranquillity will return again.

In the meantime, I must uphold my ideals, for perhaps the time will come when I shall be able to carry them out. *(Diary of Anne Frank, Amsterdam 1944)*

Filling the Cup of Redemption Ourselves

The Hassidic rebbe Naftali Tzvi Horowitz (died 1817) used to invite all the participants of the seder – in order of their place at the table – to pour from their personal cup into Elijah's cup. This symbolizes the need for everyone to make their own personal contribution to awaken the divine forces of redemption by beginning with human efforts (*heet-o-ra-rut dee-l'ta-to*).

In some families, each participant helps to fill Elijah's cup of future redemption while expressing a particular wish for a better year.

FIGURE 4.1 Anne Frank's words with Marc Chagall's painting. *Reprinted from* The Family Participation Haggadah: A Different Night *edited by Noam Zion and David Dishon (138–139), © the Shalom Hartman Institute, 1997. Marc Chagall,* Opening the Door for Elijah, *1946, © 2006 Artists Rights Society (ARS), New York / ADAGP, Paris.*

Ritual also holds multiple potential meanings which depend upon context and the experience of participants. In between Chagall's art and Frank's diary entry are two sentences that provide ritual instructions for participants. In each sentence the word that describes the desired action for the ritual appears in bold. First, "**Pour** a large cup of wine in honor of Elijah." Then, "**Open** the door expectantly for Elijah." Emotions and dispositions are made explicit as ritual actors are encouraged to be hopeful and expectant. Beneath instructions for the ritual is an explanation of the ritual actions where two phrases occur in boldface on the page. The first paragraph draws the readers' attention to the present moment and its relation to the future: "Now the seder focuses on the **hope for future redemption** symbolized by Elijah the Prophet, **bearer of good news**." The themes of hope and expectation are developed in the concluding paragraph of the

Cup of Elijah   כּוֹס אֵלִיָּהוּ

1. **Pour** *a large cup of wine in honor of Elijah.*

2. **Open** *the door expectantly for Elijah.*

Now the seder focuses on the hope for future redemption symbolized by Elijah the Prophet, bearer of good news. In Egypt the doors of the house were shut tight on the night of the Tenth Plague. Blood marked the lintels and doorposts where we now place the mezuzah. However in the contemporary seder the doors are opened wide in expectation. This is no longer a night of terror but the dawn of hope. It is, as the Torah calls it, a **Night of Watching** *in expectation of great changes for the better.*

Kadesh
Urchatz
Karpas
Yachatz
Maggid
Rochtza
Motzi
Matza
Maror
Korech
Shulchan Orech
Tzafun
Barech

Elijah's Cup

*Marc Chagall,
Opening the Door for Elijah
(1946) © ADAGP, Paris (1996)*

instructions. Whereas in ancient Egypt the doors were shut tight, at a contemporary seder "doors are opened wide in expectation" because the night is also "the dawn of hope." The ritual instructions conclude: "It is, as the Torah calls it, a Night of Watching in expectation of great changes for the better."[42] The ritual instructions create an overdetermined text and leave no room to read Frank's message outside of the redemptive frame, which powerfully shapes the range of possible meanings and constrains Frank's text within it. The haggadah has shifted from degradation to glory. This movement becomes powerfully clear on the next page, which presents the ritual: "Welcoming Elijah." Participants are instructed to "welcome Elijah with the traditional greeting 'Baruch Ha-Ba' and a prayer or song."[43] The second song suggested is Anee-ma-a-meen (*ani ma'amin*). Frank's statement "I still believe," which *A Different Night* uses as the heading of her text, resonates with the English translation of ani ma'amin: "I believe with a perfect faith."[44] Her words parallel words of messianic hope, and participants are primed through narrative and performance to read Frank's words as part of "hope for future redemption."

The Dancing with Miriam Haggadah:
A Jewish Women's Celebration of Passover

The Dancing with Miriam Haggadah: A Jewish Women's Celebration of Passover is literally meant for a different night. On the fourth night of Passover in 1994, 192 women celebrated the first Dancing with Miriam seder in Palo Alto, California.[45] The women-only seder provided an opportunity for women to gather and understand their own experiences as Jewish women in light of the Exodus story of oppression and liberation. Women-only seders and haggadot that emphasize the contributions of women in Exodus, the silencing of women throughout Jewish history, and the status of Jewish women today have become increasingly common since the first women's seder in 1975 and reflect the impact of feminism on Jewish communal and religious life over the past thirty years.[46]

Four major themes characterize most feminist haggadot, including *The Dancing with Miriam Haggadah*. First, these texts bring together feminism and Judaism. The authors acknowledge this as one of their primary reasons for holding a women's seder: "Rather than struggle with the dichotomy of Judaism versus Feminism, why not create a Jewish feminism and a feminist Judaism that speaks the language of both, and validates the authenticity of each without forcing an impossible choice?"[47] Jewish feminists strive for full inclusion of women in Jewish life and recognize that the addition of women is likely to transform Judaism itself. Second, in contrast to a traditional maggid, the telling of the Exodus story at a feminist seder highlights the role of women. Accordingly, in response to the question "Why Is This Night Different from All Other Seder Nights?" the community gathered notes, "At all other seders the heroic deeds of our sisters Miriam, Yocheved, Shifrah and Puah are kept hidden." Participants then respond in unison, "Tonight we will celebrate their courage."[48] In *The Dancing with Miriam Haggadah,* the voices of nineteen women, including Anne Frank, are heard during the seder. Third, feminist haggadot often note connections between various forms of oppression beyond the multiple exclusions faced by Jewish women both as Jews and as women. The Ten Plagues in *The Dancing with Miriam Haggadah,* for example, includes poverty, AIDS, and environmental pollution alongside the plagues of "backroom abortions," "the myth of the 'Frog Prince,'" and female infanticide.[49] Finally, feminist haggadot encourage women to take action and transform visions of liberation into reality. Thus, the reading "Why Is This Night Different from All Other Seder Nights?" includes an examination of "the pharaohs of our own day" and a celebration of "our empowerment as Jewish women."[50] Moreover, the authors repeatedly connect the dance of Miriam in Exodus 15 with the words of Emma Goldman: "If I can't dance to it, it's not my revolution."[51] The women at this seder dance and see themselves as part of a revolution.

These themes and the commitments they express, along with the traditional texts and redemptive frame of the haggadah, shape the possible readings of Anne Frank and, by extension, readings of the Holocaust. Frank appears early in the maggid. Her words are part of the third traditional passage titled here "We Have Been Enslaved." Participants familiar with Hebrew will immediately notice a difference as the traditional words *avadim hayinu* are recast in the feminine form *b'avdut hayinu*.[52] The first stanza of the one-page reading begins with an evocation of the biblical history of violence against women and their role as property in a patriarchal society:

We have been enslaved.
Like Jephthah's daughter, sacrificed on the altar of war.
Like Lot's daughters, offered upon the altar of hate.[53]

The text alludes to a history of exclusion, silence, and struggle. "We Have Been Enslaved" returns to specifics in the fourth stanza to acknowledge moments of joy even amidst sorrow: "Like Sarah, we laugh. Like Miriam, we dance. For laughter and dancing will create our freedom more than any tool of war. Let our voices ring out—'free at last.'" The passage connects the struggle of Jewish women for equal rights with the civil rights movement of African Americans through allusion to words made famous by Martin Luther King, Jr. in his "I Have a Dream" speech: "Free at last. Free at last. Thank God Almighty, we are free at last!" Like King, the Jewish women describe a journey from slavery to freedom. Like King, the Jewish women affirm a path of nonviolence.

The sixth and final stanza evokes a different reference and lexicon of meaning when it concludes: "*B'avdut hayinu*—we have been enslaved. Tonight, together, we vow: Never Again." The phrase "never again" emerged in connection to genocide following the adoption of the United Nations Convention on Genocide in 1948. Throughout the 1950s and 1960s, Jewish communities evoked the phrase to express an identity based on resistance to victimization. The phrase is also used internationally to demonstrate commitment to end genocide (although many people have noted that "again and again" more accurately represents the ongoing history of genocides in the twentieth and twenty-first centuries). In *The Dancing with Miriam Haggadah,* the words "never again" are followed by an explicit reference to Holocaust memory: "We remember the suffering and courage of those women whose lives were directly altered by the Holocaust; those who perished and those who survived to bear witness. We praise their strength and mourn their lost freedom and youth." The next line presents a single sentence, the most famous line from the diary: "Anne Frank: 'In spite of everything, I still believe that people are really good at heart.'" This appears just before the concluding words of "We Were Enslaved" at the bottom of the page: "May we be granted her hopeful optimism, and may her words prove to be true."[54]

The Dancing with Miriam Haggadah presents a more responsible use of Frank's words as several elements work in conjunction with one another to challenge a simple, redemptive reading, beginning with the location of Frank's words in this haggadah. Recall that *A Different Night* placed Frank in Barech, a section of blessing. Within Barech, Frank appeared parallel to Elijah, a strong symbol of redemption. Multiple cues within the text pulled readers toward a redemptive reading within the strong redemptive frame of the haggadah. *The Dancing with Miriam Haggadah,* by contrast, places Frank's words early in the maggid, long before the culmination of the liberatory motif. This placement mitigates the strong pull of the redemptive frame and opens up space for a fuller range of human action. The examples presented throughout "We Were Enslaved" include slavery, redemption, and the ongoing journey from one to the other. In between the violence committed against Jephthah's and Lot's daughters and the resilience displayed by Sarah's laugh and Miriam's dance, the text acknowledges the difficult and ongoing human task: "The struggle for liberation has been a long one and not easy/ And not yet over."[55] The description of struggle echoes the description of the Exodus from the biblical text, where human agency and the ongoing journey are prominent. This greater complexity of human action and motivation extends to the description of Holocaust memory as well. Victims and survivors in the brief passage endure suffering *and* display courage. Memory-work requires mourning *and* praise. Finally, the specific response to Frank's text expresses a more circumspect hope, less certain and more deliberately cautious. In contrast to the bold title "I Still Believe," which announces Frank's words in *A Different Night,* "We Were Enslaved" concludes "may her words prove to be true."

Breaking the Frame: *A Passover Haggadah*

Critics, especially Jewish critics, of the original Broadway dramatization of the diary leveled two primary complaints against the play's, and by extension the general public's, reading of Anne Frank: one, an overwhelming emphasis on Frank's optimism, and two, the universalizing of her experience from the particularity of the Holocaust to the suffering of humanity. The origins of Reform Judaism are also marked by an optimistic view of humankind and a sense of universal mission. Reform Judaism developed out of German Jewry's encounter with modernity, especially the Enlightenment belief in progress and the power of reason. A radical version of Reform Judaism known as Classical Reform took root in the United States, where its commitments and values were boldly affirmed in the 1885 "Pittsburgh Platform," a statement of eight principles of Reform Judaism. A dramatic expression of both universalism and optimism marks the Platform's fifth principle: "We recognize in the modern era of universal culture of heart and intellect the approaching of the realization of Israel's great Messianic hope for the establishment of the kingdom of truth, justice and peace among all men." In this principle, culture is "universal" and the utopian vision of "truth, justice and peace" is on the brink of becoming reality.[56]

For the leaders of Reform Judaism, as for the movement as a whole, Auschwitz radically called into question the possibility of universalism and the unbridled optimism espoused by earlier generations. The Reform movement's struggle with its legacy is reflected in an intellectual descendent of the 1885 "Pittsburgh Platform," the 1976 "Centenary Perspective," which was written in the same era as *A Passover Haggadah:* "Until the recent past our obligations to the Jewish people and to all humanity seemed congruent. At times now these two imperatives appear to conflict. We know of no simple way to resolve such tensions."[57] The Shoah provides, to recall Greenberg's terminology, "radical counter-testimony" to the existence of a "universal culture of heart and intellect" affirmed by Reform leaders of the nineteenth century. Universal ideals and particular commitments are no longer necessarily aligned. Bronstein discusses the tension between the universal and the particular when he explains how the Haggadah Committee made its decision to include the ten plagues as part of the Exodus story. Bronstein notes that the recitation of the plagues is central to the traditional haggadah. God "hardens Pharaoh's heart" through the plagues, and the tenth plague is a direct cause of Pharaoh's decision to let the Israelites go out from Egypt. However, the Reform haggadah published in the early twentieth century did not mention the plagues at all, which were considered "unworthy of enlightened sensitivities."[58] Bronstein contrasts this view with the sensibilities of *A Passover Haggadah,* where the presentation of the ten plagues, immediately following the last of the optional Holocaust readings, provides "a fusion of the particular Jewish experience of deliverance with the universal human longing for redemption."[59]

"Fusion" accurately depicts the careful back and forth between particular and universal that shapes the ten plagues ritual. The unison readings for all seder participants that precede the naming of the ten plagues serve as an example: "Though we descend from those redeemed from brutal Egypt, and have ourselves rejoiced to see oppressors overcome, yet our triumph is diminished by the slaughter of the foe."[60] The moment of rejoicing is tempered immediately by the recognition of loss of life. Participants then read that they pour ten drops from their cup of wine "to remember upheaval that follows oppression." The final participant reading recited in unison before the ritual action describes each drop removed as "hope and prayer that people will cast out the plagues that threaten everyone everywhere they are found, beginning in our own hearts."[61] The universal and particular, while not synonymous, are fused elegantly together. In contrast, universal and particular—optimism and pessimism—jostle against one another in the presentation of Anne Frank's text. An examination of how Frank's words appear in *A Passover Haggadah*—where they are placed within the narrative frame, what texts surround them, and how art functions as additional commentary—demonstrates an ambivalence about the legacy of Reform Judaism and a challenge to value-added readings of Holocaust and redemption.

In contrast to the single sentence quoted in *The Dancing with Miriam Haggadah*, *A Passover Haggadah* presents a substantive portion of Frank's July 15, 1944 entry:

> That's the difficulty in these times: ideals, dreams, and cherished hopes rise within us, only to meet the horrible truth and be shattered.
>
> It's really a wonder that I haven't dropped all my ideals, because they seem so absurd and impossible to carry out. Yet I keep them because in spite of everything I still believe that people are really good at heart. I simply can't build up my hopes on a foundation consisting of confusion, misery, and death. I see the world gradually being turned into a wilderness. I hear the ever-approaching thunder, which will destroy us too. I can feel the sufferings of millions and yet, if I look up into the heavens, I think that it will all come right, that this cruelty too will end, and that peace and tranquility will return again.
>
> In the meantime, I must uphold my ideals, for perhaps the time will come when I shall be able to carry them out.

These words appear just before the ten plagues as an optional reading titled "For More Than One Enemy Has Risen against Us."[62] This repeats the group reading, a presentation of a traditional haggadah text, which immediately precedes Frank's words: "For more than one enemy has risen against us to destroy us. In every generation, in every age, some rise up to plot our annihilation. But a Divine Power sustains and delivers us."[63] Once again, a comparison with *A Different Night* is instructive. Frank's words appear in the first half of the haggadah, not alongside the words of praise that follow the ritual meal. Moreover, the title given to her passage emphasizes the need for redemption. "For More Than One Enemy" evokes degradation, not glory.

The other texts on the page also shape possible readings of Frank's words. Immediately following the diary passage, separated by only a single asterisk, is "A Vow," by the Hebrew poet Abraham Shlonsky, who wrote several poems about the horror and devastation faced by European Jewry. This poem begins by placing the reader in proximity to witnesses to the Holocaust:

> In the presence of eyes
> which witnessed the slaughter,
> which saw the oppression
> the heart could not bear. . . .

One set of critiques about Frank's representative status in relation to the Holocaust is that her diary does not bear witness to the slaughter and oppression experienced in the concentration camps. Shlonsky's poetry reflects an encounter with the aftermath of the Holocaust. He depicts lessons learned from this encounter in a series of oaths. The first oath or vow appears in the middle of the poem: "I have taken an oath: To remember it all,/ to remember, not once to forget!" The poem concludes with a series of oaths:

> An oath: Not in vain passed over the night of the terror.
> An oath: No morning shall see me at flesh-pots again.
> An oath: Lest from this we learned nothing.

The oaths pose a stark contrast to Frank's idealism, and the attribution of the poem includes additional information about its location that further complicates the relationship between the Holocaust, Israel, and American post-Holocaust memory-work: "The original poem may be seen in the Yad Va-Shem Holocaust Memorial in Jerusalem and is recited at many S'darim, as a regular practice, in the land of Israel." These words emphasize the creation of a living Judaism emerging out of the shadow of the Holocaust. Following the attribution, a second asterisk separates the English translation

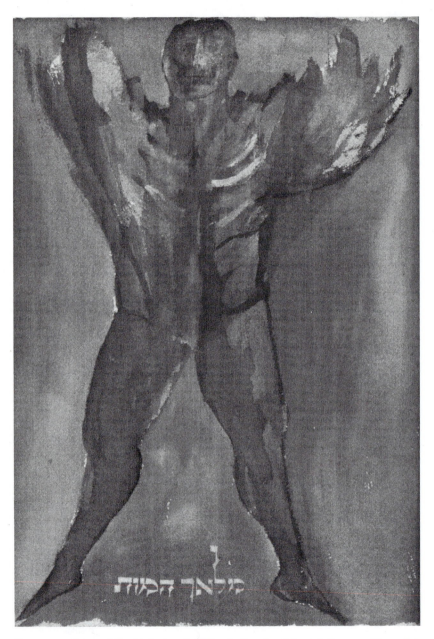

FIGURE 4.2 Leonard Baskin's Angel of Death. *Reprinted from* A Passover Haggadah *edited by Herbert Bronstein (46–47), © Central Conference of American Rabbis, 1975.*

from the original Hebrew. At the bottom left corner of the page, written in italics, the warning to "every generation" appears once again: "In every generation, in every age, some rise up to plot our annihilation."[64]

On the adjacent page, the Angel of Death rises up. Leonard Baskin's full-page drawing of the Angel of Death is an imposing figure. Against a background the color of blood orange, the angel, drawn in somber tones of green, blue, and gray, looks like a stone body builder with winged arms jutting out from his muscular body. His toes are pointed outward and barely graze the bottom of the page. In between the angel's feet appear the Hebrew words *"malach hamot"* (Angel of Death). As the transition between "In every generation" and "the ten plagues," one can read Baskin's dramatic illustration in several ways. Perhaps it is meant to lead the participant to the next page, which returns to the seder proper and the ten plagues. On this reading, the Angel of Death appears as part of the redemptive narrative in his role as slayer of the Egyptian first born. Alternately, one could read Baskin's illustration as commentary on the Holocaust texts by Frank and Shlonsky. God, through the power of the Angel of Death, destroys those who rise up "in every generation." Or, perhaps the Angel of Death occupies the role of the persecutor who "rises up" in each generation. The imposing, almost human figure could represent the murderers of six million Jews.

No single reading of Frank's words is established. No strong redemptive frame guides this collection of text, commentary, and art. Frank's idealism is muted by the call "Never Again," which is echoed by Shlonsky's disturbing phrase, "no morning shall see me at flesh-pots again." A potentially redemptive reading of Frank's words is supported by the reference to the "regular" recitation of this poem "in the land of Israel." However, any easy reading of this as an example of value-added redemption though a pairing of the Holocaust and the creation of the state of Israel is made difficult by the reminder that we are regularly—in every age and generation—threatened by destruction. The larger context calls the dominant, optimistic reading of Anne Frank into question. Taken together, the elements burst through the bounds of the redemptive frame.

CHAPTER 5

Heroism Redeemed

THE WARSAW GHETTO UPRISING

>-·+◆·-O-·◆+·-◄

*The majority of us favored an uprising. After all, humanity had
agreed that dying with arms was more beautiful than without
arms. Therefore we followed this consensus. In the Jewish
Combat Organization there were only two hundred twenty of us
left. Can you even call that an uprising? All it was about, finally,
was that we not just let them slaughter us when our turn came.*
—Marek Edelman, *Shielding the Flame*

*Like the plot of a classical tragedy, the uprisings against the
Nazis took place in a restricted space and time, and the fighters
seem tragically heroic to us because we know how they perished
and thus we can grasp the beginning and end of each uprising as
a single event, fixed in a linear progression of linked episodes.
But while it was actually happening, it was experienced instant
by instant and person by person, each with different motives and
inspirations for fighting, and each with differently formulated
explanations of his own involvement.*
—Michael Bernstein, *Foregone Conclusions:
Against Apocalyptic History*

*I*f Anne Frank is the most popular
representative of the Shoah in American Passover haggadot, the Warsaw
Ghetto Uprising comes in a close second. Many haggadot that include the
Shoah commemorate the Warsaw Ghetto Uprising when young Jews, under
the banner of the Jewish Fighting Organization, engaged in mass resistance
against the Nazis. Commemoration of the Uprising during the Passover celebration seems natural, as the Uprising began on the eve of Passover, April
19, 1943. Moreover, the symbolic force of the Uprising resonates powerfully with the redemptive theme of the seder. This chapter examines six haggadot that are representative of different ways the Warsaw Ghetto Uprising
is commemorated during Passover. In the first four haggadot the redemptive

frame contains the Uprising. Although these four present a diversity of religious and ideological perspectives, each supports a value-added redemptive reading of the Holocaust through a narrow reading of heroism born of a desire to affirm the valor of the fighters' sacrifice. The two haggadot examined at the conclusion of the chapter offer other commemorative possibilities. Their constructions of collected memory acknowledge the courage of those who participated in the Uprising on Passover eve April 19, 1943, but allow the realities of limited agency and imperfect redemption to reside uneasily within the Passover story of deliverance.

James Young writes about the symbolic value assigned to this date: "On the eve of Passover, when Jews celebrate God's deliverance of their forebears in the desert of exile, the Jewish Fighting Organization grasped fully that they were now their own deliverers."[1] The remaining Jews in the Ghetto would no longer wait for God's intervention. The image of Jews fighting back against the Nazis, rising up from the degradation of the Ghetto and redeeming themselves, provides an appealing alternative to the image of Jews being herded to their deaths like "sheep to the slaughter." Bruno Bettelheim's attack on Otto Frank provides an extreme example of the critique of passive compliance and expresses the desire to find evidence of active resistance to the Nazi regime. Although the harshness of Bettelheim's critique may be unusual, the longing that undergirds it pervades Holocaust memory. The desire to celebrate resistance, to find heroes in the midst of tragedy, shapes the majority of memory-work about the Warsaw Ghetto Uprising, including contemporary American Passover haggadot.

The fit of this commemoration, however, including the symbolic value of self-redemption attributed to the start of the Uprising, is not as natural as it first appears. Although the date has accrued great commemorative weight, the fighters did not choose the date of the Uprising, which came three months after their first instance of organized resistance in January 1943. Between January and April, the fighters maintained a constant state of readiness as they did not know when the Nazis would launch their next attack. The Nazi leadership determined the start of the Uprising on Passover eve; they often initiated actions against the Jews on Jewish holy days. For example, the announcement that the Ghetto in Warsaw would be sealed was made on Yom Kippur, and the July–September deportation that reduced the number of Jews in the Ghetto by 90 percent began on Tisha B'Av. The few survivors of the Uprising who have written about their experiences attest to their uncertainty regarding when the Uprising would begin. Vladka Meed, who worked as a member of the Jewish resistance posing as a non-Jew outside the Jewish

Ghetto, writes in her memoir, "Although all of us had anticipated the upris- ing, the actual outbreak caught us by surprise."[2] In an interview published under the title "To Outwit God," Hanna Krall asks Marek Edelman, one of the five command staff of the Jewish Fighting Organization, "Why did you choose that very day, April 19th?" His reply is simple: "We didn't choose it. The Germans chose it."[3]

The fighters did not choose the date of their resistance, but they did choose to resist. Commemorations emphasizing the fighters' heroic agency were particularly important in the 1950s and 1960s, when the dominant pub- lic discourse portrayed Jews as passive and even complicit in their own mass destruction. The Warsaw Ghetto Uprising provided an important corrective countermemory. Surviving leaders emphasize that the importance of the Up- rising was that it enabled the Jews to choose their own death. Marek Edelman, leader of the troops in the brushmakers section of the Ghetto, and Yitzhak Zuckerman, one of the leaders of the January skirmish and a contact on the Aryan side during the April Uprising, argue this most strongly. In the midst of a gruesome description of death by starvation, which Edelman witnessed often in his position as messenger in the Ghetto hospital, he says, "perhaps we are discussing all of this at too great length and in too great detail, but this is because it is vital to understand the difference between a beautiful life and an unaesthetical life, and between a beautiful death and an unaes- thetical one. It is important. Everything that happened later—everything that happened on April 19th, 1943—was a yearning for a beautiful dying."[4] And Zuckerman says in an interview given on the twenty-fifth anniversary of the Uprising, "The really important things were inherent in the force shown by Jewish youths, after years of degradation, to rise up against their destroyers and determine what death they would choose: Treblinka or Uprising."[5]

The accumulated testimonies of these fighters depict choice as the ability to choose how to die (and even then the "options" were limited). When the final heroic act is mass suicide, one's role as inheritor of memory, as a reader responding to acts that are simultaneously heroic, horrific, and heartbreaking, is complex. When the Uprising is commemorated in the hag- gadah, the temptation to create a heroic narrative and an overly simplistic, recuperative discourse of redemption is powerful. Heroic characterization of survivors, according to Dori Laub, can function as a defense mechanism to avoid truly listening to the stories survivors tell. Overwhelmed by "a flood of awe and fear, we endow the survivor with a kind of sanctity; both to pay our tribute to him and to keep him at a distance, to avoid the intimacy en- tailed in knowing."[6] Laub's observation resonates with Primo Levi's dream of "speaking and not being listened to." The language of heroism enables a value-added redemptive discourse whereby the Holocaust is made meaningful, but the experiences of the Ghetto fighters and their understandings of those experiences are obscured or even denied. To say the fighters were their own deliverers challenges common understandings of deliverance, especially in the context of Passover. Although the symbolic potency of the date of the Uprising has led to many powerful commemorations during Passover, the fighters did not see themselves as their own redeemers or deliverers in any sense that would suggest redemption or deliverance from death as the Angel of Death passed over the Israelites. Again, memoirs from the few fighters who survived the Uprising are remarkably clear on this point. The fighters knew they were going to die. They made no plans to escape because death was inevitable. They made their choice in order to make the Nazis pay for Jewish lives and to die with dignity. Instead of reducing fighters' experiences to a single narrative within the redemptive frame and thus avoiding "the intimacy entailed in knowing," commemorations of the Warsaw Ghetto Uprising in Passover haggadot should reflect fighters' distinctive understandings of choice, agency, heroism, and redemption. Before turning to the haggadot, a review of the history of the Uprising and its most famous representation, the Warsaw Ghetto Uprising Monument by Nathan Rapoport, will indicate how those who incorporated the Uprising into the haggadah primarily knew it as both historical experience and commemorative event.

The Warsaw Ghetto Uprising

The formation of ghettos was an early method used by the German government to control and reduce the Jewish population. The Nazis sealed the Warsaw Ghetto on November 16, 1940. Thirty percent of the Warsaw population, including 90,000 Jewish refugees who had been relocated there by the Nazis, resided in 2.4 percent of the city's area. Jews were forced to live, and were expected to die, in horrid conditions where diseases such as typhus ran rampant. Through Nazi manipulation of the *Judenrat,* the Jewish leadership within the Ghetto, the Jews were subjected to forced labor and starvation. The Judenrat was the official leadership within the Ghetto, and social services, as well as an underground movement, developed alongside them. The underground was made up of groups throughout the political and ideological spectrum that characterized the Jewish communities of prewar Poland, including the Zionist pioneering youth movements and socialist groups that played such a crucial role in the Uprising of April 1943.

The Final Solution became a primary goal of the war for the Nazis in mid-1941. It included the actions of the *Einsatzgruppen,* mobile killing units that conducted a campaign of terror, persecution, and slaughter in the occupied Soviet Union. When news of the mass execution of the Jews of Vilna, where more than 30,000 Jews were murdered in the nearby woods of Ponar, reached the Warsaw Ghetto in 1942, Yitzhak Zuckerman proposed forming an overall self-defense organization. Leaders within the Zionist pioneering youth organizations understood the implications of the destruction of Vilna. However, the majority of the Jews of Warsaw, including officials of the underground, believed that Vilna was unique. In their analysis, the Nazis destroyed Vilna because of its proximity to the Soviet front. There was also a sense of disbelief that precluded action: certainly the Germans did not intend to destroy all Jews when their labor was necessary for the war effort. Furthermore, leaders still believed that Jewish military action, which could not succeed in saving more than a few Jews, would bring mass retaliation and the death of workers who might otherwise survive. In 1942, the Ghetto leadership rejected Zuckerman's proposal.

The death camps became operational in the spring of 1942. Plans among the youth movements for self-defense continued. A smaller military fighting unit, the antifascist bloc, was formed in April of 1942 with great optimism and high hopes for its success, but it collapsed at the end of May when its leaders were arrested. The deportation of the Jews of Warsaw to the death camp Treblinka began July 22, 1942, the eve of Tisha B'Av. On the second day of the deportation, representatives of all the political parties met to discuss resistance, but no plan of action was agreed upon. Giving up hope of forming a larger alliance, the pioneer youth movements established the Jewish Fighting Organization on July 28, 1942. As Zivia Lubetkin, one of the leaders of the movement and a key participant in the Uprising, writes in her memoir, "we were 'an army ready for anything' whose arsenal contained only two pistols."[7] Ninety percent of the Warsaw Ghetto Jews were sent to Treblinka between July 22 and September 12, 1942, and it became tragically clear that the cost/benefit analysis calculated before the Great Deportation was no longer relevant. The Nazis intended to eliminate the Jewish population irrespective of their actions. As Israel Gutman emphasizes in his history of the Uprising, "*Only when all hope for survival was abandoned did armed resistance begin within the Ghetto. Only then could resistance enjoy widespread support.*"[8] By October 1942, all the active forces of the underground joined the Jewish Fighting Organization, with the exception of Betar and the Revisionists, who set up their own military fighting unit. Approximately five hundred fighters from twenty-two different youth movements joined together to form the Jewish Fighting Organization. The mood pervading the Ghetto was one of absolute despair. Lubetkin notes that, in contrast to the antifascist bloc, the Jewish Fighting Organization was formed under "entirely different circumstances and in a completely different mood."[9]

When the Germans began a second expulsion or *Aktion* on January 18, 1943, the fighters were taken by surprise. Although they had never discussed whether or not the time was right for active resistance, various groups resisted, including a dozen troops led by Mordecai Anielewicz, who jumped out from a line of Jews on their way to the *Umschlagplatz* (deportation point to Treblinka) and fired pistols. The Germans withdrew after four days. The Jews in the Ghetto viewed the short duration of the Nazi Aktion as a victory. Lubetkin expresses the common perception of the time when she writes, "The Germans' intention to deport the remaining Jews of Warsaw to Treblinka was foiled. They encountered unexpected armed resistance and halted the Aktion."[10] Historical records confirm that the Germans did not intend the January Aktion as a final deportation, but this was not known to those in the Ghetto at the time. Their misinterpretation gave strength to the resistance movement. A dramatic psychological change enabled new action within the Ghetto. The remaining Jewish population built bunkers underground to serve as hiding places; they would not surrender unconditionally. The fighters continued in their search to procure weapons and developed military strategies based on their recent experience.

The final deportation began on April 19, 1943, the eve of Passover. The general population descended into the bunkers, and the fighters took their positions. When the Germans entered the Ghetto, the streets were empty. As they moved from house to house, they were attacked by fighters who, although greatly outnumbered, forced the Germans to withdraw. After three days of fighting, the Germans changed their tactics and set fire to the Ghetto, building by building. The suffering was enormous as Jews became trapped in the bunkers they had built for protection. The Nazis discovered the main bunker of the Jewish Fighting Organization on May 8, 1943, and most of the leaders were killed or committed suicide to avoid capture by the Nazis. The remaining leaders and their troops descended into the sewers to escape to the Aryan side on May 10. Partisan fighting continued amid the flames and the ruins of the Ghetto until May 16, 1943, when the German SS commander, Juergen Stroop, declared victory. According to Stroop's report, the Germans killed approximately seven thousand Jews during the Uprising and transported another seven thousand to Treblinka, where they were murdered upon arrival. The remaining fifty thousand Jews of the Ghetto were sent to other camps. According to Stroop's reports, the Germans expected the elimination of the Ghetto to take three days. The fighters' resistance extended the Aktion to three months.

Heroes and Martyrs: The Warsaw Ghetto Monument

Five years after the Uprising, survivors, government officials, and other dignitaries were among the crowd of fifteen thousand gathered at the site of the former Ghetto for the dedication of a monument "To the Jewish People—Its Heroes and Its Martyrs" sculpted by Nathan Rapoport. Rapoport had fled Poland in 1939 in search of the Polish army. After traveling more than 400 kilometers he arrived in Bialystok and was placed by the Russians with a group of 120 artists who had also made their way from Warsaw. All of Rapoport's information about the fate of the Jews in Warsaw came to him while he was in Russia, first as a working artist in Bialystok and Minsk, then in a labor camp in Novosibirsk, from which he was rescued by the governor who had been one of his sponsors in Minsk. Rapoport was frustrated and horrified by the rumors of destruction that reached him. In "Memoir of the *Warsaw Ghetto Monument*," an excerpt from his recollections about events surrounding the commission of the sculpture, he notes the anxieties he felt while living in Minsk in early 1941: "Now I started to work again, but this time everything was different. The world I came from existed no more. Fear and insecurity based on dreadful rumors which arrived from conquered territories changed my whole attitude. I began to search for a new means of expression which would be strong enough to express the events. I understood that it would be almost impossible to create a form that would show the determination of human nature and its evil consequences. I had to find one, so I decided on a large group which might perhaps give a symbolic expression of a whole nation in chaos."[11] Interestingly, basic decisions about the form of the monument were derived from the massive destruction of Jewish life already underway and predate the specific events the monument commemorates.

"Memoir" presents Rapoport's vantage point decades after the events and expresses the emotional backdrop that informed his creation of the Warsaw Ghetto Monument. In 1942, the "dreadful rumors" intensified, and, Rapoport remembers, "I started to work to express my feelings of pain, anger, and sorrow. In the beginning, while the whole tragedy was not yet known, the model had a vague romantic form. But the more I heard about the camps and the ghettos, the more I understood the terrible acts of the Nazis, the more I searched for a means adequate to commemorate the tragedy of my people. I had to change the aspect of my model until I could get the compactness and strength I was looking for. I changed the model, constantly influenced by every rumor, but I felt I had to learn the truth. That is why I decided to go to Moscow."[12] In Moscow, he learned about the Uprising and was "spurred on by this event." After hearing about the burning of the Ghetto, Rapoport completed the model of the monument "trying to describe the horrors and the resistance."[13] Rapoport's memoir excerpt concludes with the day of the unveiling: "April 19, 1948, marked the day of the fifth anniversary of the Jewish Uprising in the Warsaw ghetto, the first civilian armed resistance against the Nazis in Europe. On the very site of the headquarters where the Uprising by the Jewish fighters against their persecutors erupted, my monument was erected in commemoration of that historic, tragic event and of the deportation of the Jewish people to the death camps."[14] In this brief description, Rapoport locates the Uprising in the context of European resistance. He also gives equal weight to the Uprising and deportation, a fact often lost in later commemorations.

The Warsaw Ghetto Monument has played an influential role in shaping Holocaust memory, including commemorations of the Uprising in Passover haggadot. A description of the sculpture reveals that from the earliest representations, the Ghetto Fighters appear in Jewish memory as heroes on a monumental scale. Rapoport carved figures on both sides of the sculpture. Six forms emerge from the stone on the front, the most prominent of which stands front and center. A cape is draped over his broad shoulders, framing his muscular chest and bulging right bicep, which rests in a bandage across his chest. The left arm rests down at his side with a Molotov cocktail grasped in his hand. His face is marked by a furrowed brow, deep-set eyes, clenched lips, and a square jaw, while his head tilts slightly upward, suggesting a proud and determined stance. In other words, Mordecai Anielewicz, leader of the Jewish Fighting Organization, resembles a classic heroic figure, a resemblance self-consciously chosen by the sculptor. "I needed to show the heroism, to illustrate it literally in figures everyone, not just artists, would respond to," Rapoport explained in a 1986 interview. "This was to be a public monument, after all. And what do human beings respond to? Faces, figures, the human form. I did not want to represent resistance in the abstract: it was not an abstract uprising. It was real."[15] To capture the heroic form in the carved stone, Rapoport utilized *kibbutz* workers living in Paris after the war as his models.

Moving clockwise around the sculpture, the viewer sees, crouched down by Anielewicz's right leg, a slightly older looking, bearded figure with his muscular left arm exposed, staring out from the scene with an equally determined gaze. The muscled arm of a younger man who grasps a dagger drops down over the right shoulder of the crouched figure. The younger man's face appears in side profile, revealing a classic, stunning beauty. Above these three men, a woman's right breast is prominently exposed. In contrast to the deep, determined gazes of the men, the woman's arm, raised in a protective gesture, shields her eyes, which appear to be closed. To her left, a young, cherubic child looks toward her with both arms above his head, defenseless. The woman and child are above and behind the men, and recede into the stone. An androgynous-looking young woman positioned behind the left shoulder of the first central man looks off to the left with a rifle poised for use. Finally, at Anielewicz's feet lies a fallen youth.

In contrast to the chiseled figures that emerge from the stone on the front side of the sculpture, the back is carved in bas relief. A huddled mass of stooped men, women, and children walk to the left and off the stone canvas. The eyes of almost all the figures are downcast, which adds to the reading of this scene as archetypal rather than individual, and some have noted that the number twelve evokes the twelve tribes of Israel. The most prominent exception to the downward gaze is a bearded man in the center of the group who holds a Torah in his right arm and looks upward, perhaps toward the heavens. Barely visible behind this group of despairing Jews are three Nazi helmets and two bayonets.

What relationship ensues between front and back of the sculpture? In Rapoport's memoir description, the front presents the "historic, tragic event" while the back symbolizes "the deportation of the Jewish people to the death camps." For me, the bare-breasted woman and the cherubic child serve as a visual transition between front and back. In contrast to the other fighters in the bronze relief, the woman and child recede into the stone. Also, unlike the other fighters, they are unarmed and passive. A gendered code is operative here. The young girl fighter could easily be mistaken for male, while the defenseless woman is clearly—with child, flowing hair, and exposed breast, one could say, excessively—feminine. She is a transitional figure between Uprising and deportation, hero and martyr. Like Goodrich and Hackett's screenplay of the *Diary of Anne Frank*, Rapoport's monument, through its depiction of deportation and resistance, proffers a particular reading of the Holocaust and, like the screenplay, is also open to multiple interpretations. An examination of writings by three Jewish interpreters of

FIGURE 5.1 The Warsaw Ghetto Monument. *Warsaw Ghetto Monument* © *istock-photo.com/Lukasz Gumowski*

the monument reveals the ongoing negotiation of meaning in articulations of Jewish memory-work practice.

In his meticulous study, *Against the Apocalypse: Responses to Catastrophe in Modern Jewish Culture,* David Roskies takes Rapoport to task for separating secular and religious iconography, creating a dichotomous depiction of heroes and martyrs. Viewing the monument from Roskies's perspective, the secular heroes fight back, while the religious martyrs are those "who went to their deaths unprotesting," evoking the image of sheep to the slaughter.[16] Whether or not Rapoport intended this complete bifurcation between heroes and martyrs, Roskies levels harsh criticism against Rapoport and his sculpture. In Roskies's viewing, heroism is represented solely as a secular action outside the realm of possible religious responses to persecution. Roskies and others have noted multiple secular influences on Rapoport's sculpture including "lumbering mytho-proletarian figures of the Stalinist era" and Eugène Delacroix's painting of the July 1830 Paris revolution, *Liberty Leading the People.*[17] These secular resonances of heroism have indeed lent themselves to non-Jewish commemorations. For example, Mordecai Anielewicz, the leader of the Uprising, who "couldn't have remotely resembled the heroic man who dominates the 1948 monument," was viewed in later Polish history as "a hero of Socialist labor," and the Jewish context of his struggle was erased.[18] The back of the monument, by contrast, remains within Jewish iconography that cannot access the heroic gestures of the grand figures on the front of the sculpture. According to Roskies, the bas relief presents the sole Jewish option where "exile is a permanent and predictable feature of Jewish life which no amount of heroism can ever alter."[19] The two sides of the stone block are impenetrable to one another, completely separating heroism and resistance from Jewish iconography and thus from Jewish memory. Jews are effectively and eternally denied agency in Roskies's reading of the Warsaw Ghetto Monument.

The spatial divide between the front and back of the monument also provides a physical depiction of a temporal divide between past and present. This temporal problem works in both directions: the Holocaust is separated from the present, as seen in the denial of agency, and it is also separated from the past. Jewish cultures destroyed by the Nazis are irretrievable, and the separation impoverishes Judaism as a living tradition. Roskies imagines three orders of reality: "that of the present, that of the murdered Jewish people, and that of the world they left behind."[20] Of course, he is not the first to note that the Holocaust presents a caesura, a tremendous break, with the Jewish past. Roskies's project derives from a desire to connect past to present and search out strands of continuity, "to approach the abyss as closely as possible and to reach back over it in search of meaning, language, and song."[21] After examining premodern Jewish liturgy, *Against the Apocalypse* presents modern, antitraditionalist Jewish responses to catastrophe from the nineteenth through the mid-twentieth centuries. One central argument in the text is that modern intellectuals of Eastern Europe, working in both Hebrew and Yiddish, created a set of responses to catastrophe that placed them in continuity with premodern, traditional responses. The best post-Holocaust responses to catastrophe, according to Roskies, also forge connections to the past. Roskies advocates a recuperative task, which he finds absent in a Warsaw Ghetto Monument that locates meaning in the secular forms of heroes and freedom fighters, completely outside of Jewish tradition.

Ten years after the publication of *Against the Apocalypse,* James Young questions whether the heroes and fighters depicted in the Warsaw Ghetto Monument are as outside Jewish tradition as Roskies's critique would lead one to believe. In "The Biography of a Memorial Icon: Nathan Rapoport's Warsaw Ghetto Monument," from his book-length analysis of Holocaust memorials, *The Texture of Memory: Holocaust Memorials and Meaning,* Young presents a series of facts that call the complete bifurcation of secular and Jewish into question. He notes that Rapoport's turn to secular figures for sculpture was itself a Jewish impulse informed by his religious upbringing. Rapoport was a left-wing Zionist, but he was also the grandson of a Hasidic cantor and a kosher butcher and, as such, "remained acutely aware of the Second Commandment's prohibition against making graven images—even as he resisted the taboo as a young, progressive thinker."[22] Even more significantly, Rapoport, like the fighters he commemorated, identified as a Jew, Zionist, and socialist, with the multiple aspects of identity intertwined. For example, many members of the Jewish Fighting Organization perceived their Jewish resistance in the context of resistance groups throughout Europe, a view, as we have seen, also held by Rapoport. Young concludes, "The ultimate mixing of Jewish and proletarian figures in Rapoport's monument may thus have been as inevitable as the mixed identities of the fighters themselves."[23] The unveiling and dedication of the monument also encompassed this mixed identity. As a rabbi led the dedication ceremony with a recitation of the traditional Jewish mourners' prayer, red banners of socialist and communist youth groups floated overhead, intermingled with blue-and-white star of David banners flown by Jewish and Zionist groups.

Young suggests that the two sides of the monument, both distinctly Jewish, flow into one another "from dark side to light. For as we see from a side view of the monument, the engraved martyrs recede into granite and become invisible, as if absorbed into the stone. On the western side, facing the open square, however, the heroes' profiles stand out in distinct relief. In this movement between sides, the ancient type seems to pass *into* the shaded wall only to emerge triumphantly out of the other side into the western light: one type is literally recessive, the other emergent."[24] According to Young, both are Jewish archetypes. Passivity is transformed into resistance as a new model of the strong, modern Jew comes into the world. Interestingly, the relationship between back and front in this viewing indicates a progression. The past, "the ancient type," characterized by powerlessness and exile, recedes. It literally fades away into the dark stone and a new "type" emerges—active, powerful, and heroic. Young offers a redemptive reading of the monument, one which may well be in keeping with Rapoport's intentions.

Michael Rothberg presents a rejoinder to linear, temporal readings of the Warsaw Ghetto Monument in his 2001 essay "W.E.B. Du Bois in Warsaw: Holocaust Memory and the Color Line, 1949–1952." He writes, "If, as both Young and Roskies suggest, the monument seems to put forth a narrative in which the particularity of Jewish alienation and exile is transcended in the universality of socialist resistance and insight, it also resists that narrative by freezing the two sculptures in what Walter Benjamin might have described as a tense constellation of dual claims."[25] Rothberg draws upon Du Bois's short essay "The Negro and the Warsaw Ghetto" to argue that Rapoport's monument produces a form of double consciousness that allows for contemporary agency and navigates between the two poles of absolutist and relativist forms of Holocaust memory that govern much discussion about Holocaust representation today. Du Bois developed the concept of double consciousness at the beginning of the twentieth century to describe the lack of consciousness of self felt by African Americans, to the extent that they could view themselves only though the lens of white society, which perceived them to be less human than white Americans.[26] The color line in U.S. political, legal, social, and cultural life kept whites and blacks separate and produced the duality of African American consciousness, particularly among the intellectual elite. Rothberg argues that in "The Negro and the Warsaw Ghetto" Du Bois expands the concept from a description of specifically African American consciousness to "a more general *form* for the expression of particular relationships between victimization and survival."[27] Rothberg credits the Warsaw Ghetto Monument, especially as viewed by Du Bois within the context of destruction still evident in 1949, as the impetus for the revision of this critical concept whereby "the conditions of minority life are given shape in order to ground acts of resistance."[28] In Rothberg's interpretation, inspired by Du Bois, the resistance figures of the front and the exilic figures of the back always function in relation to one another and produce a "Du Boisian double consciousness" that incorporates both "estrangement" from the dominant culture and "insight" into its workings of power.[29]

Rothberg attends to the impact of Rapoport's monument on Du Bois and draws lessons from this impact on Du Bois for contemporary representations of the Holocaust, connections to multiple histories of violence, and possibilities for resistance and hope. Sidra Ezrahi's broad designation of absolutist and relativist modes of Holocaust memory is helpful here.[30] For the extreme absolutist, the Holocaust is singular, unique, inexpressible through language, and completely discontinuous with everyday life, including other histories of suffering and violence. For the extreme relativist, the Holocaust exists in continuity with other histories and everyday life to such an extent that anything distinctive about the Nazi genocide is erased. According to Rothberg, Du Bois's understanding of the Nazi genocide and its relation to the racism perpetuated against African Americans "demonstrates another possibility for the reception of Holocaust memory beyond the universalist, de-Judaizing camp [the relativist position] and the autonomous Jewish tradition propounded with such eloquence by Roskies [the absolutist position]."[31] Finally, Rothberg credits both Rapoport and Du Bois with resources for non-redemptive agency, as "both are trying to find forms to express a post-emancipation context of extreme suffering twinned with hope for a different future."[32] The term, "twinned," echoing the double consciousness, is particularly useful because hope exists alongside of, but does not replace, the current history of suffering.

Redemptive Readings: Recasting Heroism

The heroic aspect of the Uprising, especially as presented in Rapoport's influential monument, informs many Warsaw Ghetto Uprising commemorations. The Uprising functions as a redeeming moment: At least the Jews did not go "like sheep to the slaughter." But the discourse of heroism can itself bring deleterious effects. Simple depictions of heroism without acknowledgment of the extremity of the Ghetto situation, the difficulty of making an effective response, and the emotional terror endured proffer remembrance that functions as a form of forgetting insofar as such depictions avoid the "intimacy entailed in knowing."[33] Depictions of the traditionally heroic, the individual with pistol and grenade making a last stand against all odds, encourage a diminished form of remembrance that erases the complexity of life in the Ghetto. This can also be the case when heroism is recast to fit the ideals of a new context. In other words, the qualities of a hero may change, but the reductionist quality of the discourse may remain. In the ritualizations that follow, heroic discourse functions as a metonymy for the cultural, ideological ideals of a specific haggadah, which can include ideals as diverse as ethical monotheism, an ethic of care, or religious martyrdom.

The Hero as Moral Prophet: *A Passover Haggadah*

In *A Passover Haggadah,* the Warsaw Ghetto Monument is the direct focus of the passage on the Uprising, which is drawn from the dedication ceremony that took place on the fifth anniversary of the Uprising: "The monument . . . shall serve as a reminder for us who have survived to remain loyal to our people and to the moral principles cherished by our fathers. Only through such loyalty may we hope to survive this age of moral decay. . . . Let us clearly recognize and never forget this: that mutual cooperation and the furtherance of living ties between the Jews of all lands is our sole physical and moral protection in the present situation. But for the future our hope lies in overcoming the general moral abasement which today gravely menaces the very existence of mankind."[34] The tag line following the quote identifies the speaker as "Albert Einstein before the monument to the martyred Jews of the Warsaw Ghetto, April 19, 1948." This text clearly embodies the mediated character of Warsaw Ghetto representations. The passage does not give a first-hand account of the Uprising, but, rather, an excerpt from a speech inspired by the monument that commemorates the Uprising, which, in large part due to the work of Rapoport, has come to represent the heroism of all those who died in the Holocaust. The speech and its attribution locate Holocaust memory in proximity to the date and location of the Uprising.

In this case, however, the speaker is as significant as the monument itself. Einstein's speech appears just before the maggid of the Exodus story, where the Four Children ask about Passover observance. In rabbinic tradition these children correspond to four separate injunctions in the Torah to tell the Exodus story. Mishnah tractate Pesachim 116a reports that parents should teach their children at their level of understanding. In the Reform rendering, it is the wise person who asks, "What are the precepts, laws, and observances, which the Lord our God commanded us?"[35] Einstein appears in the haggadah as the wise son. Like all the other Shoah texts in this haggadah, his words form part of a series of optional readings. In the commentary, as the wise child, Einstein gives answers. In his rabbinic thesis, Steven Leder examines the development of Einstein myths in popular Jewish culture and his position as a Jewish folk hero. In "Imagining Einstein," Leder uses the phrase *kol bo*, "all is in him," to suggest the plasticity of the Einstein myth. In popular Jewish mythology, Einstein is the *navi*, the prophet who proclaims a scientific order and, more importantly, a moral order to the universe: "By clothing Einstein in prophet's garb, Jewish culture fabricated a myth it wanted to believe: that Einstein was right because a prophet couldn't be wrong. . . . When Einstein said that God was not malicious, that order not chaos, ultimate meaning not caprice, ruled the universe, who more than the Jews needed desperately to believe him?"[36]

Each denominational, ideological, and political group can claim Einstein as "kol bo" rises above denominational debate. In this passage, Einstein's exhortation echoes classic commitments of the Reform movement. One of the hallmarks of Reform Judaism has been the privileging of ethical and moral commands over ritual obligations, and the prophetic tradition occupies a central place in its reading of tradition and text. The intellectual founders of Classical Reform carved out a distinct space for Judaism in the modern world by defining its role as a "light unto the nations" where the Jews were to live out God's will in the world by serving as moral exemplars in their home nation-states. By explicitly identifying the Warsaw Ghetto Monument in the attribution of Einstein's moral message, the heroism represented in the monument is recast. To be heroic is to be moral. The term "moral" appears four times in the brief excerpt. In an age of "moral decay" and "moral abasement," all Jews who have survived the Shoah must cooperate with one another and live by "moral principles." These are the only forms of "moral protection" available in the current degenerate age. Einstein's answers address the need for Jews to remain loyal to their people and the moral principles those people cherish. Heroism, through the authority of Einstein, is read differently. Rapoport's sculpture embodies a more explicitly moral reading.

The Hero as Mother: *Women's Passover Seder*

As illustrated by the Reform example, meanings communicated through collected memories are contested, shifting, and multiple. When the Shoah is integrated into the seder, decisions such as where to incorporate the Shoah in the traditional structure of the seder, how to include an event such as the Warsaw Ghetto Uprising, or whose voices will represent women, and for what ends, depend in part on the prior commitments of each particular haggadah. Attention to the construction of memory pays heed to all these factors. *Women's Passover Seder,* published in 1977, constructs a feminist redemptive reading. In contrast to *A Passover Haggadah,* where all the Shoah texts precede the ten plagues, *Women's Passover Seder* locates the four Holocaust passages at the end of the maggid. The editors emphasize this placement and explain their deliberate choice: "We end our story of Pesach tonight by paying homage to the victims and survivors of the holo-caust."[37] Given the earlier emphasis on the movement from degradation to glory, this may challenge expectations. Clearly, the Holocaust belongs in the realm of degradation. However, precisely because this is radically counter-intuitive to understandings of the Shoah, an examination of this text helps illustrate the way narrative emplotment is a determinative factor for reading. This passage also demonstrates that the heroism of the Uprising lends itself to a recuperative discourse in a wide range of ideological contexts.

The first of the four Holocaust texts in *Women's Passover Seder* com-memorates the Warsaw Ghetto Uprising. It is an excerpt from *In the Days of Destruction and Revolt,* a memoir by Zivia Lubetkin, a participant and leader in the Uprising. Readers are introduced to Lubetkin through a quote from Marie Syrkin's essay "Blessed Is the Match," where she writes of Lu-betkin, "Of many young women who took leading parts in the Resistance, I have heard it said, she was called 'the mother.'"[38] Motherhood was one ideal in 1970s feminism, which valorized the bond between mother and child. Before Lubetkin's words appear, she is depicted as a mother figure. The description works in two directions: Lubetkin is a hero because she is a "mother," and motherhood is affirmed as heroic. Lubetkin's text follows the attribution of a maternal role:

> We were the fighters, the leaders of the rebellion, but all our old plans were now useless. We had dreamed of a battle face to face with the enemy, like our first intoxicating victory from which the Ger-mans had fled. Patiently we had organized our ambushes and waited for the enemy to return. But the Nazis had avoided open battle, send-ing fire instead to destroy us. We had never expected this.
>
> But we knew we must go. With heavy hearts we descended into the sewer. The guides were in front, Marek and I in the rear. The sewers w[ere] an abyss of darkness. I felt the water splash around me as I jumped [and I was overcome] by a dreadful nausea there

in the cold, filthy water. I felt that nothing—not even freedom was worth this. . . . All of us were poisoned by the thought of those we had left behind, and this robbed us of all possible joy in our good fortune. More than once, one of us would fall, and beg to be left lying there. But no one in all that journey was abandoned.[39]

Lubetkin's narrative clearly evokes heroic imagery through its beginning reference to the fighters and the leaders of the rebellion against the Nazi regime. Readers are reminded of the first battle, one of the very few times Nazis actually fled from Jews. When the Nazis change their tactics and set fire to the Ghetto, however, the battle plans are of no avail. It seems that freedom is not worth what one must endure, but Lubetkin and the others refuse to give in to despair. What little hope there is, even in the absolute worst of situations, can be found in the fact that "no one in all that journey was abandoned." Even in the depths of the sewers, where death seemed preferable to freedom, an ethic of care prevailed. Through editorial selection, a feminist cultural ideal of the 1970s, and a strong redemptive turn, concludes the text.

The framing of this text promotes a reading of an ethic of care; the mother of the Ghetto ensures that all her "children" are supported. Some historians and survivors of the Holocaust suggest that women's ways of bonding provided distinctive survival skills through relationships formed in the camps.[40] While it is possible that Lubetkin's style of leadership was shaped by gender expectations, her account of this event from *In the Days of Destruction and Revolt* reads quite differently from its depiction in *Women's Passover Seder*. Specifically, it does not end with an ethic of care. Only through a strong reading—a collaborative effort between author and reader—can this episode be construed as a moment of glory. When the truck from the Polish underground arrived at the manhole, the resistance fighters exited as swiftly as possible. But one group was still far from the entrance and the truck had to leave before everyone could escape. Lubetkin says, "During the entire journey, my fear for those who were left behind in the sewer continued to plague me. They were far away from the entrance. By the time they were called and came to the exit, our comrades on the street could no longer hold off the people milling about."[41] None of those left behind in the sewers survived. Lubetkin writes that when the Jews who had been left behind exited the sewer the street was surrounded by German soldiers: "A hand-to-hand battle broke out between the weak and hungry Jewish fighters and the German soldiers. The Polish population was dumbfounded, even awe-struck, at the sight. Many stories have been told of the cruel battle in which all our people were killed."[42]

Lubetkin's text expresses the despair she felt. Her narrative also gives those who were left behind a heroic death; their deeds live on in stories told of their final battle. The ethic of care of *Women's Passover Seder,* however, cannot be sustained when the excerpt is read back into its original context. Marek Edelman, who was in the rear with Lubetkin, also recounts this event. His account shifts the discourse away from heroism toward more fundamental questions of agency, blame, and responsibility. Edelman told eight people to move to a wider sewer because "they'd been beginning to asphyxiate and die owing to the water reeking of feces and methane." Once the manhole was opened, Edelman sent a runner to fetch the others, but "Krzaczek," a member of the Polish Workers' Party who participated in the rescue, ordered the truck to drive off before the other fighters arrived at the manhole opening:

> The emergence from the sewers had been organized by Kazik. He was nineteen years old at the time, and what he accomplished was truly extraordinary, only that now he calls Marek sometimes from a city three thousand kilometers away and says that it was all his fault, because he didn't force "Krzaczek" to wait. To which Edelman answers that that's not true, that Kazik performed marvelously, and that the only one responsible was he himself, since it was he who told the others to move away from the outlet in the first place. At which point Kazik, still from his city three thousand kilometers away, says 'Stop it. After all, it's the Germans who were responsible.'[43]

The shifts between the haggadah ritualization, Lubetkin's memoir, and Edelman's interview point to fissures in the previously seamless construction of fighter as hero. Focusing on these gaps, these sites of trauma, opens up a space to reexamine a simplistic heroic discourse, regardless of how heroism is configured by the ideological commitments of the haggadah.

The Hero as Martyr: *The Bay Area Jewish Forum Haggadah*

The Bay Area Jewish Forum Haggadah, published in 1986, locates the passage commemorating the Warsaw Ghetto Uprising between the ten plagues and Elijah's cup. Whereas the Warsaw Ghetto Uprising Monument is dedicated to heroes and martyrs, in this text the heroes—along with the rest of the "six million"—are the martyrs. The first paragraph of the passage titled "Lest We Forget . . ." places seder participants in the role of witnesses and asks for a moment of remembrance: "Our people have witnessed the destruction of six million Jewish martyrs in Europe. It is therefore fitting, that in this hour of celebration of freedom, we pause for a moment in remembrance of our fallen brethren on this, the anniversary of the battle of the Warsaw Ghetto."[44] Participants in the Uprising, who most often were secular (Zionist and/or socialist), are depicted in the final paragraph of the reading as going to their deaths singing an affirmation of faith in the coming of Messiah, and other religious motifs shape the middle paragraphs:

> On this night of the Seder we remember with reverence and love the six million of our people who perished at the hands of a tyrant more wicked than the Pharaoh who enslaved our forefathers in Egypt. Come, said he to his minions, let us cut them off from being a people, that the name of Israel may be remembered no more. And they slew the blameless and pure, men and women and little ones, with vapors of poison and burned them with fire.
>
> Now, the remnants of our people who were left in the Ghettos and camps of annihilation rose up against the wicked ones for the sanctification of the Name, and slew many of them before they died. On the first day of Passover the remnants of the Ghetto of Warsaw rose up against the adversary, even as in the days of their lives, and in their death they were not divided, and they brought redemption to the name of Israel through all the world.
>
> And from the depths of their affliction the martyrs lifted their voices in a song of faith in the coming of the Messiah, when justice and brotherhood will reign among men.[45]

The martyr as hero transforms the depiction of the Ghetto fighters in terms of both the motivations and the results of their actions. Moreover, the narrative emplotment encourages a strong reading of redemption. Placed just before the cup of Elijah, and Maimonides' words "I Still Believe," the martyrdom of the Ghetto fighters becomes a moment of glory. Redemptive language and emplotment transform the secular heroes into religious martyrs, a construction of memory that may not serve those who died, those who survive, and those who want to bear witness and honor the memories of all who participated in the Uprising.

In the Hebrew Bible, God's name is made holy in the world primarily through God's actions, although there are also occasions where Israel is liable for God's honor. The rabbinic tradition develops this second model emphasizing human responsibility and *Kiddush ha-Shem* (sanctification of

God's name) that is achieved through prayer, exemplary ethical behavior, and martyrdom. This third mode of sanctification, the taking of one's own life to preserve the sanctity of God, was further developed in the medieval period in Western European Jewry, particularly after the First Crusade in the eleventh century when martyrdom became, in effect, the Jewish weapon of holy war against Christian persecution. Chronicles from the time recount entire families committing suicide as a religiously sanctioned act. Some prayer books from this period even include a benediction to be recited by a Jewish man before he kills himself and his children. The language adapted in *The Bay Area Jewish Forum Haggadah* echoes a text composed after the First Crusade. During recitation of *Av ha-Rachamim* (Merciful Father), petitioners ask God to "recall with compassion the devout, the upright, and the perfect ones; the holy congregations who gave their lives for the Sanctification of the Name—who were beloved and pleasant in their lifetime and in their death were not parted."[46] Like other liberal haggadot that incorporate Av ha-Rachamim, *The Bay Area Jewish Forum Haggadah* presents highly selective verses from the traditional prayer. These haggadot include descriptions of the Jews as "upright and blameless" and "united," while God's vengeful actions on behalf of the martyrs—"Let it be known among the nations in our sight that You avenge the spilled blood of Your servants"—are excluded.

One of the more problematic aspects of drawing on Av ha-Rachamim is the claim "in their death they were not divided," especially if one reads that claim in conjunction with the previous phrase "even as in the days of their lives." Bernstein's warning against collapsing the intentions and actions of the Nazi resistance fighters, which serves as the epigraph of this chapter, bears repeating. The Uprising "was experienced instant by instant and person by person, each with different motives and inspirations for fighting, and each with differently formulated explanations of his own involvement."[47] Furthermore, the imposed unity makes their deaths meaningful in *The Bay Area Jewish Forum Haggadah*. Redemption, according to this passage, is predicated on their rising up as one people. The fighters, as one people, sing the distinctly religious sentiment: "I believe with perfect faith in the coming of the Messiah." While individual members of the Jewish Fighting Organization may have been religious, the religious parties refused to join either the Jewish Fighting Organization or its political governing body, the Jewish National Committee. This was a principled refusal. Each group knew death was the likely outcome, no matter what choice they made. Their differences arose out of strongly held political commitments, philosophical positions, and religious worldviews. Lubetkin notes the diversity of views that competed in the Ghetto and shaped forms of action. "Despite the bitter arguments that we had with the religious parties during the first days of the Aktion," she writes, "I did not alter my attitude toward them. Then and now I hold them in great respect and know that they did a great deal to save Jews and preserve the honor of Israel—in their own way."[48]

The entry on "Kiddush ha-Shem" in volume 10 of *Encyclopedia Judaica* makes explicit the logic behind reappropriation of the Ghetto Fighters into the religious framework operative in many liberal haggadot:

> With the awakening of Jewish national feeling in later modern times, as expressed by the formation of political parties like the Bund, the organization of self-defense against pogroms, and Zionism, the principle of *Kiddush ha-Shem* reasserted its influence, consciously or subconsciously, manifested in new ideological frames for the defense of Jewish dignity and in modes of response by Jews to social and spiritual challenge. Jewish revolutionary attitudes bear its imprint in the courage and readiness to struggle and self-sacrifice for the sake of humanity even where there is no immediate prospect of victory on the horizon. In the same way, the fight and death of the rebels in the Nazi ghettos was ultimately inspired by this ancient Jewish tradition.

Given that the majority of the fighters would not make this same claim for their inspiration, it is important to honor the differences between these groups and not conflate their distinct forms of heroism. In life, they had "their own way." In death, those ways are lost if fighters are read into the religious emplotment of the haggadah as martyrs.

Secular Heroes in a Secular Haggadah

The excerpt from *Sholem Family Hagada for a Secular Celebration of Peysakh* is representative of an entire genre of unpublished haggadot used by a variety of Zionist, humanist, and secular Jewish groups. Since they are not constrained by the religious emplotment of the haggadah, these texts allow reclamation of human agency, including more accurate representation of the Warsaw Ghetto fighters. The *Sholem* haggadah devotes approximately twenty percent of the haggadah to the Holocaust, and resistance is a central focus. The Holocaust commemoration begins after the meal with a two-paragraph introduction that places the Shoah as an integral component of the Passover celebration, requiring new questions and new answers: "In a previous generation, secular Jews added a fifth question to the Hagada: Why was the first night of Passover, 1943, different from all other nights in our history?"[49] The answer to this question demands a "new Hagada." Like the Conservative haggadah, the *Sholem* haggadah says the Holocaust requires a new Maggid, a new telling.

Binem Heller's poem "Paysakh Has Come to the Ghetto Again" sets the context of commemoration. This year is different from all other years because, in the midst of starvation, there is no matzah or wine:

> Paysakh has come to the Ghetto again.
> The wine has no grape; the matza, no grain.
> But the people anew sing the wonders of old:
> The flight from the Pharaohs, so often retold.
> How ancient the story, how old the refrain![50]

At first it seems that, even in the midst of deprivation, the story of liberation and redemption holds true. But the next verse calls the viability of the story into question:

> The seyder goes on.
> And fiction and fact
> Are confused into one: which is myth? which is real?
> Come all who are hungry, invites the hagada.
> The helpless, the aged, lie starving, in fear.
> Come all who are hungry! And the children sleep, famished.
> Come all who are hungry! And the tables are bare.[51]

The poet recognizes the irony of the situation. It bursts through the frame of the traditional celebration of the seder when he comes to speak about the cup of Elijah. The reworking of Elijah is stunning, especially in comparison to commemorations that pair Holocaust texts with "I Still Believe" as a final declaration of faith:

> Paysakh has come to the Ghetto again.
> The lore-laden words of the seyder are said
> And the cup of the Prophet Elijah awaits.
> But the Angel of Death has intruded, instead.[52]

Elijah may hearken to the Messiah, but the Angel of Death appears as an uninvited, if not unexpected, guest.

In the biblical-rabbinic story, Jews put the blood of the paschal lamb on their doorposts so the Angel of Death will "pass over" their homes and kill only Egyptian first-born sons. In Heller's poem, the Angel of Death arrives, perhaps, because Jews are dying of hunger, or, perhaps, to wreak vengeance on "the Nazi [who] snarls his commands . . . As always—the fate of more Jews in his hands." In a dramatic re-reading of the story, the blood on the doorposts is not the blood of the paschal lamb, but the "blood of free Jews who will fight to the last!" They are not "sheep to the slaughter" in a passive sense, and they are not waiting for the Messiah "although he may tarry." The poem concludes with a certainty that the Ghetto fighters will die and lauds death itself as heroic:

> Listen! how death walks abroad in the fury!
> Listen! how bullets lament in their flight!
> See how our History writes End to the story
> With death heroic, this Passover night.[53]

In contrast to the religious haggadot where the experience of the fighters is read to fit with traditional meanings of redemption, here the experience of the Holocaust shifts the meanings of redemption and freedom. This ritualization seems to fit an important aspect of the self-perception of the fighters.

Shame and Survival

If death is heroic, is survival a cowardly act? The question appears absurd, but a second reading of Lubetkin's memoir in conjunction with reflections on shame and survival by Primo Levi shows that consideration and response to the question are required and urgent. Reading Lubetkin's account as traumatic and not simply heroic reveals the prominence of shame. Her memoir aptly captures the complex emotions associated with survival and demonstrates how these feelings were operative both during the Shoah and afterward. In her chapter on the deportation of July-September 1942, Lubetkin writes about a youth movement meeting held the second day of the deportation. "We were too late," she recalls: "This was the terrible feeling which overcame all of us. Crushed and dismayed, we called another meeting of our Hehalutz leadership. We sat together depressed, our eyes lowered in shame."[54] Their earlier attempts to create a defense organization had ended in failure. They were ashamed because they had been unable to take action.

Shame overwhelms them, on the one hand, because they were not able to act effectively. On the other hand, and paradoxically, the presence of shame suggests that they should have and could have acted. A presumption exists of complete agency, suggesting a fuller range of options than were truly available to most victims of the Holocaust. Michael André Bernstein makes a similar point in his analysis of how the shame of survival shapes Primo Levi's final work, *The Drowned and the Saved.* As the author of insightful works spanning several decades, Levi's writings offer reflections that can be used to understand the complexity of emotion in Lubetkin's memoir and the erasure of this emotion in the unadulterated heroism portrayed in the haggadah. In a review of a recent biography of Primo Levi, Bernstein notes how shame shaped Levi's life as well.

> Levi depicts himself as tormented by a sense of shame at having survived when so many millions died. He wrestles with the unbearable conviction that it was the noblest among the prisoners who were murdered because they refused the compromises necessary to live. . . . Psychologically, no doubt, these charges serve as a flight from the unbearable arbitrariness of survival, by moralizing the situation and positing a greater element of free choice than is warranted. . . . It is even sadder to see Levi, who made the moral indifference of *fortuna* central to *Survival in Auschwitz,* begin to blame himself for the good outcome of his bad luck, and to assign agency and choice where, as no one knew better than he himself, there was none.[55]

Levi himself elucidates the role shame plays in cultivating silence. The following passage from the opening pages of Levi's *The Reawakening* is quoted at length because it dramatically depicts this dynamic of shame amidst joy and the accompanying silence that diminishes the moment of liberation.

> They did not greet us, nor did they smile; they seemed oppressed not only by compassion but by a confused restraint, which sealed their lips and bound their eyes to the funereal scene. It was that shame we knew so well, the shame that drowned us after the selections, and every time we had to watch, or submit to, some outrage: the shame the Germans did not know, that the just man experiences at another man's crime; the feeling of guilt that such a crime should exist, that it should have been introduced irrevocably into the world of things that exist, and that his will for good should have proved too weak or null, and should not have availed in defence.
>
> So for us even the hour of liberty rang out grave and muffled, and filled our souls with joy and yet with a painful sense of pudency, so that we should have liked to wash our consciences and our memories clean from the foulness that lay upon them; and also

with anguish, because we felt that this should never happen, that now nothing could ever happen good and pure enough to rub out our past, and that the scars of the outrage would remain within us for ever, and in the memories of those who saw it, and in the places where it occurred and in the stories we should tell of it.[56]

Here shame afflicts the innocent, not those who are guilty. Shame oppresses at the very moment of freedom from oppression, and it shapes what experiences can be told and how they can be told.

In Levi's narrative, shame exists on several levels. First is the shame of having suffered various humiliations and degradations in the camp. The self is diminished by the experience. A psychological overview of research on shame emphasizes that "shame is about being in the world as undesirable self, a self one does not wish to be. Shame is an involuntary response to an awareness that one has lost status and is devalued."[57] Devaluation of the self, even though the self at that moment of extreme victimization rarely had agency to act differently, appears with regularity in Holocaust testimonies, including Lubetkin's memoir. Depictions of heroic death as the sole honorable choice buttress legacies of shame. A second source of shame, according to Levi, comes from the knowledge that survival required putting one's own needs first. Accumulated testimony suggests that luck was more determinative of survival than any general approach or particular action, but the fact remains that this self-judgment is a strong source of shame. In both cases, shame includes a strong social component, an internalizing of societal normative values. Whether it is the speaker or listener who refuses to confront the implication of this breakdown of values, silence emerges as a response to shame.

Conversely, there is the shame that exists as a response to silence. Levi's analysis suggests that, perhaps, even the innocent and the just are not completely free of blame. In *The Drowned and the Saved,* Levi returns to this passage about the moment of liberation and extends the sense of shame beyond direct survivors of the camps. He asks his readers, "Are you ashamed because you are alive in place of another? . . . It is no more than a supposition, indeed the shadow of a suspicion: that each man is his brother's Cain, that each one of us (but this time I say 'us' in a much vaster, indeed, universal sense) has usurped his neighbor's place and lived in his stead."[58] Finally, Levi speaks of the more generalized "shame of the world" that an event such as the Holocaust could occur. It is striking that Levi describes witnessing moments of humiliation and degradation as being "drowned" by shame. Those who drowned were not saved, but the distinction between drowned and saved seems blurred. The title *The Drowned and The Saved* suggests two distinct populations, and Levi often writes of them as distinct. In this passage, however, shame drowns even those who were saved; survival is incomplete. "Is this belated shame justified or not?" Levi asks. "I was not able to decide then and I am not able to decide now, but shame there was and is, concrete, heavy, perennial."[59]

Lubetkin returns to this language of shame at the end of her chapter on the deportation. She has recounted how the defense organization they formed during the first week of the deportation suffered a horrible blow when several of its leaders were arrested and their supply of weapons was confiscated: "We all sat together in silent mourning. We were ashamed to look into each other's eyes. True, we had not just sat idly by during the Aktion. We had done all that was humanly possible. The majority of our missing friends had resisted. Some had fallen with the partisans, others in various attempts at vengeance, hurrying to save Jews from the Nazis' talons or, after all hope was gone, trying to escape from the columns being led to the Umschlagplatz. They had been surrounded and thwarted on all sides, unable to take any effective action. We had remained alive and were ashamed of it."[60]

Everyday Moral Agency

The shame of survival is linked to heroic expectations. In Lubetkin's account shame pervades because members of the defense organization carry an expectation that they should have been able to do something. Of course, as she notes, the fighters did many things: formed a resistance organization, procured weapons, fought alongside the partisans, rescued underground members from the columns. Their harsh self-judgment is informed by expectations of heroism, which limits recognition of the moral agency they did exercise. Today, moral construction of collective memories must move beyond simplistic notions of heroism. The haggadot passages in this final section reframe heroism and open up other narrative possibilities. These ritualizations of the Shoah that focus on the Uprising acknowledge both the reality and limits of heroism as well as its problematic connections to redemption. Sidra Ezrahi suggests that, in contrast to Auschwitz, the Warsaw Ghetto is an alternative site to think about moral agency. She looks at writings about the Ghetto as offering the possibility to redeem not the history but "the moral discourse that was destroyed."[61] Commemorations of the Warsaw Ghetto Uprising can function as sites for moral reflection when they present a moral discourse that expresses the constrained choices of the Ghetto, acknowledges the various choices made within that context, and demands a response from the reader. Both *A Different Night: The Family Participation Haggadah* and *A Night of Questions* engage seder participants as moral agents.

A Different Night: The Family Participation Haggadah commemorates the Warsaw Ghetto Uprising after the cup of Elijah under the heading "Holocaust and Hope." The text is lengthy and a bit didactic; however, in contrast to the previous ritualizations, it gives a more nuanced and ambiguous reading of heroism, freedom, and redemption. This haggadah begins by placing the resistance in its historical location of the aftermath of the deportation: "At the darkest moment, the Warsaw Ghetto Uprising revived Jewish hope and honor. After 450,000 Jews had already been deported, the Jewish youth movements mounted armed resistance that reached its climax on seder night, 1943."[62] The presentation of the number 450,000 acknowledges the tremendous losses already incurred, and the description of the Uprising as the "climax" of armed resistance suggests it was not the beginning deliberately chosen for its confluence with Passover. The passage then instructs seder participants to "read the following dramatization, drawn from authentic memoirs by Vladislav Pavlak." The form of dramatization emphasizes the diversity of perspectives within the Ghetto. Performing the drama with separate, distinct voices encourages seder participants to consider the various perspectives presented.

N: It was April 19, 1943, the first day in the renewed defense of the Ghetto.

A: Do you know what day this is?

B: Monday. The 19th of April.

A: No, no, I don't mean that. But do you know that today is a holiday?

B: What, is he crazy? We're dying and he blabbers about holidays.

A: I am telling you, today is a great holiday. It is Passover, the Seder night.

B: If it makes you happy, why don't you conduct the Seder for yourself? Passover without matza and maror! What kind of Passover is that?

A: We need no bitter herbs. Sufficient bitterness and humiliation have been our lot. Are we not slaves? Are we not orphans who have been forsaken? We need no wine, let us drink water. We need no matzot. Our bread is the bread of affliction.

N: They read the Haggadah aloud. When they came to the words: "And the Lord freed us from the bondage of Egypt," someone interrupted.

B: It's a lie, I'm telling you. God has never freed us from bondage, for it follows us wherever we go. We were slaves by the Rivers of Babylon, in Spain and now, again we are slaves, and as slaves do we die.

Pavlak's memoirs dramatized here resemble the conflicting positions articulated by Holocaust survivors in the oral testimonies discussed in chapter two. Similar to those testimonies, this dramatization highlights the conflict between a celebration of freedom and the context of oppression. Moreover, the symbols of Passover are embodied in the experience of suffering and made present as their absence is recognized. Suffering in the ghetto is "the bitter herbs" and "the bread of affliction."

The context of ghetto rather than concentration camp becomes evident as the final speaker in the drama gives his reading of the Uprising in the context of the Passover celebration:

C: The commander spoke: Quiet! Fools! He was right when he said that today we celebrate a holiday. Passover is a holiday of freedom. Don't you see that we are free? No longer do we listen to orders. They tell us: Come out of your hiding—and we refuse to come out. They lure us with promises, and we answer with gunfire. We have thrown off the armbands which they made us wear for our humiliation, and we turned them into banners. Today is the day of freedom, and that freedom is within us. We will go down in defeat but we will die as free men and women.[63]

The commander's words contribute to revised understanding of freedom and redemption, heroism and moral agency. "The commander" in this passage speaks of Passover in terms of freedom rather than redemption. Freedom is located within the human and is not incompatible with defeat and death. The heroic gesture is to choose to die as free human beings and to resist. Resistance includes gunfire, the response of the minority Jewish Fighting Organization, as well as the refusal to come out of hiding, the response of the majority of the Jews in the Ghetto. Its format, a dialogue between multiple voices, prevents us from reading a false unity into the responses of the Jews in the Ghetto and also shows that they were unified in their resistance, now broadened to include both fighting and hiding. Moreover, the form of dialogue, dramatized by participants, opens a space for agency in the contemporary creation of Holocaust memory.

The final text comes from *A Night of Questions,* published by the Reconstructionist Press in 1999. Focused on the words and thoughts of Mordecai Anielewicz, the passage also demonstrates ambiguity of agency, complexity of emotion, and the limited nature of redemption:

> On the eve of Pesaḥ 1943, the Jews of the Warsaw Ghetto staged a revolt against the Nazis that lasted for forty-two days. Below is an account from the diary of the Commander of the Jewish Fighting Organization.
>
> It is now clear to me that what took place exceeded all expectations. Our opposition to the Germans was greater than our strength allowed—but now our forces are waning. We are on the brink of extinction. We forced the Germans to retreat twice—but they returned stronger than before. . . . I feel that great things are happening and that this action which we have dared to take is of enormous value. I cannot describe the conditions in which the Jews of the Ghetto are now "living." Only a few exceptional individuals will be able to survive such suffering. The others will sooner or later die. Their fate is certain, even though thousands are trying to hide in cracks and rat holes. It is impossible to light a candle, for lack of air. Greetings to you who are outside. Perhaps a miracle will occur and we shall see each other again one of these days. It is extremely doubtful.
>
> The last wish of my life has been fulfilled. Jewish self-defense has become a fact. Jewish resistance and revenge have become actualities. I am happy to have been one of the first Jewish fighters in the Ghetto.
>
> From where will rescue come?[64]

Anielewicz's entry clearly presents the tragic situation and the likely outcome. The conclusion of the passage with a question opens space for contemporary agency so that participants can consider both his and their responses. Anielewicz's honest assessment of the value of resistance and its limitations create a site for moral memory. Transformed from the larger than life figure of the Warsaw Ghetto Monument, Anielewicz's accomplishments can be remembered on a human scale. Irena Klepfisz, a peace activist, poet, teacher, and child survivor whose father was the first casualty of the Warsaw Ghetto Uprising, offers a vision of what a non-redemptive reading might look like during an address delivered on the forty-fifth anniversary of the Warsaw Ghetto Uprising: "What we grieve for is not the loss of a grand vision, but, rather, common things, events, and gestures. . . . I have come to believe that ordinariness is the most precious thing we struggle for, what the Jews of the Warsaw Ghetto fought for. Not noble causes or abstract theories. But the right to go on living with a sense of purpose and a sense of self-worth—an ordinary life. It is this loss we mourn today."[65] More than sixty years after the Jewish Fighting Organization fought its final battle, the search to commemorate and honor "an ordinary life" continues.

CHAPTER 6

Provisional Conclusions

⊱┈⊷┈०┈⊶┈⊰

> As the Haggadah places every Jew at Sinai, instructed to recount
> the events of the Exodus as though they had been part of his own
> life, the presence of all Jews is also fixed within the events of the
> genocide—those born after it as well as those who lived despite it.
> —Berel Lang, *Act and Idea in the Nazi Genocide*

> Perhaps the issue concerns the contradiction between two types
> of experience, which in German is expressed in the distinction
> between the raw shocks of Erlebnis and the meaningful coherence
> of Erfahrung. Whereas the victims experienced their fate largely
> in the former sense, historians tend to interpret it in the latter.
> Another way to make this point is to say that while the disaster of
> the Exodus from Egypt could be turned by the Jews into Haggadic
> truth, that of the Holocaust cannot.
> —Martin Jay, "Of Plots, Witnesses, and Judgments"

Performance at the Limits and the Limits of Performance

Chapter one described the seder as a dramatic performance of the story of slavery and redemption, and the first presentation of American haggadot in *You Shall Tell Your Children* focused on the emplotment of the Exodus story in *A Passover Haggadah* and *Feast of Freedom*. This final chapter returns to these haggadot from the Reform and Conservative movements of American Judaism and examines their performative, rather than narrative, aspect. The language of performance continues the discussion of agency begun in the previous chapter but registers a shift from consideration of the agency of victims and survivors to the agency of the performers at the Passover ritual, the seder participants. The terms "performance" and "ritual" highlight how the text of the haggadah comes to life through embodied enactment. "Cultures are most fully expressed in and made conscious of themselves in their ritual and theatrical performances," claims anthropologist Victor Turner. He provides an interesting and helpful description of performance as "a dialectic of 'flow,' that is, spontaneous movement in which action and awareness

155

are one, and 'reflexivity,' in which the central meanings, values and goals of a culture are seen 'in action,' as they shape and explain behavior."[1] Through embodied action, cultures tell stories about themselves to themselves, and through this process, performed annually in the case of the Passover seder, create and re-create themselves.

Turner uses the German term *"Erlebnis"* (also used in the epigraph by Martin Jay) to describe "unique structures of experience" that comprise the liminal stage of the ritual process.[2] The liminal stage is "betwixt and between" one form of reality and another; in some cases, such as a wedding or a graduation, performers are transformed through ritual process. In others, such as the seder, performers are momentarily transported and then return more or less to their original state. The liminal stage allows performers to experience the "as-if," and then to incorporate that experience into their individual and communal selves.[3] We live our experiences in bodies; sight, sound, taste, smell, and touch all play prominent roles in the ritual of Passover, which is structured by the series of sensory experiences participants are obligated to perform. For example, participants recline during the narration of the story to indicate their status as free persons. Knowledge of freedom is not simply a cognitive proposition; it is felt and lived through the body. Taste constitutes another important element of the seder. Wine, with its sweet taste and intoxicating effect, indicates the promises and fulfillment of redemption. Bitter herbs and salt water evoke the bitterness and tears that accompany slavery. Appeals to tradition and associations with childhood through sight, sound, smell, and taste bypass the rational to form our identities and reflect our values.[4] One need not give rational assent to a smell, a taste, a posture.

"Rituals persuade the body first," according to anthropologist and ritual theorist Barbara Myerhoff. "Behaviors precede emotions in the participants. Rituals are conspicuously physiological; witness their behavioral basis, the use of repetition and the involvement of the entire human sensorium through dramatic presentations employing costumes, masks, colors, textures, odors, foods, beverages, songs, dances, props, settings, and so forth."[5] The seder makes masterful use of ritual's potential to make a lasting impression through the use of these sensory faculties. Often from early childhood one is exposed to the taste of bitter herbs for the bitterness of slavery and salt water for the tears slavery brings. The texture of the haroset, a mix of apples, nuts, and wine eaten only during Passover, brings to life the feel of the mortar. Reclining on a pillow and partaking of elaborately prepared food and drink among family and friends imbues performers with the knowledge that they enact these rituals as free men and women. The enduring power of these embodied elements is manifest in the testimonies presented in chapter two, where survivors made critical connections between sensory elements (sitting, eating, drinking, and singing) and their conditions in the camps. Songs and illustrations also figure in the performance, adding to the emotional and aesthetic dimensions of the seder.

The epigraphs for this chapter indicate two possible relationships between those who experienced the Shoah and those who come after. Lang and Jay refer to "Jews" and "historians," respectively, but those who come after includes anyone concerned about the Nazi genocide and its legacies of remembrance. Both authors refer to the Passover haggadah, particularly its performative aspect, to consider the relationship between the Holocaust past and post-Holocaust present. Berel Lang suggests that all Jews are "fixed within the events of the genocide," regardless of their temporal relation to the Shoah. He makes a comparison between remembering the Shoah and remembering the Exodus. Martin Jay draws the opposite conclusion, uses the analogy for contrast rather than comparison, and indicates limits of the possibilities of performance. In the passages from *A Passover Haggadah* and *Feast of Freedom,* embodied and sensory aspects of ritual are in the foreground as sites for memory work. An analysis of these passages demonstrates that both relations between past victims and present performers are possible.

"The Egyptians Embittered Their Lives"

"We cried unto the Lord, the God of our Fathers, and the Lord heeded our plight, our misery, and our oppression (Deut. 26:7)." In *A Passover Haggadah,* this central text from the maggid is followed by multiple commentaries, beginning with a passage titled "The Egyptians Embittered Their Lives" that commemorates the Shoah.[6] A brief analysis of the title, given to the excerpt by the editor of *A Passover Haggadah,* suggests how the Holocaust imposes limits on its own performance. Some elements of the title repeat motifs from haggadot and testimonies already discussed: the Nazis are equated with Egyptians as harsh taskmasters; the bitter herbs of slavery represent both Egypt and Nazi Germany as they are invoked through the term "embittered." However, the use of the pronoun "their" presents a new dimension for discussion directly related to issues of performance. A comparison with the titles of the other commentaries on Deuteronomy 26:7 helps one to see the radical presence of the pronoun "their" in the title. The second and third texts in the series are traditional rabbinic expositions on the phrases "Our Misery" and "Our Oppression" respectively. Each comes from traditional collections of midrash dating back centuries and regularly found in haggadot. The first passage, entitled "Our Misery," directly echoing the words of Deuteronomy 26:7, reads: "The 'misery' refers, commentators say, to the enforced separation of husbands and wives. Husbands and wives were not allowed to live together. Nevertheless, the women of Israel were a source of strength to their husbands, bringing them food, consoling them when they visited, giving them hope of liberation."[7] The second passage, under the heading "Our Oppression," reads, "We are taught that the Egyptians taunted the Israelites for observing the circumcision of their sons. They mocked the Hebrews for this, since the infants were to be put to death anyway. But the Hebrews answered, 'We perform our duty; whatever you do later cannot affect our practice of our faith. As our ancestors were faithful to God's covenant, so shall we be.'"[8] Again the words from Deuteronomy are used for the title of the passage. Like the reference to commentators in "Our Misery," the authority of rabbinic tradition is invoked by the opening phrase "we are taught."

Given the examples of the second and third commentaries, one might reasonably expect that the first optional passage, the Holocaust text under discussion, would be titled "Our Plight." The text, however, defies this expectation; the possessive pronoun in the title of the Holocaust passage is in the third-person plural "their" rather than the first-person plural "our" of the other two texts. The shift from first to third person is no small grammatical matter; it is absolutely shocking given the pedagogical commitments of the seder and the rhetoric of presence that informs it: "I was a slave in Egypt." The assertion of slavery and redemption as a personal event in one's own life, not simply a remembrance of past events, pervades the entire ritual. One transforms the events of the past—slavery and freedom—into personal events of one's present through performance. The purpose of the seder— you shall tell your children—demands pedagogy based on performance, the presence of the child as formerly enslaved and currently redeemed. Traditionally, placing oneself outside the community impacted by slavery, as indicated here by "their" rather than "our," means placing oneself out of the community altogether, and, hence, outside the realm of redemption. The story of "the wicked child" illustrates this purpose of performance. Mishnah Pesachim 10:4 states, "According to the understanding of the son, does the father instruct him," and the haggadah presents children who represent four different modes of understanding: wise, wicked, simple, and too young to ask. The wicked child asks "What is this service to you?" The wicked child is wicked precisely because she asks about the meaning of the ritual for others, implying it is not meaningful to her personally. She shifts the grammar from first to second person. The reply to her question sanctions her severely. Tradition emphasizes that the wicked child puts herself outside the community by saying "to you" rather than "to us." By placing herself outside the community, she places herself outside the realm of redemption.

Some contemporary haggadot soften the response to the wicked child. For example, *A Night of Questions* offers a series of commentaries to interrogate tradition's verdict against the wicked child. One passage suggests the wicked child was not denied redemption but refused it, certain that the oppressor never meant to harm him. In a problematic example of backshadowing, placing blame on the victim for not acting on information that clearly could not be known at the time, Arthur Green, the author of this margin commentary, compares the wicked child with "The World War I veteran who stayed in Germany until it was too late, sure that they would never harm a German hero."[9] A second commentary asks, "Why is it so bad to choose to stand apart?" A third commentary suggests that the wicked child becomes a scapegoat as contemporary Jews react harshly in order to hide personal doubts about the worth of Passover.[10] Together these commentaries work to destabilize the rejection of the "wicked" child from the community and from redemption. The rendition of the four children in *A Passover Haggadah,* however, presents a traditional understanding of the wicked child as unredeemed. "A Participant" reads: "The wicked person says, 'What is this observance to *you?'* Since he says 'to *you*' and not 'to us,' he rejects the essentials of our faith: the unity of God and the community of Israel. To him we respond sharply: 'It is because of what the Lord did for *me* when I went forth from Egypt—'for *me,*' that is, and not 'for *you*' . . . for had you been there, you would not have known redemption.'" The other participants at the seder echo the indictment of the wicked child: "The wicked one withdraws himself from anything beyond himself; and thus, from his own redemption."[11] This reading of the wicked child brings into sharp relief the problematic of the title of the Holocaust text. Why is the title not "The Egyptians Embittered *Our* Lives"? What is it about the content of this passage that demands a shift from "our" to "their"?

The author of the text is Peter Fischl, a fourteen-year-old boy who perished in Theresienstadt, and the passage comes from the collection of children's writings, *I Never Saw Another Butterfly:*

We got used to standing in line at seven o'clock in the morning, at twelve noon, and again at seven o'clock in the evening. We stood in a long queue with a plate in our hand into which they ladled a little warmed-up water with a salty or coffee flavor. Or else they gave us a few potatoes. We got used to sleeping without a bed, to saluting every uniform, not to walk on the sidewalks, and then again to walk on the sidewalks. We got used to undeserved slaps, blows, and executions. We got accustomed to seeing piled-up coffins full of corpses, to seeing the sick amidst dirt and filth, and to seeing the helpless doctors. We got used to the fact that from time to time, one thousand unhappy souls would come here and that, from time to time, another thousand unhappy souls would go away. . . . [12]

Attention to the embodied aspects of this passage offers a possible explanation for the distance created by the grammatical shift in title. First, in contrast to most passages in haggadot, this was written in a concentration camp. Most writings about the Nazi genocide are located on either side of the camp experience, either before, like Anne Frank's diary and memoirs from the Warsaw Ghetto, or after, like memoirs by Delbo, Levi, and Wiesel. Diaries from hiding or the ghetto are temporally before the concentration camp, the primary signifier of dehumanization and mass murder. Memoirs that analyze what it was to live in and die in a concentration camp are written afterward. But this text is situated differently. Although the text is dramatically present, the text survives its author, a child murdered at the site where the text was composed.

Fischl's description is written in the past tense, but his subject is the inclusive "we," and his concrete descriptions work in conjunction with the pronoun to evoke a series of embodied sensations. The sights described by Fischl are made present. "We" got used to "seeing piled-up coffins full of corpses, to seeing the sick amidst dirt and filth, and to seeing the helpless doctors." Not only are the horrors of life in the concentration made present, they are also described as the quotidian life of the everyday. "We got used to" all of the degradation and suffering inflicted at Theresienstadt. The gerund form—standing, sleeping, saluting—describes present actions, some of which are in direct contrast to the embodied gestures of freedom emphasized at the seder. For example, the passage begins with standing in line, while the seder draws attention to sitting as an act of freedom. In Fischl's text, standing predominates. Morning, noon and night they (described as we) are forced to stand in line. This is not new information. Seder participants most likely know about the endless series of roll calls that marked life in the camps. What is gained is not informational content but, rather, a type of experience, a type of body-knowledge. Participant-performers are conscious of reclining as an act of freedom. When participant-performers are attuned to their own body posture, when they have imbued sitting with significance, standing also comes to signify. In a setting where both sitting and eating embody physical manifestations of freedom, the descriptions of standing and lack of food as an ongoing, embodied reality bring the horror of the camp closer to home. The contrasts between standing and sitting, starving and eating also mark the distance between the Holocaust and the Passover celebration.

Finally, the conclusion of Fischl's description of life in the camp suggests another reason for the shift from "our" to "their." Fischl's description of daily life in Theresienstadt is radically anti-redemptive. Martin Jay's epigraph resonates here: "Perhaps the issue concerns the contradiction between two types of experience, which in German is expressed in the distinction between the raw shocks of *Erlebnis* and the meaningful coherence of *Erfahrung*. Whereas the victims experienced their fate largely in the former sense, historians tend to interpret it in the latter. Another way to make this point is to say that while the disaster of the Exodus from Egypt could be turned by the Jews into Haggadic truth, that of the Holocaust cannot."[13] Fischl describes the daily experience of degradation, but he does not make sense of it, impose coherence upon it, or offer any form of redemption. Rather, the quotidian presence of his suffering remains. When one reads Fischl's narrative within a ritual re-enactment from a physical place of abundance, privilege, choice, and safety, it is clear that the "Egyptians [Nazis] Embittered Their [not Our] Lives." The vast majority of Jews at a seder may celebrate [as if] they have been slaves in Egypt, but they were not Jews in the death camps. The placement of Fischl's poignant text in *A Passover Haggadah* suggests the limits of performance. Whereas one can liturgically imagine one's own enslavement *and* freedom, one cannot embody one's own annihilation. Fischl's text ends unredeemed as "from time to time, another thousand unhappy souls would go away."

"We Were All in the Hell That Was the Holocaust"

Analysis of "The Egyptians Embittered Their Lives" concluded with the claim that one cannot embody one's annihilation, but another text challenges that conclusion and pairs an embodied ritual with redemptive narrative. If the passage in *A Passover Haggadah* refuses to transform the Shoah into "Haggadic truth," the following passage entitled "Remembrance of the Six Million" places contemporary seder participants "within the events of the genocide" through a performative language of presence. Reproduced in several haggadot, including the Conservative haggadah *Feast of Freedom,* the passage describes Hitler as "a tyrant more fiendish than Pharaoh" and describes the Jewish victims of the Nazi genocide as "holy innocents" and "martyrs" who should be remembered "with reverence and with pride." The final stanza directly invokes the language of performance. "We invite the souls of all who are missing, the souls of all who were snatched from our midst, to sit with us together at the Seder." Whereas the previous text distanced the "we" in Theresienstadt from the "we" at the seder table, this passage collapses the distance between here and there, then and now. The "we" who originally extended the invitation are identified as "Seder celebrants in the Vilna Ghetto in 1942." Then the givers of the invitation shift to the present as "we repeat it tonight." The repetition of "we" in conjunction with the repetition of the invitation blurs time and place. The souls were snatched from "our" midst in addition to the midst of those who remained in the Vilna Ghetto at the seder in 1942.[14]

The concluding lines of the passage further expand the collective "we": "We were all in Egypt. We were all at Sinai. We were all in the hell that was the Holocaust. And we will all be present at the final redemption."[15] Here "the hell that was the Holocaust" is immediately followed by "the final redemption" where "we will all be present." The text does not question the commensurability of Exodus and Auschwitz but links them through performance.[16] The dead are invited to sit at the seder table alongside the living. Berel Lang's observation presented in the first epigraph to this chapter speaks to this performance: "As the Haggadah places every Jew at Sinai, instructed to recount the events of the Exodus as though they had been part of his own life, the presence of all Jews is also fixed within the events of the genocide—those born after it as well as those who lived despite it." However, only the certainty of "final redemption" makes participants' presence in "the hell that was the Holocaust" possible.

Remembering When I Was Not There: Witness and Desire

Elie Wiesel draws upon the language of the seder to criticize attempts to extend the subject position of Holocaust survivors: "I did not leave Egypt, but I must think 'as if' I had been among those who did. Certain Talmudic legends explain that actually our souls were there. Or we may accept the literal interpretation, and say: Though I have not personally taken part in those events, I must live 'as if' I had. This lesson is especially relevant for those of our contemporaries who declare that all of us 'are survivors of the Holocaust.' No, all of us are not. Only those who went through the agony of Night survived that Night. Only those who knew death in Auschwitz survived Auschwitz. But all of us should think and act 'as if' we had all been there."[17] The "as if" marks a critical distance between before and after. But what exactly might it mean to think and act "as if" we experienced the Holocaust? The language of witness that pervades several decades of work in Holocaust studies illustrates an ongoing set of attempts to think through the moral imperative of the "as if" that informs the relationship between survivors of the Shoah and others who choose to put themselves in relationship to its legacy.

One of the earliest influential works to examine the role of the witness focuses specifically on survivors who bear witness to their experiences of trauma. In *The Survivor,* published in 1976, Terrence Des Pres argued that modern history, which gave birth to both the concentration camp and the gulag, also gave birth to the survivor as a moral type whose very reason for survival is to "bear witness . . . to objective conditions of evil."[18] The reversal of religious language in this notion (traditionally Jews and Christians "bear witness" to the redemptive power of God and Jesus Christ, respectively) is striking, as bearing witness itself becomes redemptive. Des Pres argues that the will to bear witness is "a typical and in some sense necessary response to extremity."[19] In the midst of extremity, the will to bear witness propels one to survive. Afterward, the eyewitness, according to Des Pres, not only attests to evil, but through the recounting of these horrific events the act of witnessing becomes "evidence that the moral self can resurrect itself from the inhuman depths through which it must pass."[20] Religious language becomes even more pronounced with the echoes of a Christian resurrection, albeit without divine intervention. Des Pres posits a moral self that "can resurrect itself," but the survivor is not alone. Here is where Des Pres's analysis is particularly relevant in the context of the seder. The moral self must recount the story, and recounting requires both a teller—a survivor who bears witness—and a listener to hear the testimony. Seder participants enact the role of listener. Des Pres's analysis articulates a problematic desire that confronts the listener in this act of witnessing. Resurrection and redemption are possible and depend upon eyewitnesses to atrocity to assure the rest of the world that goodness remains.

The redemptive role of the listener implicit in *The Survivor* becomes the subject of analysis in later works that examine the possibilities and the limitations of the witness. Twenty years after Des Pres, Shoshana Felman and

Dori Laub published a groundbreaking work that simultaneously demands less and more of the witness. Felman, a literary critic, and Laub, a psychiatrist, co-founder of the Yale Video Archive, and a child-survivor, shift the language of atrocity from "extremity" to "trauma," indicative of revised expectations and a different method of interpretation.[21] As James Berger notes in his review of *Testimony* and several other recent works that draw on the concept of trauma: "The idea of catastrophe as trauma provides a method of interpretation, for it posits that the effects of an event may be dispersed and manifested in many forms not obviously associated with the event."[22] According to those who utilize trauma theory to consider the role of the witness, there is a latency and a gap of understanding in the midst of catastrophe. On the collective level, there was a failure of cognitive recognition by those both inside and outside the Holocaust experience. In cases of trauma, however, the period of latency is followed by an emergence of the event's effects. Thus, the performance and presence of a witness afterward is critical.

Laub argues that there is a belated need, and possibility, at this historical moment for the outside witness to re-establish the possibility of an internal witness. "It is the encounter and the coming together between the survivor and the listener," writes Laub, "which makes possible something like a repossession of the act of witnessing. This joint responsibility is the source of the reemerging truth."[23] In this account the listener is explicitly named as a witness. Furthermore, and in contrast to Des Pres, it is the *outside* witness, the person who did not experience the Holocaust, who makes witnessing possible. While Laub strikingly points to the limits of the witness during the Shoah, he simultaneously imagines too much power for those who come after. In *Fantasies of Witnessing: Postwar Efforts to Experience the Holocaust,* Gary Weissman accuses Laub of looking to the Holocaust for a truth located outside everyday experience. Weissman argues that the turn in Holocaust studies to discourses of trauma and memory derives from desires to "experience the Holocaust." The fantasy of presence, according to Weissman, reflects an anxiety by nonwitnesses, who are removed from the horror and from the truth they hope to find within the horror.[24]

A desire to experience the Holocaust sounds absurd, and yet films such as *The Devil's Arithmetic* and haggadot passages such as "Remembrance of the Six Million" deliberately link nonwitnesses to the Shoah through embodied experience. Even the language of "as if" incorporates a residue of this desire. The language of witness may, as Weissman argues, harbor a misguided desire for truth found in extremity and an anxiety about distance from that "truth." Desires, however, are notoriously difficult to trace. Anxiety could also derive from recognition that the Shoah could ever have happened. Perhaps one desire inherent in the language of witness is the desire to have the power, the moral agency, to erase the stain of shame that persists—to whatever limited extent that may be possible. Numerous qualifiers have been used to describe the type of witnessing desirable and possible for those who were not there but want to tell and listen to stories after Auschwitz in order to promote remembrance and defeat forgetfulness. Laub uses the term "belated witness." Dominick LaCapra talks about the "secondary witness" to emphasize that listeners are even further from the experience, which even the original witness cannot access directly.[25] James Young considers the possibility that one does not remember but "remember[s] to others" so that to testify "means to make others into witnesses," although he also warns that the experience of the Shoah belongs to the survivor alone.[26] The subject position of the witness that best captures the possibilities and limits of witnessing the Shoah during the Passover seder is offered by Geoffrey Hartman, co-founder of the Fortunoff Archive for Holocaust Video Testimony, who uses the term "intellectual witness" to indicate "active reception" of Holocaust memory. The intellectual witness engages in conversation with another, which prevents an "intimacy" with the primary witness that moves beyond empathy to "over-identifying with victims or a victimized generation, to the point of seeking a mystical correspondence with the dead."[27] After Auschwitz, intellectual witnesses who choose to put their resources into remembrance have the privilege of time, a true possibility for reflection and conversation.

"A Hermeneutic of Trauma"

I am a seder participant and a witness. Throughout these past chapters, I have referred to seder participants in the third person. To conclude this book, I return to the first person, to my own voice, to consider what I have learned from this project and what I hope you, readers of this work, might be able to take from it. The project began with a question: "What will help them [contemporary participants in the seder] to tell and absorb stories about the Holocaust in a manner that will defeat forgetfulness?" This question led to more questions (considerably more than four), many of which you have seen throughout these chapters:

- How could remembrance of the Holocaust be voluntary?
- Whose voices were included in commemorations and whose voices were missing?
- Where in the haggadah did the Holocaust appear?

- When were Holocaust passages read during the seder?
- What kinds of remembrance were enabled by the conjunction of the Holocaust and the Exodus from Egypt?
- What forms of remembrance were foreclosed?
- What happens when the Holocaust is inserted into the emplotment that begins with degradation and ends with glory?
- How can Jews remember and memorialize the Shoah during the celebration of freedom-redemption without adding redemptive value to the Final Solution?
- What counts as knowledge of the Holocaust?
- How do post-Holocaust generations evaluate the assertion of subjectivity and resistance?
- What remains of the possibility of hope?

So many questions. And I wanted answers. Both for myself and to share with you. I considered concluding this book with what I called a "hermeneutic of trauma," a set of principles or rules for reading Holocaust narratives within the narrative frame of the haggadah. In this formulation, I argued that a hermeneutic of trauma opens up additional ways of reading the commemoration of the Shoah in Passover haggadot by approaching Holocaust passages as diffuse and mediated reemergences of the traumatic event over time so as to consider both the significance of the event itself and the effects of its representations. Now I find the hermeneutic of trauma inadequate to the task of offering a final response to my questions. Several factors influenced the shift in my thinking. The term "hermeneutic" comes from biblical studies and refers to methods of textual interpretation, which misses the element of performance and embodiment that is essential to consideration of Holocaust commemoration in the haggadah. Furthermore, a set of principles or rules strikes me as too closed. One key value of Passover as a site of remembrance is precisely the openness of the ritual: its yearly repetition; its emphasis on questions. I include the principles of my "hermeneutic of trauma" in case you find them of use, but they no longer constitute the final word, since I no longer believe final answers to questions of Holocaust memory are possible or desirable:

1. A hermeneutic of trauma requires one to read "against the frame." The reader must both acknowledge and resist the desire for coherence in narrative and the lure of redemptive memory.
2. A hermeneutic of trauma calls for a genealogy of the text. Through attention to history, ideology, construction of memory in the Shoah

text, and the decision-making process for its inclusion in the haggadah, one can open a space to allow mourning and prevent forgetting. It is a way to remember, a telling, that works against collusion
toward silence.

3. A hermeneutic of trauma, through its deliberate resistance to silence,
attempts to break the link between silence and shame.

4. A hermeneutic of trauma must acknowledge its limits. Reading using
this hermeneutic should preserve a margin of unsayability and recognize that any telling is only a partial account of traumatic experience.

5. A hermeneutic of trauma should preserve the tension between Exodus
and Auschwitz.

Rereading these principles, I recognize that they guided my process in writing *You Shall Tell Your Children,* and played a valuable role in helping me
consider what commemorations of the Shoah I wanted to advocate in this
text. That said, I eschew a prescriptive conclusion because taking seriously
the seder as performance, and not simply as written text, means the questions participants bring to the table will change over time.

How Is This Passover Different?

The Passover haggadah recognizes that in every generation different
questions will be salient, and that the meaningfulness of the event—whether
"the event" is the Exodus from Egypt or the Holocaust—requires a willingness to encounter both the possibility and the limits of meaning. Engaging (or engagement with) multiple pasts and wrestling with their legacies
for the present takes place throughout the seder in the form of questions,
especially questions posed "as if" the event personally matters to the one
who asks. The haggadah also recognizes that in every generation multiple
perspectives, which generate diverse questions, enrich the seder. Each of the
Four Children inspires a set of questions. Moreover, as many contemporary
haggadot note, each seder participant has elements of the wise, the wicked,
the simple, and the child who does not know how to ask inside of her. Finally, the Passover haggadah recognizes the provisional conclusion of any
yearly ritual performance of the seder. The haggadah concludes with the
wish, "*next year,* may we be free." Final redemption remains outside of history, which leaves open the question for next year: how do I make historical
memories part of the Passover ritual in meaningful ways?

Although haggadot are often used without attention to their historicity, each haggadah was created at a particular moment in time and

engages the issues of Holocaust memory salient at the moment of its creation. This is true of the postwar American texts I have analyzed here. Haggadot from the mid-1970s, for example, faced a public silence about the Final Solution, whereas in the early twenty-first century some cultural critics worry about too much Holocaust representation. Thus, what worked in the past may not meet current needs. Needs change on the personal level as well. For me, engaging Holocaust commemoration during the Passover seder as more than a perfunctory act required coming to terms with my own desire to offer up "the right answer." I began this project with an anxiety about forgetfulness and a sense that Holocaust commemoration in the haggadah was often too easily redemptive. Placing myself in conversation with critics such as Michael André Bernstein, Lawrence Langer, and James Young, I argued for non-redemptive commemoration of the Shoah in Passover haggadot. This led me to interrogate idealized representations of Holocaust victims. I maintained that idealizations often violate rather than preserve memory by erasing the value of the everyday life that was lost, and collapsing the diversity of responses to what occurred both during the Shoah and afterwards. Thinking about how to commemorate the Shoah by privileging non-idealized representations led to a focus on sites of agency, both in the past and in the contemporary moment.

The dual focus on past and present is, of course, also in keeping with the haggadah itself, and I return for the last time to Hannah and *The Devil's Arithmetic* for the value of illustration. When Hannah refuses to read at the seder, her father reads in her place: "A tale is told of Rabbi Eliezer, Rabbi Joshua, Rabbi Eleazar ben Azariah, Rabbi Akiba, and Rabbi Tarfon, who once reclined together at Bene Berak telling about the departure from Egypt all night, until their disciples came to them and said, 'Masters, the time has come to read the morning Shema.'" In most haggadot this passage is presented with two additional texts. One is another reference to Eleazar ben Azariah, who emphasizes one should remember the Exodus through the nights as well as the days of one's life. The other usually appears as commentary in the margins and divulges that the five rabbis may actually have been plotting a rebellion against Rome, the Egypt of their day. When Hannah refuses to read this text, she refuses to participate in the ongoing conversation about the Exodus as relevant to her own life. The set of questions I have asked throughout this project are meant to continue a conversation in the spirit of the rabbis of Bene Berak and as an intellectual witness to the Shoah.

As a witness in an ongoing conversation about Passover, the Shoah, their representations, and their legacies, I conclude by considering my own seder practice, and what "next year" might mean to me. Last year, I began my seder on the front porch of my home in Bakersfield, California, with a series of readings on Judaism and the environment in recognition of my brother's presence at the seder. Josh practices environmental law, and last year was our first seder together since childhood. As we enjoyed the temperate evening and drew attention to the often downplayed connections to nature present in the holiday of Passover, we considered the resources religion can offer in our current environmental crisis. I finished the seder with Primo Levi's poem "Passover," which concludes the Reconstructionist haggadah and is reprinted in the latest Reform haggadah as well. Levi begins with questions:

> Tell me: how is this night different
> From all other nights?
> How, tell me, is this Passover
> Different from all other Passovers? [28]

But by the end of the seder, at least at the end of my seder, bellies are full and the time for questions has passed. Primo Levi speaks throughout *You Shall Tell Your Children*, but received short shrift at my last seder.

Perhaps next year I will bring concerns about environmental justice and Holocaust legacies together and pair environmental readings from rabbinic tradition with Anne Frank's diary entry of February 23, 1944: "The best remedy for those who are afraid, lonely, or unhappy, is to go outside, somewhere where they can be quite alone with the heavens, nature, and God. Because only then does one feel that all is as it should be and that God wishes to see people happy, amidst the simple beauty of nature. As long as this exists, and it certainly always will, I know that then there will always be comfort for every sorrow, whatever the circumstances may be. And I firmly believe that nature brings solace in all troubles." [29] Or perhaps, I will move Levi's poem from the end to the beginning of my seder:

> And time reverses its course,
> Today flowing back into yesterday,
> Like a river enclosed at its mouth.
> Each of us has been a slave in Egypt,
> Soaked straw and clay with sweat,
> And crossed the sea dry-footed.

You too, stranger.
This year in fear and shame,
Next year in virtue and justice.[30]

Perhaps the poem will spark a conversation about links between fear, shame, virtue and justice. I would like to ask guests at my seder what these terms mean to them. How do they envision moving from fear and shame to virtue and justice? How do you?

NOTES

Introduction

1. Sara Horowitz, "Voices from the Killing Ground," in *Holocaust Remembrance: The Shapes of Memory,* ed. Geoffrey H. Hartman (Cambridge, Mass.: Blackwell, 1994), 57. At this point a short note on transliteration is in order. There are a variety of methods for transliterating Hebrew into the Latin alphabet, and the one which I have adopted should be familiar to American readers. The Hebrew letter ח is represented by "ch"; thus—Pesach. I have also used the common spelling of "haggadah." I have not changed the transliteration in quoted text.
2. Herbert Bronstein, ed., *A Passover Haggadah: The New Union Haggadah prepared by the Central Conference of American Rabbis,* rev. ed. (New York: CCAR, 1975), 7.
3. For an extended description of the textual embrace see Laura Levitt, "(the Problem with) Embraces," in *Judaism since Gender,* ed. Miriam Peskowitz and Laura Levitt (New York: Routledge, 1997).
4. Horowitz, "Voices from the Killing Ground," 58.
5. Barry A. Kosmin et al., *American Religious Identification Survey 2001* (New York: Graduate Center of the City University of New York, 2001). The National Jewish Population Survey (NJPS) was conducted by the Council of Jewish Federations, an association of 189 federations serving approximately 800 localities in the United States and Canada. The sample survey included almost 2,500 "households containing at least one person identified as currently or previously Jewish." The sample represents about 3.2 million American households. For an overview of the survey methodology see their website: www.jewishdatabank.com/njps90/njps90.html.
6. Far more Jews continue to attend seders and light Hanukkah candles than light candles on the Sabbath or observe the dietary laws. See Sidney Goldstein and Calvin Goldscheider, *Jewish Americans: Three Generations in a Jewish Community* (Englewood Cliffs, N.J.: Prentice-Hall, 1968). This pattern of core religious practices continued at least through the 1980s. See Steven M. Cohen, *American Assimilation or Jewish Revival?* (Bloomington: Indiana University Press, 1988).

7. Samuel C. Heilman, *Portrait of American Jews: The Last Half of the 20th Century.* (Seattle: University of Washington Press, 1995), 128–129; Gary A. Tobin and Julie A. Lipsman, "A Compendium of Jewish Demographic Studies," in *Perspectives in Jewish Population Research,* ed. Steven M. Cohen, Jonathan S. Woocher, and Bruce A. Phillips (Boulder, Colo.: Westview Press, 1984).

8. Cohen, *American Assimilation or Jewish Revival;* Heilman, *Portrait of American Jews;* Tobin and Lipsman, "A Compendium of Jewish Demographic Studies."

9. Marshall Sklare and Joseph Greenblum, *Jewish Identity on the Suburban Frontier: A Study of Group Survival in the Open Society* (New York: Basic Books, 1967).

10. Marshall Sklare, *America's Jews* (New York: Random House, 1971), 114.

11. Ibid., 115.

12. Ibid.

13. Ibid., 117.

14. Charles Silberman, *A Certain People: American Jews and Their Lives Today* (New York: Summit Books, 1985), 233–235.

15. Joel Gereboff, "With Liberty and Haggadahs for All," in *Key Texts in American Jewish Culture,* ed. Jack Kugelmass (New Brunswick, N.J.: Rutgers University Press, 2003), 275.

16. Bernard Lazerwitz et al., *Jewish Choices: American Jewish Denominationalism* (New York: State University New York Press, 1998), 74–75.

17. Steven M. Cohen and Arnold M. Eisen, *The Jew Within: Self, Family, and Community in America* (Bloomington: Indiana University Press, 2000), 187.

18. Ibid., 65.

19. Ibid., 83.

20. For the social and religious context of postmodern spirituality see Richard W. Flory and Donald E. Miller, ed. *GenX Religion* (New York: Routledge, 2000); Wade Clark Roof, *A Generation of Seekers: The Spiritual Journeys of the Baby Boom Generation,* (San Francisco: HarperSanFrancisco, 1993).

21. Beatrice S. Weinreich, "The Americanization of Passover," in *Studies in Biblical and Jewish Folklore,* ed. Raphael Patai, Francis Lee Utley, and Dov Noy (Bloomington: Indiana University Press, 1960), 354.

22. Yosef Hayim Yerushalmi, *Haggadah and History: A Panorama in Facsimile of Five Centuries of the Printed Haggadah from the Collections of Harvard University and the Jewish Theological Seminary of America,* 2nd ed. (Philadelphia: Jewish Publication Society of America, 1997), 84.

23. Theodore Wiener, *Addenda to Yaari's Bibliography of the Passover Haggadah from the Library of Congress Hebraica Collection* (New York, 1971); Abraham Yaari, *Bibliography of the Passover Haggadah from the Earliest Printed Edition to 1960, with Twenty-five Reproductions from Rare Editions and a Facsimile of a Unique Copy of the First Printed Haggadah in the Jewish National and University Library, Jerusalem* (Jerusalem: Bamberger & Wahrman, 1960).

24. The Reform and Conservative movements are the largest denominations within American Judaism. In the 2000–01 National Jewish Population Survey, 27 percent of Jewish adults surveyed identified as Conservative and 35 percent said they belong to the Reform movement. Egon Mayer, Barry A. Kosmin, and Ariela

Keysar, "American Jewish Identity Survey 2001," (New York: The Center for Cultural Judaism, 2003), 7.

25. Saul Friedländer, "Trauma, Memory, and Transference," in *Holocaust Remembrance: The Shapes of Memory,* ed. Geoffrey H. Hartman (Cambridge, Mass.: Blackwell, 1994), 253. In *Fantasies of Witnessing: Postwar Efforts to Experience the Holocaust,* Gary Weissman writes, "It has become customary in writings on the Holocaust to begin by making amends for using the term 'the Holocaust.' With some variation, the writer first points out the deficiency of this term, then names a few terms that may be preferable ('Shoah,' 'Churban,' 'the Final Solution,' etc.), then briefly considers how each of these terms is also problematic, and concludes by resolving to use 'the Holocaust' in the text despite its inappropriateness, since it remains the term most familiar to readers." Gary Weissman, *Fantasies of Witnessing: Postwar Efforts to Experience the Holocaust* (Ithaca, N.Y.: Cornell University Press, 2004), 24. For a concise description of these terms and a history of the word "holocaust," see question two, "What is the origin of the word 'Holocaust'?" in the frequently asked questions section of the website for the United States Holocaust Memorial Museum: *http://www.ushmm.org/research/library/faq/details. php?topic=01#02.* For an analysis of the implications of various namings see James E. Young, *Writing and Rewriting the Holocaust: Narrative and the Consequences of Interpretation* (Bloomington: Indiana University Press, 1988), 88–93.

CHAPTER 1   *Passover and the Challenge of Holocaust Memory*

1. Joy Levitt and Michael Strassfeld, eds., *A Night of Questions: A Passover Haggadah* (Elkins Park, Pa.: The Reconstructionist Press, 1999), 51.
2. Donna Deitch, *The Devil's Arithmetic* (Showtime Entertainment, 1999).
3. Primo Levi, *The Drowned and the Saved,* (New York: Vintage International, 1989), 201–204.
4. Ibid., 120.
5. Lisa Schiffman, *Generation J,* (San Francisco: HarperSanFrancisco, 1999).
6. Dora Apel, *Memory Effects: The Holocaust and the Art of Secondary Witnessing* (New Brunswick, N.J.: Rutgers University Press, 2002).
7. Schiffman, *Generation J,* 85.
8. Oren Baruch Stier, *Committed to Memory: Cultural Mediations of the Holocaust,* 1st ed. (Amherst: University of Massachusetts Press, 2003).
9. Ibid., 47.
10. Sidra DeKoven Ezrahi, "Representing Auschwitz," *History and Memory* 7, no. 2 (1996), 121–156.
11. Lore Segal, "Memory: The Problems of Imagining the Past," in *Writing and the Holocaust,* ed. Berel Lang (New York: Holmes and Meier, 1988), 58.
12. Charlotte Delbo, *Auschwitz and After* (New Haven: Yale University Press, 1995); Anne Frank, *The Diary of a Young Girl: The Definitive Edition,* (New York: Anchor Books/Doubleday, 1996); Primo Levi, *Survival in Auschwitz: The Nazi Assault on Humanity,* (New York: Simon and Schuster, 1996); Elie Wiesel, *Night,* (New York: Bantam Books, 1986). The diary and memoirs by these authors shaped Holocaust consciousness.

13. Levi, *The Drowned and the Saved,* 16–17.
14. Shoshana Felman and Dori Laub, *Testimony: Crises of Witnessing in Literature, Psychoanalysis, and History* (New York: Routledge, 1992), 80.
15. Delbo, *Auschwitz and After,* 142.
16. Ibid., 145.
17. Saul Friedländer, *Probing the Limits of Representation: Nazism and the "Final Solution"* (Cambridge, Mass.: Harvard University Press, 1992), 3. See also Terrence Des Pres, *The Survivor: An Anatomy of Life in the Death Camps* (New York: Oxford University Press, 1976).
18. Ibid., 5.
19. Ezrahi, "Representing Auschwitz," 134–135.
20. Ibid., 122.
21. Ibid.
22. Saul Friedländer, "Trauma, Memory, and Transference," in *Holocaust Remembrance: The Shapes of Memory,* ed. Geoffrey H. Hartman (Cambridge, Mass.: Blackwell, 1994), 261. One could make similar claims about most historical documents and narratives, but historiography of the Nazi genocide particularly engages the ideas of excess and opaqueness in representations.
23. United States Holocaust Memorial Museum, "Auschwitz" in *Holocaust Encyclopedia* (accessed August 12, 2005); http://www.ushmm.org/wlc/article.php?lang=en&ModuleId=10005189.
24. Primo Levi, *The Reawakening* (New York: Simon and Schuster, 1995), 55.
25. See also Michael André Bernstein, "Primo Levi (Book Review)," *The New Republic* 221, no. 13 (1999), 35–42
26. Levi, *The Reawakening,* 52.
27. Ibid., 54.
28. Ibid., 55.
29. Baruch M. Bokser, *The Origins of the Seder: The Passover Rite and Early Rabbinic Judaism* (Berkeley: University of California Press, 1984), 83; Irving Greenberg, *The Jewish Way: Living the Holidays* (New York: Simon and Schuster, 1988), 34–65.
30. Bokser, *The Origins of the Seder,* 99.
31. Barry Holtz, "Midrash," in *Back to the Sources: Reading the Classic Jewish Texts,* ed. Barry Holtz (New York: Summit Books, 1984), 179.
32. Daniel Boyarin, *Intertextuality and the Reading of Midrash* (Bloomington: Indiana University Press, 1990), 14.
33. Ibid., 28.
34. David Stern, *Midrash and Theory: Ancient Jewish Exegesis and Contemporary Literary Studies* (Evanston, Ill.: Northwestern University Press, 1996), 18.
35. Rachel Anne Rabinowicz, ed., *The Passover Haggadah: The Feast of Freedom* (New York: Rabbinical Assembly, 1982), 45.
36. Ibid., 49.
37. Ibid.
38. Jonathan Rosen, *The Talmud and the Internet: A Journey between Worlds* (New York: Picador, 2000), 9–10.
39. Rabinowicz, ed., *The Passover Haggadah: The Feast of Freedom,* 44.

40. Joy Levitt and Michael Strassfeld, eds., *A Night of Questions: A Passover Haggadah,* 43.

41. See the classic study by Lawrence A. Hoffman, *Beyond the Text: A Holistic Approach to Liturgy* (Bloomington: Indiana University Press, 1989).

42. Yosef Hayim Yerushalmi, *Zakhor: Jewish History and Jewish Memory* (Seattle: University of Washington Press, 1982), 43.

43. I use the term "performance" in conjunction with ritual to emphasize the embodied, interactive, and reflexive qualities of the seder. I examine performative implications of the integration of the Shoah into the seder in chapter six. For an introduction to the relatively new, multidisciplinary field of performance studies see Richard Schechner, *Performance Studies: An Introduction* (New York: Routledge, 2002).

44. Elie Wiesel's commentary on Had Gadya appears in *A Night of Questions: A Passover Haggadah* as part of the section "In Every Generation": "We recited the customary blessings, the Psalms, and to finish we sang Had Gadya, that terrifying song in which, in the name of justice, evil catches evil, death calls death, until the angel of destruction, in his turn, has his throat cut by the Eternal. I loved this naïve little song in which everything seemed so simple, so primitive: the cat and the dog, the water and the fire, executioners and victims turn and turn about, all undergoing the same punishment inside the same scheme. But that evening the song upset me. I rebelled against the resignation it implied. Why does God always act too late? Why didn't God get rid of the Angel of Death before he even committed his first murder?" Joy Levitt and Michael Strassfeld, eds., *A Night of Questions: A Passover Haggadah,* 106.

CHAPTER 2 *Collected Memories*

1. Ester R., Interview by the USC Shoah Foundation Institute for Visual History and Education, University of Southern California, Jerusalem, Israel, 27 July 1998, 47236.

2. Abba B., Interview by the USC Shoah Foundation, Brooklyn, N.Y., U.S.A., 26 November 1998, 47582.

3. Halina L., Interview by the USC Shoah Foundation, Pembroke Pines, Fla., U.S.A., 12 April 1995, 2023.

4. Irma H., Interview by the USC Shoah Foundation, Hoofdorp, Noord-Holland, Netherlands, 10 December 1996, 24685.

5. Abraham T., Interview by the USC Shoah Foundation, New York, N.Y., U.S.A., 6 February 1997, 25959.

6. Margaret G., Interview by the USC Shoah Foundation, Lakewood, N.J., U.S.A., 12 September 1996, 19751.

7. Andrew G., Interview by the USC Shoah Foundation, Bondi Junction, Sydney, N.S.W., Australia, 28 June 1995, 3597.

8. Natan L., Interview by the USC Shoah Foundation, Rosswell, Ga., U.S.A., 21 May 1997, 29339.

9. Lawrence L. Langer, "The Dilemma of Choice in the Deathcamps," in *Holocaust: Religious and Philosophical Reflections,* ed. John K. Roth and Michael Berenbaum (New York: Paragon House, 1989), 224.

10. Joan Ringelheim, "The Unethical and the Unspeakable: Women and the Holocaust," *The Simon Wiesenthal Center Annual* 1 (1984): 79.

11. Helen R., Interview by the USC Shoah Foundation, Cranbury, N.J., U.S.A., 26 October 1997, 34684.

12. Zuzi B., Interview by the USC Shoah Foundation, Philadelphia, Pa., U.S.A., 18 September 1997, 33619.

13. Abraham Maslow, "A Theory of Human Motivation," *Psychological Review* 50 (1943); Erich Fromm, *The Sane Society* (Greenwich, Conn.: Fawcett, 1965).

14. Helen K., Interview by the USC Shoah Foundation, Philadelphia, Pa., U.S.A., 11 November 1996, 22639.

15. Edith K., Interview by the USC Shoah Foundation, London, England, U.K., 13 March 1997, 26900.

16. Abram H., Interview by the USC Shoah Foundation, Brooklyn, N.Y., U.S.A., 18 March 1997, 27715.

17. Thomas S., Interview by the USC Shoah Foundation, Thornhill, Ont., Canada, 16 February 1995, 1029.

18. Tova F., Interview by the USC Shoah Foundation, Highland Park, N.J., U.S.A., 22 November 1998, 47647.

19. William W., Interview by the USC Shoah Foundation, Los Angeles, Calif., U.S.A., 27 November 1995, 9269.

20. Regina P., Interview by the USC Shoah Foundation, Brooklyn, N.Y., U.S.A., 12 August 1996, 18602.

21. Shoshana Felman and Dori Laub, *Testimony: Crises of Witnessing in Literature, Psychoanalysis, and History* (New York: Routledge, 1992), 59.

22. Ibid., 60.

23. Quoted in David Arnow, *Creating Lively Passover Seders: A Sourcebook of Engaging Tales, Texts, and Activities* (Woodstock, Vt.: Jewish Lights Publishing, 2004), 193.

24. Fay P., Interview by the USC Shoah Foundation, Tucson, Ariz., U.S.A., 13 July 1997, 30681.

25. Alfred P., Interview by the USC Shoah Foundation, Los Angeles, Calif., U.S.A., 15 February 1995, 896.

26. Yosef Dov Sheinson and Saul Touster, *A Survivors' Haggadah* (Philadelphia: Jewish Publication Society, 2000), 7.

27. Ibid., 8.

28. Ibid., 9.

29. Ibid., 10.

30. Ibid., 7.

31. Ibid., 9.

32. Ibid., 29, 31.

33. Ibid., 24.

34. Ibid., 37.

35. Ibid., 63.

36. Ibid., 29.

37. Ibid., 66.

38. Ibid., 68.

39. Alon Confino, "Collective Memory and Cultural History: Problems of Method," *American Historical Review* 102, no. 5 (1997): 1402.
40. Maurice Halbwachs and Lewis A. Coser, *On Collective Memory* (Chicago: University of Chicago Press, 1992).
41. James E. Young, *The Texture of Memory: Holocaust Memorials and Meaning* (New Haven: Yale University Press, 1993), xi.
42. See also Iwona Irwin-Zarecka, *Frames of Remembrance: The Dynamics of Collective Memory* (New Brunswick, N.J.: Transaction Publishers, 1994).
43. Young, *The Texture of Memory: Holocaust Memorials and Meaning,* viii.

CHAPTER 3   *Wrestling with Redemption*

1. Yosef Hayim Yerushalmi, *Haggadah and History: A Panorama in Facsimile of Five Centuries of the Printed Haggadah from the Collections of Harvard University and the Jewish Theological Seminary of America,* 2nd ed. (Philadelphia: Jewish Publication Society of America, 1997), 15.
2. Joy Levitt and Michael Strassfeld, eds., *A Night of Questions: A Passover Haggadah* (Elkins Park, Pa.: The Reconstructionist Press, 1999), 11.
3. Ibid., 46.
4. Ibid., 50.
5. March of the Living International, *March of the Living International* [Web site] (accessed October 23, 2005); available from http://www.motl.org/mission.htm.
6. Saul Friedländer, "Trauma, Memory, and Transference," in *Holocaust Remembrance: The Shapes of Memory,* ed. Geoffrey H. Hartman (Cambridge, Mass.: Blackwell, 1994).
7. Friedländer attributes the idea of multiple, simultaneous, but incompatible forms of Holocaust memory to Lawrence Langer. In *Holocaust Testimony: the Ruins of Memory,* Langer credits this conception of memory to survivor Charlotte Delbo.
8. Friedländer, "Trauma, Memory, and Transference," 254.
9. Ibid., 262.
10. Ibid., 254.
11. Norman Lamm, "The Face of God: Thoughts on the Holocaust," in *Theological and Halakhic Reflections on the Holocaust,* ed. Richard H. Rosenberg and Fred Heuman (Hoboken, N.J.: KTAV, 1992).
12. Lawrence L. Langer, "Pre-Empting the Holocaust," *The Atlantic Monthly,* November 1998.
13. Lamm, "The Face of God: Thoughts on the Holocaust," 120.
14. Ibid.
15. Ibid., 125–126.
16. Ibid., 122.
17. Ibid., 123.
18. *Yalkut Shimoni,* Isaiah chap. 6 cited in ibid., 124.
19. *Midrash Shir ha-Shirim* cited in ibid.
20. Lamm, "The Face of God: Thoughts on the Holocaust," 125.
21. Ibid., 133.

22. Of course the thesis that God does not act in history was also the conclusion reached by Richard Rubenstein twenty years earlier, but he was writing from outside the boundaries of Orthodox Judaism. See Richard L. Rubenstein, *After Auschwitz: Radical Theology and Contemporary Judaism* (Indianapolis: Bobbs-Merrill, 1966).

23. Lawrence L. Langer, *Admitting the Holocaust: Collected Essays* (New York: Oxford University Press, 1995), 184.

24. Langer, "Pre-Empting the Holocaust," 105.

25. Langer, *Admitting the Holocaust,* 6.

26. Langer, "Pre-Empting the Holocaust," 112.

27. Quoted in Langer, "Pre-Empting the Holocaust," 110.

28. Quoted in ibid.

29. Levitt and Strassfeld, eds., *A Night of Questions: A Passover Haggadah,* 70.

30. Rabinowicz, ed., *The Passover Haggadah: The Feast of Freedom,* 25.

31. Levitt and Strassfeld, eds., *A Night of Questions: A Passover Haggadah,* 121.

32. Morris Silverman, ed., *Passover Haggadah* (Hartford, Conn.: Prayer Book Press, 1959; reprint, 1967).

33. "Pour Out Your Wrath" is not included in the Reconstructionist haggadah. This version is quoted from the Conservative haggadah.

34. Ellen Sue Levi Elwell, ed., *The Open Door: A Passover Haggadah* (New York: Central Conference of American Rabbis Press, 2002), 85–87.

35. Levitt and Strassfeld, eds., *A Night of Questions: A Passover Haggadah,* 80.

36. Ibid.

37. Ibid., 85. Kelman is Director of Educational Initiatives at the Hebrew Union College–Jewish Institute of Religion in Jerusalem.

38. Ibid., 85. Spitzer is Rabbi of Congregation Dorshei Tzedek in West Newton, Massachusetts.

39. Irving Greenberg, "Cloud of Smoke, Pillar of Fire: Judaism, Christianity, and Modernity after the Holocaust," in *Auschwitz: Beginning of a New Era?*, ed. Eva Fleischner (New York: The Cathedral Church of St. John the Divine, 1977), 8.

40. Greenberg says that the norms of Christians and secular humanists must also be informed by the experience of the Holocaust.

41. Ibid.

42. Ibid.

43. Ibid., 11.

44. Ibid., 27.

45. Ibid.

46. Irving Greenberg, *The Jewish Way: Living the Holidays* (New York: Simon and Schuster, 1988), 92.

47. Michael L. Morgan, *Beyond Auschwitz: Post-Holocaust Jewish Thought in America* (New York: Oxford University Press, 2001), 139.

48. Greenberg, "Cloud of Smoke, Pillar of Fire: Judaism, Christianity, and Modernity after the Holocaust," 50.

49. Greenberg, *The Jewish Way: Living the Holidays,* 421.

50. Taking White beyond what he asserts in "Historical Emplotment and the Problem of Truth," James Young and Martin Jay suggest that "the facts" are always already

embedded in interpretation. Jay characterizes White's position as "a failure of nerve" and asserts "the factual record is not . . . entirely prior to its linguistic mediation, or indeed its figural signification. What distinguishes the events and facts that later historians reconstruct is precisely their being often already inflected with narrative meaning for those who initiate or suffer them in their own lives." I agree with Jay's critique but focus here on White's contribution regarding the heuristic value of emplotment. See Martin Jay, "Of Plots, Witnesses, and Judgments," in *Probing the Limits of Representation: Nazism and the "Final Solution,"* ed. Saul Friedländer (Cambridge, Mass.: Harvard University Press, 1992), 99; James E. Young, *Writing and Rewriting the Holocaust: Narrative and the Consequences of Interpretation* (Bloomington: Indiana University Press, 1988).

51. Hayden White, "Historical Emplotment and the Problem of Truth," in *Probing the Limits of Representation: Nazism and the "Final Solution,"* ed. Friedländer, 43.

52. Hayden White, *The Content of the Form: Narrative Discourse and Historical Representation* (Baltimore: The Johns Hopkins University Press, 1987), xi.

53. Aristotle, *Poetics,* trans. Stephen Halliwell (Cambridge, Mass.: Harvard University Press, 1995), 50.

54. Ibid., 54.

55. Ibid., 52.

56. Seymour Chatman, *Story and Discourse: Narrative Structure in Fiction and Film* (Ithaca, N.Y.: Cornell University Press, 1978), 47.

57. Gary Saul Morson, *Narrative and Freedom: The Shadows of Time* (New Haven: Yale University Press, 1994), 38.

58. J. Hillis Miller, "Narrative," in *Critical Terms for Literary Study,* ed. Frank Lentricchia and Thomas McLaughlin (Chicago: University of Chicago Press, 1990), 69.

59. White, *The Content of the Form: Narrative Discourse and Historical Representation,* 21.

60. I thank Tim Vivian for pointing out this meaning of interpolate.

61. Primo Levi, *The Reawakening* (New York: Macmillan, 1993), 40.

62. I thank Shauna Eddy-Sanders for leading me to think about the difference in these two Exodus narratives.

63. Robert Goldenberg, "Talmud," in *Back to the Sources: Reading the Classic Jewish Texts,* ed. Barry Holtz (New York: Summit Books, 1984); Michael Chernick, ed., *Essential Papers on the Talmud* (New York: New York University Press, 1994).

64. Louis Jacobs, "The Talmudic Argument," in *Essential Papers on the Talmud,* ed. Michael Chernick (New York: New York University Press, 1994), 53, 60.

65. Goldenberg, "Talmud," 156.

66. This reading of Rav and Samuel is indebted to David Arnow. See David Arnow, *Creating Lively Passover Seders: A Sourcebook of Engaging Tales, Texts, and Activities* (Woodstock, Vt.: Jewish Lights Publishing, 2004).

67. Levitt and Strassfeld, eds., *A Night of Questions: A Passover Haggadah,* 47.

68. Ibid., 46.

69. Ibid., 47.

70. Cited in Paul R. Mendes-Flohr and Jehuda Reinharz, *The Jew in the Modern World: A Documentary History,* 2nd ed. (New York: Oxford University Press, 1995), 158.
71. Rabinowicz, ed., *The Passover Haggadah: The Feast of Freedom,* 6.
72. Herbert Bronstein, ed., *A Passover Haggadah: The New Union Haggadah prepaed by the Central Conference of American Rabbis,* rev. ed. (New York: CCAR, 1975), 6; Rabinowicz, ed., *The Passover Haggadah: The Feast of Freedom,* 9.
73. A. Stanley Dreyfus, "The Gates Liturgies: Reform Judaism Reforms Its Worship," in *The Changing Face of Jewish and Christian Worship in North America,* ed. Paul Bradshaw and Lawrence Hoffman (Notre Dame, Ind.: University of Notre Dame Press, 1991), 146.
74. Bronstein, ed., *A Passover Haggadah: The New Union Haggadah,* 6.
75. Ibid.
76. Several of these passages are examined in detail in the following chapters.
77. Bronstein, ed. *A Passover Haggadah: The New Union Haggadah,* 33.
78. Ibid.
79. Ibid., 41.
80. Ibid., 45–46.
81. Ibid., 48.
82. Ibid., 77–79.; See also Menahem Kasher, *Israel Passover Haggadah* (New York: American Biblical Encyclopedia Society, 1956) for an early Orthodox haggadah that includes the fifth cup and the state of Israel as "the beginning of our redemption."
83. Jacob Neusner, *Stranger at Home: "The Holocaust," Zionism, and American Judaism* (Chicago: University of Chicago Press, 1981), 86.
84. Ibid., 63.
85. Rabinowicz, ed., *The Passover Haggadah: The Feast of Freedom,* 9.
86. Ibid.
87. Langer, "Pre-Empting the Holocaust," 105.
88. Rabinowicz, ed., *The Passover Haggadah: The Feast of Freedom,* 94.
89. Ibid.
90. Ibid., 95.
91. Ibid.
92. Ibid., 96.
93. Ibid.
94. Ibid., 99–100. This passage also appears in a 1976 anthology with the attribution: "Inscription on the walls of a cellar in Cologne, Germany, where Jews hid from Nazis." See Jacob Glatstein et al., eds., *Anthology of Holocaust Literature* (New York: Atheneum, 1976), 340.

CHAPTER 4   *Anne Frank, Hope, and Redemption*

1. Anne Frank, *The Diary of a Young Girl: The Definitive Edition,* ed. Otto H. Frank and Mirjam Pressler (New York: Doubleday, 1995), 1.
2. Ibid., 6.
3. Ibid., 290.

4. Ibid., 239.
5. A full account of the controversies surrounding the multiple versions is beyond the scope of this chapter. See Hyman Aaron Enzer and Sandra Solotaroff-Enzer, *Anne Frank: Reflections on Her Life and Legacy* (Urbana: University of Illinois Press, 2000) and Anne Frank et al., *The Diary of Anne Frank: The Critical Edition* (New York: Viking, 1989).
6. Frank, *The Diary of a Young Girl: The Definitive Edition,* 323–327.
7. Ibid., 238.
8. Ibid., 326.
9. Ibid., 323–327.
10. Barbara Chiarello, "The Utopian Space of a Nightmare: The Diary of Anne Frank," in *A Scholarly Look at the Diary of Anne Frank,* ed. Harold Bloom (Philadelphia: Chelsea House Publishers, 1999), 97.
11. Rachel Feldhay Brenner, *Writing as Resistance: Four Women Confronting the Holocaust: Edith Stein, Simone Weil, Anne Frank, Etty Hillesum* (University Park: Pennsylvania State University Press, 1997), 104.
12. Rachel Feldhay Brenner, "Writing Herself against History: Anne Frank's Self-Portrait as a Young Artist," in *Anne Frank: Reflections on Her Life and Legacy,* 91.
13. Alvin Rosenfeld, "Popularization and Memory: The Case of Anne Frank," in *Lessons and Legacies: The Meaning of the Holocaust in a Changing World,* ed. Peter Hayes (Evanston, Ill.: Northwestern University Press, 1991), 251.
14. Quoted in ibid., 246.
15. Ibid., 272.
16. Frank, *The Diary of a Young Girl: The Definitive Edition,* 257. It is cited in Rosenfeld, "Popularization and Memory: The Case of Anne Frank"; Meyer Levin, *The Obsession* (New York: Simon and Schuster, 1973); and Henry Pommer, "The Legend and Art of Anne Frank," *Judaism* 9, no. 1 (1960).
17. Quoted in Rosenfeld, "Popularization and Memory: The Case of Anne Frank," 257.
18. Levin, *The Obsession.*
19. Lawrence Graver, *An Obsession with Anne Frank* (Berkeley: University of California Press, 1995); Ralph Melnick, *The Stolen Legacy of Anne Frank: Meyer Levin, Lillian Hellman, and the Staging of the Diary* (New Haven: Yale University Press, 1997).
20. Molly Magid Hoagland, "Anne Frank On and Off Broadway," in *A Scholarly Look at the Diary of Anne Frank,* ed. Harold Bloom (Philadelphia: Chelsea House Publishers, 1999).
21. Bruno Bettelheim, "The Ignored Lesson of Anne Frank," in *A Scholarly Look at the Diary of Anne Frank,* 6.
22. Ibid., 9.
23. Ibid.
24. Ibid., 7.
25. Ibid., 6.
26. John Berryman, "The Development of Anne Frank," in *Anne Frank: Reflections on Her Life and Legacy,* ed. Enzer and Solotaroff-Enzer, 80.
27. See also Michael André Bernstein, *Foregone Conclusions: Against Apocalyptic History,* (Berkeley: University of California Press, 1994).

28. Ronald Reagan, "Never Again: Speech at Bergen Belsen, May 5, 1985," in *Bitburg and Beyond: Encounters in American, German, and Jewish History,* ed. Ilya Levkov (New York: Shapolsky Publishers, 1987), 134. See also Geoffrey H. Hartman, ed., *Bitburg in Moral and Political Perspective* (Bloomington: Indiana University Press, 1986).

29. Frank, *The Diary of a Young Girl: The Definitive Edition,* 74, 150.

30. Lawrence L. Langer, "The Uses—and Misues—of a Young Girl's Diary: 'If Anne Frank Could Return from among the Murdered, She Would Be Appalled,'" in *Anne Frank: Reflections on Her Life and Legacy,* ed. Enzer and Solotaroff-Enzer, 204.

31. Judith Doneson, "The American History of Anne Frank's Diary," *Holocaust and Genocide Studies* 2, no. 1 (1987), 156. In a similar vein, see also Colijn, who critiques the Dutch affinity for the diary and the ways it has been used throughout the Netherlands to perpetuate the myth of the "good Dutch." G. Jan Colijn, "Review Essay: Anne Frank Remembered," in *Anne Frank: Reflections on Her Life and Legacy;* G. Jan Colijn, "Toward a Proper Legacy," in *Anne Frank in the World,* ed. Carol Rittner (Armonk, N.Y.: M. E. Sharpe, 1998).

32. Rittner, ed., *Anne Frank in the World.*

33. Victoria J. Barnett, "Reflections on Anne Frank," in *Anne Frank in the World,* ed. Rittner, 6.

34. Ibid.

35. Ibid., 7–8.

36. Rosenfeld, "Popularization and Memory: The Case of Anne Frank," 275.

37. Noam Zion and David Dishon, ed., *A Different Night: The Family Participation Haggadah* (Jerusalem: Shalom Hartman Institute, 1997), 3.

38. Ibid.

39. Herbert Bronstein, ed., *A Passover Häggadah: The New Union Haggadah,* rev. ed. (New York: CCAR, 1975), 5; Rachel Anne Rabinowicz, ed., *The Passover Haggadah: The Feast of Freedom* (New York: Rabbinical Assembly, 1982), 6; Zion and Dishon, ed., *A Different Night: The Family Participation Haggadah,* 3.

40. Zion and Dishon, ed., *A Different Night: The Family Participation Haggadah,* 138–141.

41. Frank, *The Diary of a Young Girl: The Definitive Edition,* 152.

42. Zion and Dishon, ed., *A Different Night: The Family Participation Haggadah,* 138.

43. Ibid., 140.

44. Ibid., 139.

45. Elaine Moise and Rebecca Schwartz, ed., *The Dancing with Miriam Haggadah: A Jewish Women's Celebration of Passover,* 3rd ed. (Palo Alto, Calif.: Rikudei Miriam, 1999), vi.

46. For the story of the first women's seder and haggadah see E. M. Broner and Naomi Nimrod, *The Telling,* (San Francisco: HarperSan Francisco, 1993). For additional information on feminist haggadot see Lee Bycel, "'To Reclaim Our Voice': An Analysis of Representative Contemporary Feminist Haggadot," *CCAR Journal,* (Spring 1993).

47. Moise and Schwartz, ed., *The Dancing with Miriam Haggadah: A Jewish Women's Celebration of Passover,* ix.

48. Ibid., 10.

49. Ibid., 17.
50. Ibid., 10.
51. Ibid., vi, ix, 8.
52. Hebrew is a gendered language. Masculine forms of the plural are used for groups of men and for groups that include men and women. Feminine forms of the plural are reserved for groups of women only.
53. Moise and Schwartz, ed., *The Dancing with Miriam Haggadah: A Jewish Women's Celebration of Passover,* 11.
54. Ibid.
55. Ibid.
56. Central Conference of American Rabbis, *Declaration of Principles* (October 1997 / 1885 [accessed July 31 2006]); available from http://data.ccarnet.org/platforms/pittsurgh.html.
57. Central Conference of American Rabbis, *Reform Judaism: A Centenary Perspective* (October 1997 / 1976 [accessed July 31 2006]); available from http://data.ccarnet.org/platforms/centenary.html.
58. Bronstein, ed., *A Passover Haggadah: The New Union Haggadah,* 7.
59. Ibid.
60. Ibid., 49.
61. Ibid.
62. Ibid., 45.
63. Ibid.
64. Ibid., 46.

CHAPTER 5   *Heroism Redeemed*

1. Young also notes, "This was to be a day of redemption all around: Christians redeemed by the sacrifice of their Jews in the Ghetto, Jews redeemed, if not by their God, then by themselves. For the Germans, there was the further inspiration of Hitler's birthday, 20 April, a day for delivering to their leader the present of a 'Judenrein' (Jew-free) Warsaw." James E. Young, *The Texture of Memory: Holocaust Memorials and Meaning* (New Haven: Yale University Press, 1993), 162–163.
2. Vladka Meed, *On Both Sides of the Wall* (New York: Holocaust Library, 1979), 140.
3. Hanna Krall and Marek Edelman, *Shielding the Flame: An Intimate Conversation with Dr. Marek Edelman, the Last Surviving Leader of the Warsaw Ghetto Uprising,* (New York: Henry Holt, 1986), 133.
4. Ibid., 149.
5. Yitzhak Zuckerman and Barbara Harshav, *A Surplus of Memory: Chronicle of the Warsaw Ghetto Uprising* (Berkeley: University of California Press, 1993), xii.
6. Shoshana Felman and Dori Laub, *Testimony: Crises of Witnessing in Literature, Psychoanalysis, and History* (New York: Routledge, 1992), 72.
7. Zivia Lubetkin, *In the Days of Destruction and Revolt* (Tel Aviv: Hakibbutz Hameuchad Publishing House: Am Oved Publishing House, 1981), 99.
8. Israel Gutman, *Resistance: The Warsaw Ghetto Uprising* (Boston: Houghton Mifflin, 1994), 150.

9. Lubetkin, *In the Days of Destruction and Revolt,* 83.

10. Ibid., 159.

11. Nathan Rapoport, "Memoir of the *Warsaw Ghetto Monument,*" in *The Art of Memory: Holocaust Memorials in History,* ed. James E. Young (Munich and New York: Prestel-Verlag, 1994), 103.

12. Ibid., 105–106.

13. Ibid., 106.

14. Ibid.

15. Young, *The Texture of Memory: Holocaust Memorials and Meaning,* 168.

16. David G. Roskies, *Against the Apocalypse: Responses to Catastrophe in Modern Jewish Culture* (Cambridge, Mass.: Harvard University Press, 1984), 301.

17. Young, *The Texture of Memory: Holocaust Memorials and Meaning,* 155.

18. Roskies, *Against the Apocalypse: Responses to Catastrophe in Modern Jewish Culture,* 297.

19. Ibid., 301.

20. Ibid., 7.

21. Ibid., 9.

22. Young, *The Texture of Memory: Holocaust Memorials and Meaning,* 157.

23. Ibid., 161–162.

24. Ibid., 174.

25. Michael Rothberg, "W. E. B. Du Bois in Warsaw: Holocaust Memory and the Color Line, 1949–1952," *The Yale Journal of Criticism* 14, no. 1 (2001): 185.

26. Craig Calhoun, ed., *Dictionary of the Social Sciences* (New York: Oxford University Press, 2002), 129.

27. Rothberg, "W. E. B. Du Bois in Warsaw: Holocaust Memory and the Color Line, 1949–1952," 186.

28. Ibid.

29. Ibid., 184.

30. Sidra DeKoven Ezrahi, "Representing Auschwitz," *History and Memory* 7, no. 2 (1996). See also discussion in chapter 1.

31. Ibid.

32. Ibid., 185.

33. Felman and Laub, *Testimony: Crises of Witnessing in Literature, Psychoanalysis, and History,* 72.

34. Herbert Bronstein, ed., *A Passover Haggadah: The New Union Haggadah,* rev. ed. (New York: CCAR, 1975), 32–33.

35. Ibid., 30.

36. Steven Leder, "Imagining Einstein." Unpublished thesis (Hebrew Union College—Jewish Institute of Religion, 1987), 159.

37. Sharon Abramowitz et al., eds., "Women's Passover Seder." Unpublished manuscript (Los Angeles: Hebrew Union College Library 1977), 18.

38. Ibid.

39. Ibid.

40. For a thorough introduction to the issues surrounding the study of women during the Shoah, see Dalia Ofer and Lenore J. Weitzman, eds., *Women in the Holocaust* (New Haven: Yale University Press, 1998).

41. Lubetkin, *In the Days of Destruction and Revolt*, 253.
42. Ibid., 254.
43. Krall and Edelman, *Shielding the Flame: An Intimate Conversation with Dr. Marek Edelman, the Last Surviving Leader of the Warsaw Ghetto Uprising*, 76.
44. Ralph Kramer and Philip Schild, ed., *The Bay Area Jewish Forum Haggadah* (Berkeley, Calif.: Benmire Books, 1986), 46.
45. Ibid.
46. Nosson Scherman, ed., *The Complete Artscroll Siddur*, 3rd ed. (New York: Mesorah Publications, 1989), 455.
47. Michael André Bernstein, *Foregone Conclusions: Against Apocalyptic History* (Berkeley: University of California Press, 1994), 12.
48. Lubetkin, *In the Days of Destruction and Revolt*, 134.
49. Sholem Community Organization, ed., *Sholem Family Hagadah for a Secular Celebration of Peysakh* (Los Angeles: Sholem Community Organization, 1992), 11.
50. Ibid.
51. Ibid.
52. Ibid.
53. Ibid., 12.
54. Lubetkin, *In the Days of Destruction and Revolt*, 99.
55. Michael André Bernstein, "Primo Levi (Book Review)," *The New Republic* 221, no. 13 (1999), 37–38.
56. Primo Levi, *The Reawakening* (New York: Simon and Schuster, 1995), 16.
57. Paul Gilbert, "What Is Shame? Some Core Issues and Controversies," in *Shame: Interpersonal Behavior, Psychopathology, and Culture*, ed. Paul Gilbert and Bernice Andrews (New York: Oxford University Press, 1998), 22.
58. Primo Levi, *The Drowned and the Saved* (New York: Summit Books, 1988), 81–82.
59. Ibid., 81.
60. Lubetkin, *In the Days of Destruction and Revolt*, 121.
61. Ezrahi, "Representing Auschwitz," *History and Memory* 7, no. 2 (1996), 131.
62. Noam Zion and David Dishon, eds., *A Different Night: The Family Participation Haggadah* (Jerusalem: Shalom Hartman Institute, 1997), 141.
63. Ibid.
64. Joy Levitt and Michael Strassfeld, eds., *A Night of Questions: A Passover Haggadah* (Elkins Park, Pa.: The Reconstructionist Press, 1999), 112.
65. Irena Klepfisz, "Yom Hashoah, Yom Yerushalayim: A Meditation," in *Jewish Women's Call for Peace, a Handbook for Jewish Women on the Israeli/Palestinian Conflict*, ed. Rita Falbel, Irena Klepfisz, and Donna Nevel (Ithaca, N.Y.: Firebrand Books, 1990), 42.

CHAPTER 6   *Provisional Conclusions*

1. Victor Turner quoted in "Introduction," in *By Means of Performance: Intercultural Studies of Theatre and Ritual*, ed. Richard Schechner and Willa Appel (Cambridge: Cambridge University Press, 1990), 1.

2. Victor Turner, "Are There Universals of Performance?" in *By Means of Performance: Intercultural Studies of Theatre and Ritual,* 11.

3. On the ritual process see Arnold van Gennep, *The Rites of Passage* (Chicago: University of Chicago Press, 1960); Victor Turner, *The Ritual Process* (Chicago: Aldine, 1969).

4. Barbara Myerhoff, "A Death in Due Time: Construction of Self and Culture in Ritual Drama," in *Rite, Drama, Festival, Spectacle: Rehearsals toward a Theory of Cultural Performance,* ed. John J. MacAloon (Philadelphia: Institute for the Study of Human Issues, 1984).

5. Barbara Myerhoff, "We Don't Wrap Herring in a Printed Page: Fusion, Fictions, and Continuity in Secular Ritual," in *Secular Ritual,* ed. Sally F. Moore and Barbara G. Myerhoff (Amsterdam: Van Gorcum, 1977), 199.

6. Herbert Bronstein, ed., *A Passover Haggadah: The New Union Haggadah,* rev. ed. (New York: CCAR, 1975), 41.

7. Ibid.

8. Ibid.

9. Joy Levitt and Michael Strassfeld, eds., *A Night of Questions: A Passover Haggadah* (Elkins Park, Pa.: The Reconstructionist Press, 1999), 50. On the problem of backshadowing see Michael André Bernstein, *Foregone Conclusions: Against Apocalyptic History* (Berkeley: University of California Press, 1994).

10. Levitt and Strassfeld, eds., *A Night of Questions: A Passover Haggadah,* 50.

11. Bronstein, ed., *A Passover Haggadah: The New Union Haggadah,* 30.

12. Ibid., 41.

13. Martin Jay, "Of Plots, Witnesses, and Judgments," in *Probing the Limits of Representation,"* ed. Friedländer, 356. I also thank Glenn Libby for helping me clarify this insight.

14. Rabinowicz, ed., *The Passover Haggadah: The Feast of Freedom,* 96; see also Beth Chayim Chadashim Liturgy Committee, ed., *Haggadah Shel Pesach,* 2nd ed. (Los Angeles: Beth Chayim Chadashim, 1990), 65.

15. Ibid.

16. In *Haggadah Shel Pesach* from Beth Chayim Chadashim, this passage is titled "Remembrance of the Six Million" and is placed just before the cup of Elijah, which further collapses the vast space between Exodus and Auschwitz, bringing both into the realm of redemption.

17. Elie Wiesel, Mark Podwal, and Marion Wiesel, eds., *A Passover Haggadah* (New York: Simon and Schuster, 1993), 69.

18. Terrence Des Pres, *The Survivor: An Anatomy of Life in the Death Camps,* 49.

19. Ibid., 33. Des Pres develops his notion of extremity in his opening chapter: "The first condition of extremity is that there is no escape, no place to go except the grave. . . . Extremity requires an attitude which allows men and women to act, and thereby to keep faith in themselves as something more than victims." Des Pres, *The Survivor: An Anatomy of Life in the Death Camps,* 7–8.

20. Des Pres, *The Survivor: An Anatomy of Life in the Death Camps,* 50.

21. Peter Novick vociferously critiques dependence on trauma theory as an explanatory device in histories of the Holocaust. See Peter Novick, *The Holocaust in American Life* (Boston: Mariner Books, 1999). However, his position does not

mitigate the value of the concept of trauma in analysis of representations of the Holocaust. Whether or not trauma theory is accurate as a causal explanation for the relative silence immediately following the Holocaust and through the mid-sixties, it presents a useful discourse for rethinking the possibilities of witnessing as it brings heightened awareness about the mediated character of witnessing.

22. James Berger, "Trauma and Literary Theory," *Contemporary Literature* 38, no. 3 (1997).

23. Shoshana Felman and Dori Laub, *Testimony: Crises of Witnessing in Literature, Psychoanalysis, and History* (New York: Routledge, 1992), 85.

24. Gary Weissman, *Fantasies of Witnessing: Postwar Efforts to Experience the Holocaust* (Ithaca, N.Y.: Cornell University Press, 2004). Lawrence Langer, Elie Wiesel, Steven Spielberg, Irving Greenberg, and Claude Lanzmann are also subject to Weissman's scathing critique.

25. Dominick LaCapra, *History and Memory after Auschwitz* (Ithaca, N.Y.: Cornell University Press, 1998), 21.

26. James E. Young, *Writing and Rewriting the Holocaust: Narrative and the Consequences of Interpretation* (Bloomington: Indiana University Press, 1988), 171.

27. Geoffrey H. Hartman, "Shoah and Intellectual Witness," *Partisan Review* 65, no. 1 (1998).

28. Primo Levi, *The Collected Poems of Primo Levi,* translated by Ruth Feldman and Brian Swann (Boston: Faber and Faber, 1988).

29. Anne Frank, *Anne Frank: The Diary of a Young Girl* (New York: Bantam Books, 1993), 143.

30. Levi, *Collected Poems of Primo Levi.*

GLOSSARY

afikomon: The hidden matzah that children ransom to end the Passover meal.

aliyah: Emigration to pre-1948 Palestine or the State of Israel.

ani ma'amin: "I still believe"; Maimonides' declaration of faith.

Auschwitz: A complex of concentration camps in southwestern Poland where Nazis murdered 1.1 million Jews and others. Often used as a synonym for the Holocaust.

Av ha-Rachamim: "Merciful father"; A prayer for Jewish martyrs written in the eleventh or twelfth century.

Avadim hayinu (fem. b'avadut hayinu): "We Have Been Enslaved"; A passage from the Passover haggadah.

b'tzelem elohim: "In the image of God"; A theological concept affirming the value of human life.

Barech: A ritual action of the seder. Recite grace after the meal. Drink third cup of wine.

baruch ha ba: A traditional greeting to welcome the prophet Elijah.

bracha (pl. brachot): A blessing said before eating food or to sanctify other experiences.

Bricha: "Escape" or "Flight"; An illegal organized exodus of some 250,000 refugees from Europe to Palestine after the Shoah.

Bund: Jewish secular socialist political party active from the 1890s through the 1930s. Members of the Bund were key leaders in the Warsaw Ghetto Uprising.

chametz (also chametzin, chametzke, chametzick): Leaven; any food made of grain and water that has been allowed to ferment. Chametz is forbidden during Passover.

Classical Reform: Early period of Reform Judaism; Also current practitioners of Reform Judaism who adopt Classical ideology, place ethics over ritual, and stress personal autonomy.

Conservative Judaism: One of the main movements or denominations of Judaism. It generally accepts the binding nature of Jewish law, but also believes the law can and should adapt to the modern world.

Dayenu: A passage from the Passover haggadah; literally, "it would have been sufficient," Dayenu recounts the many gifts God has given to the Jews.

diaspora Judaism: The religion of Jews who live outside the land of Israel.

Einsatzgruppen: Mobile killing units of German SS and police personnel who murdered more than one million Jews and other victims, usually through mass shootings.

Elijah: Prophet understood to be the harbinger of the messiah; it is customary to open the door to welcome Elijah during the Passover seder.

erev Pesach: Passover eve.

Exodus: 1) The second book of the Torah; 2) The event recounted in the Torah when the Israelites flee Egypt after 400 years of enslavement.

Final Solution: A synonym for Holocaust. A term coined by the Nazis to describe their planned genocide of the Jews in Europe.

First Fruits Festival: A time when Israelites would bring their harvest to the Temple; several verses from Leviticus that describe the festival are incorporated into the haggadah.

The Four Children: A passage from the Passover haggadah. The responses to questions by the four children (wise, wicked, simple, and does not know how to ask) teach that people must be taught the meaning of the seder in ways that match their ability.

The Four Questions: A passage from the Passover haggadah. Questions traditionally asked by the youngest child at the seder.

frummeh, frum: Yiddish for observant Jews.

galut: Hebrew term which refers to Jews exiled from the Holy Land.

ghettos: An early method used by the German government to control and reduce the Jewish population.

haggadah (also hagada; pl. haggadot, haggadoth): "The telling"; the ritual book used during the Passover seder meal.

Hallel: A ritual action of the seder. Recite psalms of praise. Drink fourth cup of wine.

haroset: a food that symbolizes the mortar used by the slaves.

Hasidic Judaism: A form of Orthodoxy begun by charismatic leaders who emphasized joy, faith, and ecstatic prayer.

hester panim: "the hiding face"; a theological concept referring to a perceived absence or eclipse of God from history.

Holy Land: Religious term for Palestine.

Israelites: Ancestors of present-day Jews.

Jewish feminism: Jewish feminists strive for inclusion of women in Jewish life and recognize that the addition of women is likely to transform Judaism itself.

Jewish Fighting Organization: Leaders of the Warsaw Ghetto Uprising.

Judenrat: Administrative councils the Nazis required Jews to form in each ghetto.

Kadesh: A ritual action of the seder. Say a blessing to sanctify the festival. Drink the first cup of wine.

Karpas: A ritual action of the seder. Dip celery or parsley, often understood as a sign of spring, in salt water, which represents the tears shed by the Israelites.

kashrut (also kosher): Jewish dietary laws.

kibbutz: Jewish communal settlements, usually agrarian, in Palestine and Israel.

kiddush: A blessing of sanctification, usually said over wine.

Kiddush ha-Shem: Sanctification of God's name.

kohlrabi: Turnip-like cabbage.

Korech: A ritual action of the seder. Eat matzah and bitter herbs together. This ritual emphasizes the bitterness of slavery.

liberal Judaism: An umbrella term for non-Orthodox movements within Judaism.

Maggid: 1) "Telling"; central narrative and commentary in the haggadah; 2) A ritual action of the seder. Recite the story of the Exodus. Drink second cup of wine.

Malach hamot: "Angel of Death."

manna: Food provided by God during forty years in wilderness.

Ma-os tsur: Song about God as the rock whose power saves that Jews sing during Hanukkah.

Maror: A ritual action of the seder. Dip bitter herbs, which represent the bitterness of slavery, in haroset, a food that symbolizes the mortar used by the slaves.

martyr: A person who dies because of their faith. Derived from the Greek work for "witness." The Hebrew term for martyrdom is Kiddush ha-Shem, "sanctification of God's name."

matchil bigenut umesayem beshevach: "From degradation/shame to praise/glory"; phrase from the Talmud used to describe the narrative structure of the Exodus story in the haggadah.

matzah: 1) The unleavened bread eaten at Passover; 2) A ritual action of the seder. Recite special blessing for eating matzah.

messiah: "Anointed one"; contemporary traditional Jews believe a person will come in the future to bring peace and justice to the world.

midrash (plural midrashim): From the biblical Hebrew *lidrosh,* which means "to search" or "to examine." 1) Rabbinic stories written down between the fifth and thirteenth centuries C.E.; 2) the process of using a story for searching out meaning in a text.

mi-panei chata'einu: "Because of our sins"; theological concept used to explain persecution of Jews throughout history.

Mishnah: A foundational rabbinic text from the third century C.E., which is part of the Talmud.

mitzrayim: Hebrew term for Egypt; literally "narrow straits."

Motzi: A ritual action of the seder. Recite blessing for eating bread.

navi: Hebrew word for a prophet.

Nirtzah: A ritual action of the seder. Conclude the seder.

Orthodox Judaism: Generic term to differentiate the movements following traditional practices from the liberal Jewish movements. Orthodox Judaism affirms the revelatory status of both written Torah and oral Torah (the Talmud).

Palestine: Geographical area of the Holy Land.

Passover, Pesach: Holiday when Jews are commanded to tell the Exodus story of slavery and freedom to their children.

pikuakh nefesh: "Where life is at stake"; Jewish law places supreme importance on pikuakh nefesh—the preservation of human life—which takes precedence over almost all other commandments.

rebbe, rabbi: A Jewish teacher.

rebbetzin: Term used to refer to a rabbi's wife.

Reconstructionist Judaism: One of the main movements or denominations of Judaism. Founded in the United States in the twentieth century, it is the smallest of the liberal denominations.

Reform Judaism: One of the main movements or denominations of Judaism. Reform Judaism recognizes the historical origin of Torah and affirms personal choice in the context of tradition. It is the largest Jewish denomination in the United States.

Rohtzah: A ritual action of the seder. Wash hands and recite blessing.

Sabbath (also Shabbat): Weekly day of rest from Friday evening to Saturday sundown.

"The Secret Annex" (or the Annex): The hiding place of the Frank family.

seder (also s'darim, pl. sederim): Ritual meal traditionally held on the first and second nights of Passover; literally means "order."

she'erit hapletah: "The surviving remnant," Holocaust survivors.

Sh'ma (also Shema): A central prayer of Jewish faith that affirms God is one.

Shoah: A synonym for Holocaust, describing the extermination of the Jews in Europe.

Shulchan-Orech: A ritual action of the seder. Eat the holiday meal.

state of Israel: Modern nation-state created in 1948.

Talmud (also Oral Torah): An important text studied by Jews that shapes Jewish belief and practice.

The Ten Plagues: Sufferings inflicted on the Egyptians by God in the book of Exodus.

theodicy: A branch of theology and philosophy concerned with perceived contradiction between an all-powerful, good God and the presence of evil in the world.

Tisha B'Av: Traditional holiday for mourning tragedies throughout Jewish history.

Torah: 1) The term usually used by Jews to refer to the Hebrew Bible. Technically, it refers to the first five books—Genesis, Exodus, Leviticus, Numbers, and Deuteronomy. 2) The sacred texts of the Jewish people. 3) Jewish learning.

Tzafun: A ritual action of the seder. Eat the afikomon, the piece of matzah hidden earlier, at the end of the meal.

Urchatz: A ritual action of the seder. Wash hands.

Warsaw Ghetto Uprising: Waged from April 19 to May 16, 1943, the largest and symbolically most important Jewish uprising during World War II.

Yachatz: A ritual action of the seder. Break the middle matzah from the three pieces of matzah that have been placed on the table. An adult hides half of the middle matzah, which children search for at the end of the meal.

yiddin: Colloquial Yiddish word for Jews

Yom Kippur: The Day of Atonement; an important Jewish holy day.

Zeman heiruteinu: "Season of Our Liberation;" another name for Passover.

Zionist: A person who supports the creation of the modern state of Israel.

BIBLIOGRAPHY

Abramowitz, Sharon, Diane Gelon, Anna Rubin, and Sheila Ruth, eds. *Women's Passover Seder.* Unpublished mansucript. Los Angeles: Hebrew Union College Library, 1977.

Apel, Dora. *Memory Effects: The Holocaust and the Art of Secondary Witnessing.* New Brunswick, N.J.: Rutgers University Press, 2002.

Aristotle. *Poetics.* Translated by Stephen Halliwell. Cambridge, Mass.: Harvard University Press, 1995.

Arnow, David. *Creating Lively Passover Seders: A Sourcebook of Engaging Tales, Texts, and Activities.* Woodstock, Vt.: Jewish Lights Publishing, 2004.

Barnett, Carol J. "Reflections on Anne Frank." In *Anne Frank in the World,* edited by Carol Rittner, 3–9. Armonk, N.Y.: M.E. Sharpe, 1998.

Berger, James. "Trauma and Literary Theory." *Contemporary Literature* 38, no. 3 (1997): 569–82.

Bernstein, Michael André. "Primo Levi (Book Revew)." *The New Republic* 221, no. 13 (1999): 35–42.

———. *Foregone Conclusions: Against Apocalyptic History.* Berkeley: University of California Press, 1994.

Berryman, John. "The Development of Anne Frank." In *Anne Frank: Reflections on Her Life and Legacy,* edited by Hyman Enzer and Sandra Solotaroff-Enzer, 76–80. Urbana, Ill.: University of Illinois Press, 2000.

Beth Chayim Chadashim Liturgy Committee, ed. *Haggadah Shel Pesach.* 2nd ed. Los Angeles: Beth Chayim Chadashim, 1990.

Bettelheim, Bruno. "The Ignored Lesson of Anne Frank." In *A Scholarly Look at the Diary of Anne Frank,* edited by Harold Bloom, 5–14. Philadelphia: Chelsea House Publishers, 1999.

Blair, Jon. *Anne Frank Remembered.* Sony Pictures, 1995.

Bokser, Baruch M. *The Origins of the Seder: The Passover Rite and Early Rabbinic Judaism.* Berkeley: University of California Press, 1984.

Boyarin, Daniel. *Intertextuality and the Reading of Midrash.* Bloomington: Indiana University Press, 1990.

Brenner, Rachel Feldhay. *Writing as Resistance: Four Women Confronting the Holocaust: Edith Stein, Simone Weil, Anne Frank, Etty Hillesum.* University Park: Pennsylvania State University Press, 1997.

———. "Writing Herself against History: Anne Frank's Self-Portrait as a Young Artist." In *Anne Frank: Reflections on Her Life and Legacy,* edited by Hyman Enzer and Sandra Solotaroff-Enzer, 86–93. Urbana, Ill.: University of Illinois Press, 2000.

Broner, E. M., and Naomi Nimrod. *The Telling.* San Francisco: HarperSan Francisco, 1993.

Bronstein, Herbert, ed. *A Passover Haggadah: The New Union Haggadah.* 2nd rev. ed. New York: Central Conference of American Rabbis (CCAR), 1982.

Bycel, Lee. "'To Reclaim Our Voice': An Analysis of Representative Contemporary Feminist Haggadot." *CCAR Journal,* Spring 1993.

Calhoun, Craig, ed. *Dictionary of the Social Sciences.* New York: Oxford University Press, 2002.

Central Conference of American Rabbis. 1976. Reform Judaism: A Centenary Perspective. http://data.ccarnet.org/platforms/centenary.html. (accessed July 31, 2006).

———. 1885. Declaration of Principles. http://data.ccarnet.org/platforms/pittsburgh. html. (accessed July 31, 2006).

Chatman, Seymour. *Story and Discourse: Narrative Structure in Fiction and Film.* Ithaca, N.Y.: Cornell University Press, 1978.

Chiarello, Barbara. "The Utopian Space of a Nightmare: The Diary of Anne Frank." In *A Scholarly Look at the Diary of Anne Frank,* edited by Harold Bloom, 85–100. Philadelphia: Chelsea House Publishers, 1999.

Cohen, Steven M. and Arnold M. Eisen. *The Jew Within: Self, Family, and Community in America.* Bloomington: Indiana University Press, 2000.

Colijn, G. Jan. "Review Essay: Anne Frank Remembered." In *Anne Frank: Reflections on Her Life and Legacy,* edited by Hyman Enzer and Sandra Solotaroff-Enzer, 173–84. Urbana: University of Illinois Press, 2000.

———. "Toward a Proper Legacy." In *Anne Frank in the World,* edited by Carol Rittner, 95–104. Armonk, N.Y.: M.E. Sharpe, 1998.

Confino, Alon. "Collective Memory and Cultural History: Problems of Method." *American Historical Review* 102, no. 5 (1997): 1386–1403.

Deitch, Donna. *The Devil's Arithmetic.* Showtime Entertainment, 1999.

Delbo, Charlotte. *Auschwitz and After.* New Haven: Yale University Press, 1995.

Des Pres, Terrence. *The Survivor: An Anatomy of Life in the Death Camps.* New York: Oxford University Press, 1976.

Doneson, Judith. "The American History of Anne Frank's Diary." *Holocaust and Genocide Studies* 2, no. 1 (1987): 149–60.

Dreyfus, A. Stanley. "The Gates Liturgies: Reform Judaism Reforms Its Worship." In *The Changing Face of Jewish and Christian Worship in North America,* edited by Paul Bradshaw and Lawrence Hoffman, 141–56. Notre Dame, Ind.: University of Notre Dame Press, 1991.

Elwell, Ellen Sue Levi, ed. *The Open Door: A Passover Haggadah.* New York: Central Conference of American Rabbis Press, 2001.

Enzer, Hyman Aaron, and Sandra Solotaroff-Enzer, eds. *Anne Frank: Reflections on Her Life and Legacy.* Urbana: University of Illinois Press, 2000.

Epstein, Isidore, ed. *Hebrew-English Edition of the Babylonian Talmud.* Mo'ed, Pesachim 116. London: Soncino Press, 1967.

Ezrahi, Sidra DeKoven. "Representing Auschwitz." *History and Memory* 7, no. 2 (1996).

Felman, Shoshana, and Dori Laub. *Testimony: Crises of Witnessing in Literature, Psychoanalysis, and History.* New York: Routledge, 1992.

Frank, Anne. *Anne Frank: The Diary of a Young Girl.* New York: Bantam Books, 1993.

———. *The Diary of a Young Girl: The Definitive Edition.* Edited by Otto H. Frank and Mirjam Pressler. New York: Doubleday, 1995.

Friedländer, Saul. "Trauma, Memory, and Transference." In *Holocaust Remembrance: The Shapes of Memory,* edited by Geoffrey H. Hartman. Cambridge, Mass.: Blackwell, 1994.

———. *Probing the Limits of Representation: Nazism and The "Final Solution."* Cambridge, Mass.: Harvard University Press, 1992.

Gilbert, Paul. "What Is Shame? Some Core Issues and Controversies." In *Shame: Interpersonal Behavior, Psychopathology, and Culture,* edited by Paul Gilbert and Bernice Andrews, 3–38. New York: Oxford University Press, 1998.

Glatstein, Jacob et al., eds. *Anthology of Holocaust Literature.* New York: Atheneum, 1976.

Goldenberg, Robert. "Talmud." In *Back to the Sources: Reading the Classic Jewish Texts,* edited by Barry Holtz, 129–75. New York: Summit Books, 1984.

Goodrich, Frances, and Albert Hackett. *The Diary of Anne Frank: A Random House Play.* Based on the translation by B.M. Mooyaart-Doubleday. New York: Random House, 1955.

———. *The Diary of Anne Frank.* Adapted by Wendy Kesselman. Performance Manuscript. New York, 1997.

Graver, Lawrence. *An Obsession with Anne Frank.* Berkeley: University of California Press, 1995.

Greenberg, Irving. "Cloud of Smoke, Pillar of Fire: Judaism, Christianity, and Modernity after the Holocaust." In *Auschwitz: Beginning of a New Era?,* edited by Eva Fleischner, 7–55. New York: The Cathedral Church of St. John the Divine, 1977.

———. *The Jewish Way: Living the Holidays.* New York: Simon and Schuster, 1988.

Gutman, Israel. *Resistance: The Warsaw Ghetto Uprising.* Boston: Houghton Mifflin, 1994.

Halbwachs, Maurice, and Lewis A. Coser. *On Collective Memory.* Chicago: University of Chicago Press, 1992.

Hartman, Geoffrey H., ed. *Bitburg in Moral and Political Perspective.* Bloomington: Indiana University Press, 1986.

———. "Shoah and Intellectual Witness." *Partisan Review* 65, no. 1 (1998): 37–48.

Hoagland, Molly Magid. "Anne Frank On and Off Broadway." In *A Scholarly Look at the Diary of Anne Frank,* edited by Harold Bloom, 75–84. Philadelphia: Chelsea House Publishers, 1999.

Hoffman, Lawrence A. *Beyond the Text: A Holistic Approach to Liturgy.* Bloomington: Indiana University Press, 1989.

Holtz, Barry. "Midrash." In *Back to the Sources: Reading the Classic Jewish Texts,* edited by Barry Holtz, 177–211. New York: Summit Books, 1984.

Irwin-Zarecka, Iwona. *Frames of Remembrance: The Dynamics of Collective Memory.* New Brunswick, NJ: Transaction Publishers, 1994.

Jacobs, Louis. "The Talmudic Argument." In *Essential Papers on the Talmud,* edited by Michael Chernick, 52–69. New York: New York University Press, 1994.

Jay, Martin. "Of Plots, Witnesses, and Judgments." In *Probing the Limits of Representation: Nazism and The "Final Solution,"* edited by Saul Friedländer, 97–107. Cambridge, Mass.: Harvard University Press, 1992.

Kasher, Menahem. *Israel Passover Haggadah.* New York: American Biblical Encyclopedia Society, 1956.

Klepfisz, Irena. "Yom Hashoah, Yom Yerushalayim: A Meditation." In *Jewish Women's Call for Peace, a Handbook for Jewish Women on the Israeli/Palestinian Conflict,* edited by Rita Falbel, Irena Klepfisz and Donna Nevel, 39–45. Ithaca, N.Y.: Firebrand Books, 1990.

Krall, Hanna, and Marek Edelman. *Shielding the Flame: An Intimate Conversation with Dr. Marek Edelman, the Last Surviving Leader of the Warsaw Ghetto Uprising.* New York: Henry Holt and Co., 1986.

Kramer, Ralph, and Philip Schild, eds. *The Bay Area Jewish Forum Haggadah.* Berkeley: Benmire Books, 1986.

LaCapra, Dominick. *History and Memory after Auschwitz.* Ithaca, N.Y.: Cornell University Press, 1998.

Lamm, Norman. "The Face of God: Thoughts on the Holocaust." In *Theological and Halakhic Reflections on the Holocaust,* edited by Richard H. Rosenberg and Fred Heuman, 119–36. Hoboken, N.J.: KTAV, 1992.

Langer, Lawrence L. *Admitting the Holocaust: Collected Essays.* New York: Oxford University Press, 1995.

———. "The Dilemma of Choice in the Deathcamps." In *Holocaust: Religious and Philosophical Reflections,* edited by John K. Roth and Michael Berenbaum, 222–32. New York: Paragon House, 1989.

———. *Holocaust Testimonies: The Ruins of Memory.* New Haven: Yale University Press, 1991.

———. "Pre-Empting the Holocaust." *The Atlantic Monthly,* November 1998, 105–15.

———. "The Uses—and Misuses—of a Young Girl's Diary: "If Anne Frank Could Return from among the Murdered, She Would Be Appalled."" In *Anne Frank: Reflections on Her Life and Legacy,* edited by Hyman Enzer and Sandra Solotaroff-Enzer, 203–05. Urbana: University of Illinois Press, 2000.

Leder, Steven. "Imagining Einstein." Unpublished dissertation. Hebrew Union College—Jewish Institute of Religion, 1987.

Levi, Primo. *The Drowned and the Saved.* New York: Vintage International, 1989.

———. *The Reawakening.* New York: Maxwell Macmillan International, 1993.

Levi, Primo. *The Collected Poems of Primo Levi.* Translated by Ruth Feldman and Brian Swann. Boston: Faber and Faber, 1988.

Levin, Meyer. *The Obsession.* New York: Simon & Schuster, 1973.

Levitt, Joy, and Michael Strassfeld, eds. *A Night of Questions: A Passover Haggadah.* Elkins Park, Penn.: The Reconstructionist Press, 1999.

Lubetkin, Zivia. *In the Days of Destruction and Revolt.* Tel Aviv: Hakibbutz Hameuchad Publishing House: Am Oved Publishing. House, 1981.

March of the Living International. http://www.motl.org/mission.htm. (accessed October 23, 2005).

Maslow, Abraham. "A Theory of Human Motivation." *Psychological Review* 50 (1943): 370–96.

Meed, Vladka. *On Both Sides of the Wall.* New York: Holocaust Library, 1979.

Melnick, Ralph. *The Stolen Legacy of Anne Frank: Meyer Levin, Lillian Hellman, and the Staging of the Diary.* New Haven: Yale University Press, 1997.

Mendes-Flohr, Paul R., and Jehuda Reinharz. *The Jew in the Modern World: A Documentary History.* 2nd ed. New York: Oxford University Press, 1995.

Miller, J. Hillis. "Narrative." In *Critical Terms for Literary Study,* edited by Frank Lentricchia and Thomas McLaughlin, 66–79. Chicago: University of Chicago Press, 1990.

Moise, Elaine, and Rebecca Schwartz, ed. *The Dancing with Miriam Haggadah: A Jewish Women's Celebration of Passover.* 3rd ed. Palo Alto, Calif.: Rikudei Miriam, 1999.

Morgan, Michael L. *Beyond Auschwitz: Post-Holocaust Jewish Thought in America.* New York: Oxford University Press, 2001.

Morson, Gary Saul. *Narrative and Freedom: The Shadows of Time.* New Haven: Yale University Press, 1994.

Myerhoff, Barbara. "A Death in Due Time: Construction of Self and Culture in Ritual Drama." In *Rite, Drama, Festival, Spectacle: Rehearsals toward a Theory of Cultural Performance,* edited by John J. MacAloon, 149–78. Philadelpha: Institute for the Study of Human Issues, 1984.

———. "We Don't Wrap Herring in a Printed Page: Fusion, Fictions and Continuity in Secular Ritual." In *Secular Ritual,* edited by Sally F. Moore and Barbara G. Myerhoff, 199–208. Amsterdam: Van Gorcum, 1977.

Neusner, Jacob. *Stranger at Home: "The Holocaust," Zionism, and American Judaism.* Chicago: University of Chicago Press, 1981.

Novick, Peter. *The Holocaust in American Life.* Boston: Mariner Books, 1999.

Ofer, Dalia, and Lenore J. Weitzman, eds. *Women in the Holocaust.* New Haven: Yale University Press, 1998.

Pommer, Henry. "The Legend and Art of Anne Frank." *Judaism* 9, no. 1 (1960): 37–46.

Rabinowicz, Rachel Anne, ed. *The Passover Haggadah: The Feast of Freedom.* New York: Rabbinical Assembly, 1982.

Rapoport, Nathan. "Memoir of the *Warsaw Ghetto Monument.*" In *The Art of Memory: Holocaust Memorials in History,* edited by James E. Young, 103–07. Munich and New York: Prestel-Verlag, 1994.

Reagan, Ronald. "Never Again: Speech at Bergen Belsen, May 5, 1985." In *Bitburg and Beyond: Encounters in American, German, and Jewish History,* edited by Ilya Levkov, 131–34. New York: Shapolsky Publishers, 1987.

Ringelheim, Joan. "The Unethical and the Unspeakable: Women and the Holocaust." *The Simon Wiesenthal Center Annual* 1 (1984): 69–87.

Rittner, Carol, ed. *Anne Frank in the World.* Armonk, N.Y.: M.E. Sharpe, 1998.

Rosen, Jonathan. *The Talmud and the Internet: A Journey between Worlds.* New York: Picador, 2000.

Rosenfeld, Alvin. "Popularization and Memory: The Case of Anne Frank." In *Lessons and Legacies: The Meaning of the Holocaust in a Changing World,* edited by Peter Hayes, 243–78. Evanston, Ill.: Northwestern University Press, 1991.

Roskies, David G. *Against the Apocalypse: Responses to Catastrophe in Modern Jewish Culture.* Cambridge, Mass.: Harvard University Press, 1984.

Rothberg, Michael. "W. E .B. Du Bois in Warsaw: Holocaust Memory and the Color Line, 1949–1952." *The Yale Journal of Criticism* 14, no. 1 (2001): 169–89.

Rubenstein, Richard L. *After Auschwitz: Radical Theology and Contemporary Judaism.* Indianapolis: The Bobbs-Merrill Company. 1966.

Schechner, Richard. *Performance Studies: An Introduction.* New York: Routledge, 2002.

Scherman, Nosson, ed. *The Complete Artscroll Siddur,* 3rd ed: New York: Mesorah Publications, 1989.

Schiffman, Lisa. *Generation J.* San Francisco: HarperSanFrancisco, 1999.

Segal, Lore. "Memory: The Problems of Imagining the Past." In *Writing and the Holocaust,* edited by Berel Lang. New York: Holmes and Meier, 1988.

Sheinson, Yosef Dov, and Saul Touster. *A Survivors' Haggadah.* Philadelphia: Jewish Publication Society, 2000.

Sholem Community Organization, ed. *Sholem Family Hagada for a Secular Celebration of Peysakh.* Los Angeles: Sholem Community Organization, 1992.

Skolnik, Fred, ed. *Encyclopedia Judaica.* 2nd ed. New York: Macmillan, 2006.

Stern, David. *Midrash and Theory: Ancient Jewish Exegesis and Contemporary Literary Studies.* Evanston, Ill.: Northwestern University Press, 1996.

Stevens, George. *The Diary of Anne Frank.* 20th Century Fox, 1959.

Stier, Oren Baruch. *Committed to Memory: Cultural Mediations of the Holocaust.* Amherst: University of Massachusetts Press, 2003.

Tanakh, a new translation of the Holy Scriptures according to the traditional Hebrew text. Philadelphia: Jewish Publication Society, 1985.

Turner, Victor. "Are There Universals of Performance in Myth, Ritual, and Drama?" In *By Means of Performance: Intercultural Studies of Theatre and Ritual,* edited by Richard Schechner and Willa Appel, 8–18. Cambridge: Cambridge University Press, 1990.

United States Holocaust Memorial Museum. "Auschwitz" in *Holocaust Encyclopedia.* http://www.ushmm.org/wlc/article.php?lang=en&ModuleId=10005189. (accessed August 12, 2005).

Weissman, Gary. *Fantasies of Witnessing: Postwar Efforts to Experience the Holocaust.* Ithaca, N.Y.: Cornell University Press, 2004.

White, Hayden. *The Content of the Form: Narrative Discourse and Historical Representation.* Baltimore: The John Hopkins University Press, 1987.

———. "Historical Emplotment and the Problem of Truth." In *Probing the Limits of Representation: Nazism and The "Final Solution,"* edited by Saul Friedländer, 37–53. Cambridge, Mass.: Harvard University Press, 1992.

Wiesel, Elie, Mark Podwal, and Marion Wiesel. *A Passover Haggadah.* New York: Simon & Schuster, 1993.

Yerushalmi, Yosef Hayim. *Haggadah and History: A Panorama in Facsimile of Five Centuries of the Printed Haggadah from the Collections of Harvard University and the Jewish Theological Seminary of America.* 2nd ed. Philadelphia: Jewish Publication Society of America, 1997.

———. *Zakhor, Jewish History and Jewish Memory.* Seattle: University of Washington Press, 1982.

Young, James E. *The Texture of Memory: Holocaust Memorials and Meaning.* New Haven: Yale University Press, 1993.

———. *Writing and Rewriting the Holocaust: Narrative and the Consequences of Interpretation.* Bloomington: Indiana University Press, 1988.

Zion, Noam, and David Dishon, eds. *A Different Night: The Family Participation Haggadah.* Jerusalem: Shalom Hartman Institute, 1997.

Zuckerman, Yitzhak, and Barbara Harshav. *A Surplus of Memory: Chronicle of the Warsaw Ghetto Uprising.* Berkeley: University of California Press, 1993.

INDEX